Heidemarie Wawrzyn

Nazis in the Holy Land

1933–1948

Heidemarie Wawrzyn

Nazis in the Holy Land 1933–1948

DE GRUYTER MAGNES

Co-published by
The Hebrew University Magnes Press (Jerusalem)
and De Gruyter (Berlin/Boston)
for the Vidal Sassoon International Center for the Study of Antisemitism

ISBN 978-3-11-048567-7
e-ISBN 978-3-11-030652-1

Library of Congress Cataloging-in-Publication Data
A CIP catalog record for this book has been applied for at the Library of Congress.

Bibliographic information published by the Deutsche Nationalbibliothek
The Deutsche Nationalbibliothek lists this publication in the Deutsche Nationalbibliografie; detailed bibliographic data are available in the Internet at http://dnb.dnb.de.

Typesetting: Dr. Rainer Ostermann, München
Printing: Hubert & Co. GmbH & Co. KG, Göttingen
♾ Printed on acid free paper
Printed in Germany

www.degruyter.com
www.magnespress.co.il

Preface

> It is very important to me to start a Nazi country group in Palestine. I am sure it will be possible to do so. My official in charge knows from his own experience that many racial German comrades have settled down in the *Judenland*. These Germans, who have been living far away from their fatherland for many years, should not be abandoned. It is the holy task of National Socialism to help and support them to maintain their German mind-set.[1]

Ernst Wilhelm Bohle, the future head of the *Auslands-Abteilung* (Overseas Department), sent these words in a letter from his office in Hamburg to Karl Ruff, a German architect from Haifa. It was in July 1932 that the Overseas Department began encouraging Germans in Palestine to establish a Nazi branch in the Holy Land. At that time, Palestine[2] already counted six NSDAP members – four men and two women.[3] The foundation of a Nazi party in Palestine seems bizarre and contradictory. Even more astonishing is that no extensive research written in English has been done on this interesting and intriguing subject until today.

In 1952, H. Schmidt published a short article on National Socialist organizations in Palestine and the Middle East.[4] Donald McKale, in a 1977 book provided roughly two pages of information on the Country Group Palestine and its anti-Jewish policy.[5] Historian Paul Sauer,[6] who published a comprehensive work on the history of the Temple Society in 1985, addressed one chapter to the issue of National Socialism but showed an excessively sympathetic attitude towards the Templers' involvement. Francis Nicosia, writing on the *Third Reich and the Palestine Question* (1998), came to the conclusion that a thorough study of the Christian groups in Palestine and their involvement in the NSDAP was at that

---

1 Ernst Wilhelm Bohle, Hamburg to Karl Ruff, Hamburg, 16 July 1932, Israel State Archives (hereafter ISTA), 821/1-פ: "Es liegt mir viel daran, besonders in Palästina eine Landesgruppe ins Leben zu rufen, und dies ist möglich. Aus eigener Erfahrung weiss mein Sachbearbeiter, dass in dem Judenland sich viele völkische Volksgenossen angesiedelt haben, und gerade diese Deutschen, die vom Vaterlande schon lange Jahre fern sind, dürfen nicht verlassen werden, und es ist die heilige Pflicht des Nationalsozialismus, dafür zu sorgen, dass diesen ihre Deutschgesinnung auch erhalten bleibt."

2 Palestine here refers to the region and borders of the British Mandate of Palestine from 1920 to 1948 (without Transjordan). The term *Holy Land,* sometimes used in this study, refers to the same area.

3 Ernst Wilhelm Bohle, Hamburg to Karl Ruff, Hamburg, 16 July 1932, ISTA, 821/1-פ.

4 H. Schmidt, "The Nazi Party in Palestine and the Levant, 1932–9," *International Affairs* 28, no. 4 (1952): 460–69.

5 Donald M. McKale, *The Swastika outside Germany* (Kent State, 1977), 125–26.

6 Paul Sauer, *Uns rief das Heilige Land. Die Tempelgesellschaft im Wandel der Zeit* (Stuttgart, 1985).

time still lacking and should be done.[7] Ralf Balke's dissertation, *Hakenkreuz im Heiligen Land* (2001), was the first book to provide extensive data and new details on the beginnings and development of the NS groups in Palestine, with a thorough examination of the relationship of the Nazis in Palestine with the *Auslands-Organisation* (AO) in Germany and its impact on Hitler's foreign policy.[8] Thanks to his groundbreaking study, the present work can concentrate on elaborating the attitude of the Palestine-Germans[9] towards their Arab and Jewish neighbors and their relationship with them, as well as the reactions they evoked by "planting" a Nazi organization in Palestine.

Balke's book was published in German and is therefore limited to German-speaking readers. In the last ten years, several articles on Nazi activities in Palestine have appeared in Hebrew in Israeli newspapers.[10] This volume, *Nazis in the Holy Land, 1933–1948,* will hopefully find an extensive English readership. Because most of the previous publications concentrated on the members of the Temple Society, this study includes Protestant and Catholic Germans as well. Numerous Protestant newsletters and correspondence were surveyed to demonstrate the Protestants' engagement in the NSDAP in Palestine; the involvement of a few Catholics in the Nazi party in Palestine in the 1930s was a new discovery, deserving of further research.

What is completely new in this work is the documentation of the NS women's organization abroad, the *Arbeitsgemeinschaft der Deutschen Frau im Ausland*, a substitute for the *NS Frauenschaft* (NS Women's League) in Germany. As it is often confused with the *NS Frauenschaft*, I decided to devote more attention to the overseas work group for women in particular, and to the women's National Socialist involvement in general, than to other NS groups in Palestine.

Nazi activities drastically decreased with the beginning of the Second World War, but did not completely cease. Therefore, this study also covers the period of 1939 to 1945 and the years between the end of the war and the departure of the last group of Germans in 1950. In order to show the decisions and actions of the Nazis in Palestine in a broader context, and to put them into the perspective of the Jewish reality, sources, data, and testimonies from Jewish contemporaries were integrated into this work. A survey of NS groups worldwide was conducted to

---

7 Francis R. Nicosia, *The Third Reich and the Palestine Question* (London, 2000), 93.

8 Ralf Balke, *Hakenkreuz im Heiligen Land. Die NSDAP-Landesgruppe Palästina* (Erfurt, 2001).

9 Palestine-Germans refers to all Germans residing in Palestine, the region of the British Mandate of Palestine (excluding Transjordan).

10 Dalia Karpel, "Swastika in Jerusalem" *Haaretz,* 28 Feb. 2008; Alex Carmel, "What's This? Making Fun of Nazis?," *Haaretz,* 29 Oct. 1999; Moshe Temkin, "The History of the Hitler Youth in Jerusalem" (in Hebrew), *Yediot Achronot,* 1 Oct. 1999; L. Bahat, "Hitler Boulevard at the Corner of Kaplan" (in Hebrew), *Yediot Achronot,* 3 Mar. 2006.

compare the *Landesgruppe Palästina* to other NS groups abroad, and to analyze the similarities and differences between them.

As mentioned above, the founding of NS groups in Palestine seems bizarre and contradictory, especially if one takes in account that the initial contact between Palestine-Germans and National Socialists in Germany was not made by the Auslands-Abteilung in Germany but by a Palestine-German, born in Haifa. Among German consulate documents, one can find letters expressing "how awful it was to live as a good, pure German among Jews." Why did Nazi party members and sympathizers remain in Palestine as long as possible? What was their relationship with local Jews and Arabs? How could they – living among Jews and Arabs – accept the racial theory of the Third Reich? Was their antisemitism different from that of those who lived in Germany?

Compared to the figure of 2,000 to 2,500 Germans living in Palestine, the Nazi party in Palestine was of small size and limited significance.[11] Nevertheless, a miniature Third Reich with local NS groups, Hitler Youth program, and associations for women, teachers, and others, was established by ambitious NS officials living in Palestine. Did local Jews and Arabs take note of the Nazi party and its activities? How did they respond to German National Socialism in their country? How did this influence their perception of Palestine-Germans in general? This book will address these questions. Furthermore, it will hopefully motivate historians and other researchers to conduct further studies on this topic. More than seven hundred names of those who joined the NS groups in Palestine were collected, along with data about age, gender, and profession (See Appendix II), in order to facilitate additional research, on, for example, the social components of the Nazi branches abroad.

11 Yad Vashem Archives (hereafter YVA), R 3/11, data of 6 June 1937; YVA, R 3/27 and R3/30, correspondence of the German Consul General, Jerusalem, 1937 and 1938.

Acknowledgments

First of all, I want to thank the Vidal Sassoon International Center for the Study of Antisemitism in Jerusalem, which provided a grant over a period of two years, and without which this research would not have been possible.

Furthermore, I want to express my thanks to the friendly and supportive employees and assistants of the archives and libraries in Israel, Germany, and the United States: the Israel State Archives, the Yad Vashem Archives, the Central Zionist Archives, the Leo Baeck Institute, the Dormition Abbey, the Albright Institute, the German Institute of Archaeology, the Lutheran Church of the Redeemer, Jerusalem, and the National Library of Israel, Givat Ram, Jerusalem; the Schumacher Institute, Haifa; the *Bundesarchiv Berlin* and the *Politisches Archiv des Auswärtigen Amtes*, as well as the Central Archives of the Protestant Church (*Evangelisches Zentralarchiv*), the *Jerusalemsverein*, and the *Diakonisches Werk* in Berlin; the Library of Congress and the U.S. Holocaust Memorial Museum in Washington, D.C.

Special thanks go to Prof. Ezra Mendelsohn, Dr. Michael Silber, Dr. Ralf Balke, and Yossi Bezark, as well as to Brigitte Kneher and Peter Lange from the Temple Society, Germany for their advice and help. Last but not least, my thanks to colleagues and friends who helped improve this book by listening and giving advice.

Contents

List of Illustrations

Illustrations appear following Chapter 3.

Introduction

An Overseas Organization for a Worldwide Nazi Network

The NSDAP (National Socialist German Workers' Party) was founded in Germany in 1920 and came to power in January 1933. At this time approximately thirty million Germans, that is, German citizens and those of German descent *(Volksdeutsche)* lived outside Germany.[12] The strong concern of the NSDAP was the continuation of the German language, traditions, and character summarized in the term *Deutschtum*. Hitler and his followers believed that "it was Germany's mission to unify the thirty million Germans outside the Reich into a world-wide German *Volksgemeinschaft* (racial community)."[13] They were obsessed with the idea of saving the Germanic population and preserving it from anti-German "elements" ("world Jewry," communism, and liberalism). Nazi groups outside Germany were established "as bases from which the historic struggle against the alleged plot could be carried on worldwide. The Jew, Nazi officials firmly believed, was out to enslave the world's Aryan population; thus, it was crucial in fighting such a menace to confront it not only in Germany but throughout the world."[14] As a consequence, the Nazis established agencies to care for those Germans who lived in foreign countries, one of which was the Auslands-Organisation (AO),[15] supporting the Nazis' efforts abroad and encouraging the formation of NS groups. Its propaganda, training program, and political agitation were aimed at increasing the number of *Landesgruppen* (country groups), expanding Germany's influence in foreign countries and building a strong Pan-German movement in each country.[16]

According to McKale's study on Nazi party organizations in foreign countries, Nazi members abroad first developed their activities in the Americas, South

12 Donald M. McKale, *The Swastika Outside Germany* (Kent State, Ohio, 1977), 4. *Volksdeutsche* were defined as people whose language and culture had German origins but who did not hold German citizenship. Used by Hitler and his followers, the term *Volksdeutsche* carried racial implications; the National Socialists also introduced the term *Auslandsdeutsche*, which generally referred to German citizens residing abroad.

13 Ibid., 7.

14 Ibid., 8.

15 *Auslands-Organisation* — Overseas Organization of the NSDAP from February 1934 to 1945. From May 1931 to Feb. 1934, the organization was called *Auslands-Abteilung* — Overseas Department. Rolf Balke, *Hakenkreuz im Heiligen Land. die NSDAP-Landesgruppe Palästina* (Erfurt, 2001), 31–34; McKale, *Swastika Outside Germany*, xiv.

16 McKale, *Swastika Outside Germany*, 3–8; cf. Frank Foerster, *Mission im Heiligen Land. Der Jerusalems-Verein zu Berlin 1852–1945* (Gütersloh, 1991), 177.

Africa, and China as early as the end of the 1920s – long before the Overseas Department was founded. "Nazi activities in the United States also began in the 1920s. The large number of Germans who had migrated to the United States ... offered promising recruitment possibilities for the National Socialists ... In Latin America, nearly 1.5 million persons of German descent and roughly 180,000 Reich citizens lived chiefly in southern Brazil, Argentina ..., Chile, Paraguay, and Uruguay."[17] The very first Nazi group abroad to officially receive the rank of a local NS group (Ortsgruppe), in July 1928, was in Timbó in Brazil.[18]

Party branches for German citizens outside Germany were often created by private individuals who felt politically frustrated by the Weimar regime but nevertheless had a strong loyalty to their homeland.[19] Wherever they could find "political friends" (*Gesinnungsgenossen*), they founded groups to inform others about Hitler and encourage them to contact the offices of the NSDAP in Germany.[20] According to a statistical analysis by the Auslands-Organisation, the social composition of NS groups abroad was little different from the largely young, middle-class party membership inside Germany itself. The majority (90 percent) of party members abroad were male, under thirty-eight years of age, "and engaged in some type of business activity or other middle class profession."[21] They persistently used the German language in daily conversation, and they formed close-knit communities with their own cultural groups, clubs, and schools.[22]

Most Landesgruppen consisted of several departments and various offices. The *Landesgruppenleiter* (country group head) engaged party members to handle membership and financial records, and work with the press, radio, films, local economic affairs, the harbor service, and welfare organizations. To support their propaganda and indoctrination work, the AO sent NS films, short wave radio sets, pamphlets, books, and even swastika banners.[23] In general, the established party branches abroad were small and of limited significance. In order to encourage party members to recruit new members, the Overseas Department in Hamburg gave everyone who had recruited five new members a copy of Hitler's

17 McKale, *Swastika Outside Germany*, 12–13.

18 Jürgen Müller, *Nationalsozialismus im Lateinamerika: Auslandsorganisation der NSDAP in Argentinien, Brasilien, Chile und Mexiko, 1931–1945* (Stuttgart, 1997), 95.

19 McKale, *Swastika Outside Germany*, 12–13; Emil Ehrich, *Die Auslands-Organisation der NSDAP* (Berlin, 1937), 8–9.

20 McKale, *Swastika Outside Germany*, 12.

21 Ibid., 120. See also Müller, *Nationalsozialismus im Lateinamerika*, 128–34 (collective biography of NSDAP members in Argentina, Brazil, and Chile).

22 McKale, *Swastika Outside Germany*, 12.

23 Ibid., 123.

Mein Kampf.[24] Over the years, however, the propaganda and political agitation showed results. By 1937, the Auslands-Organisation was administering approximately 30,000 Nazi party members, organized in roughly forty-nine Landesgruppen around the world.[25]

24 ISTA, 821/1-פ, circular, 2 Dec. 1932.
25 McKale, *Swastika Outside Germany*, 120, 122.

1 Establishing and Developing the NSDAP in Palestine

The beginning of the Landesgruppe Palestine was similar to that of the other NS groups abroad. German architect Karl Ruff began a regular correspondence with the Nazis in Germany in November 1931.[26] He had been born in Haifa in 1904 to parents who were part of the Temple Society. In the 1920s, he spent several years in Germany studying architecture and civil engineering *(Bauingenieurwesen)*; he returned to Haifa in 1929–30. A letter of December 1930 shows him to be a German patriot with an anti-Jewish, anti-Polish attitude, someone who hoped for Germany to increase its political strength. Ruff called Germany his beloved fatherland and referred to Palestine as "*our* beautiful Palestine." In 1930, he planned to found sports clubs in Haifa and Sarona to organize German youth in Palestine.[27] At the beginning of 1932, he requested application forms from Germany in order to officially join the NSDAP. He and one of his friends (Walter Aberle) were accepted as party members retroactive to 1 January 1932.[28] In July of that year, the Overseas Department encouraged Karl Ruff to introduce an organizational network for Nazis in Palestine.[29] Ruff and his friends were soon ambitiously engaged in lecturing on NS theories and recruiting new members, so 1932 can be seen as the beginning of the Nazi movement in Palestine.

In July of that year, Karl Ruff received a letter from the Overseas Department in Hamburg, Germany. Ernst Bohle, the future head of the Auslands-Organisation, wrote:

> It is very important to me to start a Nazi branch in Palestine. I am sure it will be possible to do so. My official in charge knows from his own experience that many racial German comrades settled down in the *Judenland* (the Jews' land). These Germans, who have been living far away from their fatherland for many years, should not be abandoned. It is the holy task of National Socialism to help and support them to maintain their German mind-set. I think the number of our fellow Germans is three thousand. They successfully established German settlements and erected German churches and schools. Not far from Jerusalem there is the German Colony SARONA with approximately two hundred people who strongly uphold *Deutschtum*. Most of the settlers come from Wuerttemberg. Not far from Haifa at the bottom of the Mount Carmel, there is another German colony with almost five hundred settlers. Should not Dr. Hoffmann, a son of old German settlers, help organize our movement of freedom? Just as in Haifa, there are also German colonies in Rephaim/Jerusalem and in

26 Correspondence 1931/32, ISTA, 821/1-פ; Rolf Balke, *Hakenkreuz im Heiligen Land. Die NSDAP-Landesgruppe Palästina* (Erfurt, 2001), 41, 79–80.

27 Schumacher Institute, P-RK-63, P-RK-66 (correspondence).

28 Rolf Balke, *Hakenkreuz im Heiligen Land*, 41.

29 Ernst Bohle, Hamburg to Karl Ruff, Haifa, 16 July 1932, ISTA, 821/1-פ.

> Wilhelma near Jaffa. You probably know everything which I have written to you; but my information is intended to stimulate your recruitment campaign. All the locations mentioned above have to be preserved for us, especially in the coming Third Reich.[30]

At this time, six Palestine-Germans (*Palästina-Deutsche*) were members of the NSDAP, scattered in different areas such as the German colonies in Haifa, Bethlehem in the Galilee, Jaffa, and Jerusalem. The new NS group consisted of two women and four men: Walter Aberle, Karl Bez, Rudolf Gassmann, Gertrud Koch, Karl Ruff, and Maria Wohlfarth.[31]

Karl Ruff, the leading figure at that time, wrote to Bohle in September 1932 about the motivation of the very first party members in Palestine,

> The newly recruited, small circle feels loyal to our great movement. This loyalty is mainly based on their love for their homeland and the understanding that our fatherland greatly depends on unity and concord, especially to demonstrate its power abroad. They know that such unity can only be achieved by subordination under a responsible leader.[32]

Ruff also informed Bohle about a gathering of the party members on the day of the *Reichstagswahl* (election) in November 1932. The party members had come together in Haifa to hear the election results on the radio, arriving from Jerusalem,

---

30 Ibid., "Es liegt mir viel daran, besonders in Palästina eine Landesgruppe ins Leben zu rufen, und dies ist möglich. Aus eigener Erfahrung weiss mein Sachbearbeiter, dass in dem Judenland sich viele völkische Volksgenossen angesiedelt haben, und gerade diese Deutschen, die vom Vaterlande schon lange Jahre fern sind, dürfen nicht verlassen werden, und es ist die heilige Pflicht des Nationalsozialismus, dafür zu sorgen, dass diesen ihre Deutschgesinnung auch erhalten bleibt. Ich glaube, nicht fehl zu gehen, wenn ich die Zahl unserer Volksgenossen auf annähernd 3000 Kopf zähle. Diese haben es verstanden, deutsche Siedlungen erstehen zu lassen und deutsche Kirchen und Schulen zu bauen. Nicht weit entfernt von Jerusalem ist die deutsche Siedlung SARONA, die etwa 200 Kopf zählt; das Deutschtum wird dort immer sehr hoch gehalten. Die meisten Siedler sind Württemberger. Auch nicht weit entfernt von Haifa liegt eine etwa 500 Köpfe zählende deutsche Kolonie am Fuße des Karmelberges. Sollte denn Dr. Hoffmann dort, der doch ein Sohn alter deutscher Palästina-Siedler ist, nicht mit dazu beitragen können, unsere Freiheitsbewegung mit zu organisieren? Ebenso wie in Haifa sind deutsche Kolonien in Rephaim b/Jerusalem und in Wilhelma b/Jaffa.
Alles, was ich Ihnen hier schreibe, wissen Sie ja bestimmt auch, aber meine Mitteilungen sollen Ihnen neue Anregung geben zum Werben; denn alle die erwähnten Plätze müssen besonders im kommenden Dritten Reich uns erhalten bleiben."

31 Ibid.

32 Karl Ruff, Haifa, to Ernst Bohle, 30 Sept. 1932, ISTA, 821/1-פ: "Die Zugehörigkeit des bisher geworbenen kleinen Kreises zu unserer großen Bewegung gründet sich vor allem auf Liebe zum Vaterlande und dann auf die Erkenntnis, dass unserem Vaterlande Einigkeit, ganz besonders zum Zwecke der Macht nach außen hin, sehr not tut, und dass eine solche Einigkeit nur durch Unterordnung unter einen verantwortungsbewussten Führer zustande kommen kann."

Jaffa, and Bethlehem. Two members of the SA also joined this "radio meeting." Bohle from the Overseas Department in Hamburg (1932) wrote back to Ruff expressing his pleasure in hearing about this event.[33]

Six members were still too few to establish a local Nazi group (*Ortsgruppe*) or support point (*Stützpunkt*), since a local group was supposed to have at least twenty-five members.[34] Ruff decided to hold lectures on National Socialist issues in winter 1932 in order to attract more Germans to the NSDAP.[35] The German Society (*Deutscher Verein*) in Jaffa and the Schwarz family often hosted propaganda events as well.[36] After the Nazis' accession to power in 1933, the number of party members in Palestine increased.

In November 1933, Dr. Iven of the ministry of propaganda was sent to Palestine, where he gave speeches to Germans in Haifa, Jaffa-Sarona, and Jerusalem. He visited the German community in Jerusalem on November 16, and the next day gave a talk on "National Socialist Germany" at the Templers' community hall in Sarona.[37] Party membership was increasing; in Jerusalem, it had expanded to 30–50 persons.[38] Ludwig Buchhalter, head of the NS group in Jerusalem, informed Ruff about the successful evening with Dr. Iven, adding with delight that Dr. Rohrer,[39] an influential member of the Temple Society in Jerusalem, had become a member even before the propaganda meeting took place, and was a useful addition to the Nazi party in Palestine.[40]

In autumn 1933, the Auslands-Abteilung began developing a strong organizational network for Palestine with Karl Ruff nominated as confidential NS agent for Palestine (*Landesvertrauensmann*), an expression of gratitude for his early engagement on the behalf of the NSDAP in Palestine. The new position made Ruff head of the growing NS organization in the region which included Palestine, Transjordan, Syria, and Lebanon.[41] Due to the political situation and organizational problems (Palestine and Transjordan were under British rule, while Syria and Lebanon belonged to the French Mandate), this regulation was valid only

33 Ernst Wilhelm Bohle, Hamburg to Ruff, Haifa, 22 Nov. 1932, ISTA, 821/1-פ.

34 A support point was supposed to have seven members; Balke, *Hakenkreuz im Heiligen Land*, 47–48.

35 Ernst Wilhelm Bohle, Hamburg to Ruff, Haifa, 21 Oct. 1932, ISTA, 821/1-פ.

36 Balke, *Hakenkreuz im Heiligen Land*, 51.

37 *Die Warte des Tempels*, 15 Dec. 1933, 180.

38 The data varies from source to source. Cf. Monthly Report, NS support point in Jerusalem, Nov. 1933, ISTA, 821/5-פ; Buchholz to Ruff, 17 Nov. 1933, ISTA, 823/8-פ; Balke, *Hakenkreuz im Heiligen Land*, 51.

39 Probably Dr. Herbert Rohrer, see list of names, appendix.

40 Buchholz to Ruff, 17 Nov. 1933, ISTA, 823/8-פ.

41 Correspondence, 1933, ISTA, 823/8-פ; correspondence, Mar. 1934, ISTA, 822/15-פ.

for a year, after which Syria and Lebanon received the status of a country group (Landesgruppe), separate from Palestine and Transjordan.[42]

When Ruff was nominated in November 1933, the NS groups in Haifa and Jaffa had enough members to be named a support group (Stützpunkt), led by Karl Ruff in Haifa and Cornelius Schwarz in Jaffa, both members of the Temple Society.[43] Encouraged by the new, local hierarchy, Ruff and Schwarz decided in a high-handed manner to upgrade the local support points to local groups, a decision later confirmed in 1934 by the Auslands-Organisation (AO).[44] Subsequently, the NS units in the German settlements in Haifa, Jaffa, Jerusalem, and Sarona were officially given the rank of local Nazi groups (Ortsgruppen). Support points (Stützpunkte) were named in Wilhelma and Bethlehem-Waldheim in the Galilee.[45] In October 1934 the NS groups Sarona and Jaffa were united to one local group and subsequently became the largest and most substantial NS group in Palestine.[46]

According to the monthly report of the NS group in Jerusalem, it had started in June 1933. As a result of Karl Ruff's encouragement and recruitment, Ludwig Buchhalter, H. Kirchner, and E. Herrmann of the German Colony in Jerusalem decided to join the NSDAP. In their twenties at the time, they were members of the Temple Society who had been born in Egypt or Palestine. Only a few days afterward, a *Mitgliedersperre* (ban on new members) was ordered in Germany and abroad, blocking the new, small NS group in Jerusalem from growing, but the ban was lifted in October or November 1933.[47] Following Dr. Iven's November propaganda mission, several new members joined the group. On December 4, 1933 the first *Pflichtabend* (compulsory evening) for NSDAP members took place in Jerusalem, attended by more than forty members and four friends. Party member Nikolai Schmidt gave a speech on the latest developments in Germany.[48]

Thus, by the end of 1933, Jerusalem had forty-two party members and four members of the Hitler Youth; at least 114 German Nazis could be found in the

---

42 Balke, *Hakenkreuz im Heiligen Land*, 51.
43 Ibid., 51–52.
44 Correspondence, AO, 28 Feb. 1934, ISTA, 822/15-פ.
45 Balke, *Hakenkreuz im Heiligen Land*, 51–53; Roland Löffler, "Die Gemeinden des Jerusalemsvereins in Palästina im Kontext des kirchlichen und politischen Zeitgeschehens in der Mandatszeit," in *Seht, wir gehen hinauf nach Jerusalem. Festschrift zum 150jährigen Jubiläum von Talitha Kumi und des Jerusalemsvereins*, edited by Almut Nothnagle, Hans-Jürgen Abromeit, and Frank Foerster (Leipzig, 2000), 185–212, 207.
46 Balke, *Hakenkreuz im Heiligen Land*, 53, 59.
47 Karl Ruff, circular, 4 Nov. 1933, YVA, R 3/25; Monthly Report, local NS group Jerusalem, n.d., ISTA, 821/5-פ; Balke, *Hakenkreuz im Heiligen Land*, 48, 53.
48 Monthly Report, local NS group in Jerusalem, Dec. 1933, ISTA, 821/5-פ.

whole of Palestine.[49] Membership lists at the Archives of Yad Vashem show the following figures[50]:

By the end of 1933:	
Jerusalem:	42 + 4 Hitler Youth
Jaffa:	24 + 3 Hitler Youth
Sarona:	29
Haifa:	19
Total:	114 + 7 Hitler Youth

After a morning gathering of the Sarona and Jaffa NS groups on *Heldengedenktag* (memorial day for heroes, February 25, 1934), the party members met again in the afternoon at the German consulate in Jaffa. The swearing-in ceremony saw the installation of Theodor Samuel Hoffmann as leader of the NS group in Sarona, Ewald Glenk as treasurer (*Kassenwart),* Oswald Knoll as secretary, Cornelius Schwarz as head of the NS group in Jaffa, Eugen Faber as his vice-leader and head of the Hitler Youth, Friedrich Bulach as treasurer in Jaffa, and Bruno Wieland as secretary and *Propaganda-Pressewart* (officer for press and propaganda).[51] The following month, the Nazi organization in Palestine recognized an additional thirty new party members, including fourteen people in Sarona, ten in Haifa, and six in Jerusalem.[52]

By the end of 1934, almost two hundred Germans in Palestine had received their party membership books, including employees of the German consulates like Martha Eppinger and Marie-Luise Hess, who had applied for party membership in 1933.[53] Templers, Kirchlers, and a few Protestants and Catholics belonged as well.[54] The entire NS leadership in Palestine was recruited from the Temple Society except for Eugen Faber, leader of the Hitler Youth, and Dr. Kurt Hegele, the

49 Membership lists, containing the names of party members and applicants, YVA, R3/25.
50 Ibid.
51 Report by the local NS groups Sarona and Jaffa on the events of Feb. 1934, ISTA, 822/15-פ; Karl Ruff to the local NS groups in Palestine, 21 and 22 Feb. 1934, ISTA, 822/15-פ.
52 Karl Ruff, correspondence, 7 Mar. 1934, ISTA, 822/15-פ.
53 ISTA, 822/15-פ; YVA, R 3/25.
54 Kirchler were former members of the Temple Society who had rejoined the German Protestant denomination in 1885–86; see E. Jakob Eisler, "'Kirchler' im Heiligen Land. Die evangelischen Gemeinden in den württembergishchen Siedlungen Palästinas," in *Dem Erlöser der Welt zur Ehre. Festschrift zum hundertjährigen Jubiläum der Einweihung der evangelischen Erlöserkirche in Jerusalem*, edited by Karl-Heinz Ronecker (Leipzig, 1998), 81–100.

representative of the *Nationalsozialistischer Lehrerbund* (NSLB, National Socialist Teachers' Alliance).[55]

In 1935, Temple Society member Cornelius Schwarz replaced Karl Ruff. Under his leadership, the Nazi branch in Palestine underwent political and organizational changes. Ambitious and very loyal to Hitler's policies, the new leader used his position and power to turn the German settlements into an outpost of the Third Reich in Palestine. He set the rules and goals for his *Landeskreis* (regional group) and dominated its activities, marking a turning point in the history of Palestine's NS organization.[56] In the same year (1935), the German Consul General, Heinrich Wolff, was obliged to give up his position because he was married to a Jew. He was replaced by Walter Doehle, a loyal Nazi who cooperated with Cornelius Schwarz and gave more attention to the NS groups than to the German Christian groups in Palestine.[57]

Under Schwarz's aegis, organizational improvements were made. His recommendations of Alfred Hoenig as support point leader (Stützpunktleiter) of Wilhelma and Hans Sus as political leader of the united settlements of Bethlehem and Waldheim were accepted by the AO in Germany. By the end of 1936, the NS group in Wilhelma counted twenty-two party members, with eighteen in Bethlehem-Waldheim.[58] Schwarz's engagement for the NSDAP was so successful that the regional NS group Palestine (*Landeskreis Palästina*) was upgraded to the rank of a NS country group (Landesgruppe) on Hitler's birthday in 1937, and the support points Wilhelma and Bethlehem-Waldheim officially became Ortsgruppen with Sus and Hoenig as their leaders (Ortsgruppenleiter).[59] In summer 1937, Schwarz even went to Germany to participate in the NSDAP Reichsparteitag. His participation was negatively perceived by the Jewish press in Palestine.[60]

In summary, the NS country group in Palestine showed the same organizational system as the home NSDAP in Germany: Each local NS group and support point had its own leader. Celebrations for new members were held and German national holidays were observed. Swastika flags and Nazi-style uniforms could be seen at such occasions. Camps and hiking tours were organized for the Hitler Youth program. German teachers joined the Nationalsozialistischer Lehrerbund, women became members of the Arbeitsgemeinschaft der Deutschen Frau im

55 Balke, *Hakenkreuz im Heiligen Land*, 79.
56 Ibid., 66–67.
57 Ibid., 67–68.
58 Ibid., 68.
59 Correspondence, 29 Apr. 1937, ISTA 18/19-חת; A. Dyck to C. Schwarz, 25 June 1937, ISTA, 821/11-פ; Balke, *Hakenkreuz im Heiligen Land*, 69.
60 Balke, *Hakenkreuz im Heiligen Land*, 68.

Ausland (AGdFA, Work Group of the German Woman Abroad), and employed persons participated in the Deutsche Arbeitsfront (DAF, German Labor Front). Winter Relief collections (Winterhilfe) were organized to support needy Germans. National Socialist books, brochures, and pamphlets were distributed throughout Palestine. Nazi films and shortwave radio sets that could receive broadcasts from Germany were sent out by the AO.[61]

It is clear that Palestine-Germans were being offered many avenues to participation in the goals of the Third Reich.

61 McKale, *Swastika Outside Germany*, 122f; Balke, *Hakenkreuz im Heiligen Land*, 56–58, see also YVA: R3/11, R3/18, R3/26; *Evangelisches Gemeindeblatt* (May 1933): 38; *Palestine Post*, 2 May 1934, 7; 2 May 1935, 1; 23 Sept. 1935, 5; 3 May 3, 1936, 12; *Die Warte des Tempels*, 15 Oct. 1935, 149; 31 May 1938, 76.

2 Propaganda Activities

Speeches, lectures, and propaganda agents

As the number of party members was still very low at the end of 1932, Ruff decided to hold lectures in order to attract Germans to the NSDAP.[62] Numerous informational talks and publicity campaigns were conducted in Wilhelma, Jaffa, and Sarona in spring 1934.[63] The German Society (Deutscher Verein) in Jaffa and the Schwarz family often hosted such publicity evenings.[64] Erwin Schwarz, son of Cornelius Schwarz and a leading NSDAP figure in Cairo, spoke on "Hitler's German Mission" at the Templer community hall in Jaffa, attended by Templers from Haifa, Jaffa, Sarona, Wilhelma, and Jerusalem.[65] On January 9, 1936, Dr. Richard Hoffmann lectured on the Nuremberg Laws in Sarona, pointing out the hostility and wrong interpretation with which the legislation had been received.[66] Recruitment meetings were held not only for the NSDAP but also for its related groups and organizations. The German Labor Front (Deutsche Arbeitsfront [DAF]) invited Wilhelm Baumert of the NS group in Jaffa to speak in order to encourage all party members in Haifa to join the DAF.[67]

Campaign efforts were supported by the Reichsminister for Propaganda, who sent specially trained agents to Palestine to recruit new members. Over the next few years, the following agents were authorized to conduct NS propaganda among the Germans in Palestine: Fritz Wegebauer, Ernst Riehl, Rolf Jordau, Peter Wuest, Kurt Daumer, Georg von Kolst in Haifa; Hans Dunkel, Erich Arens, Walter Mehrer, Richard Groehl, and Paul Gregor in Jerusalem; Willy Menzel, Hans Menger, Kurt Gruner, Ernst Obertuer, Bernt Frieder, and Karl Dreher in Jaffa.[68]

Dr. Iven, mentioned earlier, arrived in Palestine from Kabul, and gave talks in Jerusalem, Sarona, and other places. One of his speeches was titled "National Socialist Germany" (Das nationalsozialistische Deutschland).[69] Reverend Krause was also sent from Germany; on April 23, 1934, he spoke at the sports club in Jerusalem on "The Ideological Basis of National Socialism" (Die weltanschaulichen

62 Ernst Bohle to Karl Ruff, 21 Oct. 1932, ISTA, 821/1-פ.

63 Karl Ruff, correspondence, Mar.–Apr. 1934, YVA, R 3/25.

64 Rolf Balke, *Hakenkreuz im Heiligen Land. Die NSDAP-Landesgruppe Palästina* (Erfurt, 2001), 51.

65 *Die Warte des Tempels*, 31 Aug. 1934, 127.

66 *Die Warte des Tempels*, 29 Feb. 1936, 31.

67 Wilhelm Baumert to Oskar Beck, 7 Jan. 1937, ISTA, 821/11-פ.

68 British Public Record Office London, Foreign Office (henceforth, BPRO, FO) 371/21887.

69 *Die Warte des Tempels*, 15 Dec. 1933: 180; Balke, *Hakenkreuz im Heiligen Land*, 51.

Grundlagen des Nationalsozialismus). Two days later, he lectured before the local NS group in Sarona, considered a well-attended and succesful evening.[70]

Guest speakers from Germany were invited to Palestine on German holidays. In December 1935, a circular sent to German missionary organizations and consulates informed them that the travel costs of guest speakers would be covered by the AO, while further expenses for accommodation, meals, and other things were to be covered by the local NS group.[71]

NS pamphlets and books

NS literature and German newspapers were also distributed among Palestine-Germans in order to spread the ideology of the Third Reich. Such propaganda material was usually shipped by the AO to a port in Palestine, although it was often met with obstruction by British custom officers and Jewish dock-workers.[72] Once the NS literature had reached the German settlers, it was widely circulated. Hans Frank, assisted by his daughter Hulda, for example, passed NS literature to his friends and neighbors in an attempt to convince them of the virtues of National Socialism and persuade them to join the new movement, yet in October 1933, he noted that there were only a few Germans in Palestine who felt close to the Nazi movement, the rest being hostile or indifferent.[73] Cornelius Schwarz circulated his newspapers, and copied articles to send to various people.[74] Hermann Schneller, the director of the Syrian Orphanage, was very active in distributing letters, bills, and delivery notes throughout Palestine. Nazi party members received a ten percent reduction if they ordered their books and pamphlets at the Syrian Orphanage bookstore on Mamilla Road in Jerusalem.[75] Sheets and letterhead of the local NSDAP were printed at Schneller's print shop.[76] Special material concerning official party issues and information for speakers was ordered from the Overseas Department of the NSDAP by Ludwig Buchhalter, the chairman of the NS group in Jerusalem, and by Karl W. Ehmann, the vice-chairman of the NS group in Sarona.[77]

---

70 Monthly Report, local NS group in Jerusalem, April 1934, ISTA, 821/5-פ; *Die Warte des Tempels*, 31 May 1934, 77–78.

71 Correspondence, 23 Dec. 1935, ISTA, 497/1049-פ.

72 Correspondence, 23 Feb. 1934, ISTA, 822/15-פ; Balke, *Hakenkreuz im Heiligen Land*, 50.

73 Hans Frank to Mr. Seiz, Mergentheim, 25 Oct. 1933, ISTA, 3160/9-פ.

74 Balke, *Hakenkreuz im Heiligen Land*, 50.

75 YVA, R3/26.

76 YVA, R3/18, R3/25, R3/26.

77 Letter of the Overseas Department, 28 Feb. 1934 and order (*Bestellung*) of 18 Feb. 1934, ISTA, 822/15-פ.

The YMCA, which had opened in Jerusalem in 1933, became the locus of a quarrel between its German and Jewish members.[78] *Die Warte des Tempels* reported in February 1935 that Germans, supported by Arab members, insisted on having a regular subscription to the *Völkischer Beobachter* in the reading room. Jews opposed it on grounds of the paper's blatant antisemitism. In the end, the Germans gave in and the journal was not ordered.[79]

Haifa's local group had a library of some one hundred volumes of NS literature. Some items were addressed to German women, such as *Den deutschen Frauen* by the Reich Women's Leader Gertrud Scholtz-Klink, and *Die Frauenfrage und ihre Lösung durch den Nationalsozialismus* by Paula Siber.[80]

Franz Reichert of the *Deutsches Nachrichtenbüro* (DNB, German News Agency) provided typed transcripts of German radio news to be posted on information boards at the German consulates, the Temple Society colonies, and other public locations.

The "Volksempfänger"

As the majority of Germans did not have radios on which to follow the German news, they were dependent on local and foreign services. Officials in Germany feared that their fellow Germans abroad would be influenced by the news service of their enemies.[81]Thus the "people's receiver" (*Volksempfänger*), a low-cost radio, was introduced in 1933 in order to keep Germans living abroad informed about events in the Reich, to encourage them with political speeches, and to cheer them with German songs and marches; in short, to help maintain German pride and identification with the homeland wherever they lived. Naturally, the broadcasts available portrayed non-German media reports as lies not to be believed.[82] The German Protestant Church, especially its Overseas Department (*Kirchliches Außenamt*) promoted the purchase of the sets by Protestant organizations abroad, as well as German churches, schools, clubs, and restaurants. As fellow Germans (*Volksgenossen*) gathered to listen to Nazi speeches, their sense of a common German destiny would be strengthened.[83]

---

78 *EvGB* (May 1933): 38; ISTA: 497/1049-פ.

79 *Die Warte des Tempels*, 15 Feb. 1935, 19–20.

80 Schooling report by G. Ruff, 28 Feb. 1939, and list of books, Mar. 1939, ISTA, 821/9-פ.

81 Letter of Consul General in Jerusalem, 16 Feb. 1935, ISTA, 3160/9-פ; *Front der Heimat*, part 2, published by the *Gaupropagandaamt* Oberdonau, Linz (Oct. 1939).

82 Fritz H. Reimesch, "Auslanddeutschtum und Deutscher Rundfunk," in *Auslanddeutschtum und evangelische Kirche, Jahrbuch 1935*, edited by Ernst Schubert (Munich, 1935), 69–83.

83 Ibid., 76, 82.

Palestine-Germans loved to listen to the Volksempfänger. In the 1930s, they followed political events in Germany with great interest, and often gathered to hear speeches by Hitler, Goebbels, Rudolf Hess, and other Nazi officials.[84] Cornelius Schwarz opined that Hitler's speeches on the radio were like a true Christian service.[85] On the occasion of the Saar Plebiscite in 1935, students of the German school in Sarona gathered around a radio to hear the results of the referendum, followed by speeches by Hitler and Goebbels and ending with the *Saarlied* and the German anthem.[86] The NS group in Jerusalem also waited excitedly by a radio for the announcement of the Saar ballot, as reported in their monthly report:

> And then, it was announced. With growing excitement and enthusiasm, the rapt audience heard what the administrator of the Saarland reported to the Führer, what the Führer and Reichsminister Goebbels had to say at this historical moment. Everywhere, you met Germans; you saw happy faces and heard cheers and congratulations.[87]

NS films

NS groups abroad were responsible for most of their own propaganda. The AO augmented this by sending them short wave radio sets and Nazi films such as *Triumph of the Will*.[88] The first film evening of the NSDAP in Palestine took place in summer 1935. Inhabitants of the German colonies were invited to attend the German Evening (Deutscher Abend) at the Orient movie theater in Jerusalem, owned by the architect Gottlob Bäuerle.[89] The event was announced in the newsletter of the Lutheran Church of the Redeemer in Jerusalem, and Germans from all the colonies except Haifa participated. The NS movies screened that evening included *Unser Führer eröffnet das Winterhilfswerk*, *Hindenburg-Gedächtnisfilm*, and

84 See *EvGB* (May 1933): 38; *Die Warte des Tempels*, 31 Jan. 1938, 16; *Die Warte des Tempels*, 30 Nov. 1937, 185–86; Paul Sauer, *Uns rief das Heilige Land. Die Tempelgesellschaft im Wandel der Zeit* (Stuttgart, 1985), 252.

85 Balke, *Hakenkreuz im Heiligen Land*, 44.

86 *Die Warte des Tempels*, 15 Feb. 1935, 19–20.

87 "Und es kam! Mit wachsender Spannung und Begeisterung vernahmen die Lauschenden, was der Saarbevollmächtigte dem Führer meldete, was der Führer und der Reichsminister Goebbels in dieser historischen Stunde zu sagen hatten. Überall, wo man Deutsch traf, sah man strahlende Gesichter, hörte man frohe Zurufe und Glückwünsche." Monthly Report of the local NS group, Jerusalem, 31 Jan. 1935, ISTA, 821/5-פ.

88 Donald M. McKale, *The Swastika Outside Germany* (Kent State, Ohio, 1977), 123.

89 Sauer, *Uns rief das Heilige Land*, 248; David Kroyanker, *The German Colony and Emek Refaim Street* (Jerusalem, 2008), 59–72.

Unser Führer. Furthermore, poems were recited by members of the HJ and BDM; there were musical performances by choirs and solo singers, as well as lectures added to the program. The party member Haigis organized the entire event, in which about 500 Germans took part.[90]

In January 1936, an evening with silent movies was organized by the NSDAP in Sarona; the film projector being provided by the Syrian Orphanage in Jerusalem. Vicar Daxer spoke some words of welcome to the audience.[91] In February 1936 the Nazi film *Eva* was screened in Tel Aviv.[92]

In 1939, Gottlieb Ruff, the *Schulungswart* (training officer) of the NS group in Haifa, complained in his report about the difficulties in training the NS members, in part because there were often delays in delivering the documentary films provided by the AO. As a result, many Germans were returning to the Jewish movie theaters. To prevent this, he suggested improving the delivery system, and offering movies for entertainment and the *Wochenschau*.[93] The same year (April 1939), Consul Dr. Melchers from the local NS group in Haifa even sent a film to the Nazi branch in Beirut.[94]

Screening of Nazi movies and the spread of NS propaganda via journals, movies, pamphlets, and other means caused great concern among the Jewish population.[95] Subsequently, German movies were banned from Jewish movie theaters.[96] A general censorship of German films was discussed in 1939 but not carried out. The Hebrew daily newspaper, *Haboker*, reported "that the Palestine Administration has agreed to the request of German residents of Palestine not to censor German propaganda films intended for showing exclusively to German audiences in German residential centers."[97] A heated discussion in the press in Palestine frequently raised the question of whether the NS campaign was confined to Germans only. While in April 1936 the British concluded there was no indication of Nazi propaganda spreading outside the German community of Palestine, news reports and articles by the *Palestine Post* and the *Palestinian Telegraphic Agency* (P.T.A.) drew a different picture.[98] The P.T.A. informed its readers on March 10, 1936 that two agents of the NSDAP had left Germany for Palestine

90 Monthly Report, local NS group in Jerusalem, July 1935, ISTA, 821/5-פ; *EvGB* (Aug. 1935): 87.
91 *Die Warte des Tempels*, 29 Feb. 1936, 31.
92 *Palestine Post*, 2 Feb. 1936, 10.
93 G. Ruff, Schooling report, 28 Feb. 1939, ISTA, 821/9-פ.
94 Correspondence, 27 Apr. 1939 about the film *Petermann ist dagegen*, ISTA, 821/9-פ.
95 *Palestine Post*, 13 Aug. 1934, 5; 28 Sep. 1934, 5; 26 Sep. 1934, 2; 1 Jan. 1935, 3; 2 Feb. 1936, 10; 24 Mar. 1936, 5; 17 May 1936, 2; 24 July 1939, 1–2.
96 *Die Warte des Tempels*, 30 Apr. 1933, 62.
97 Quoted by *Palestine Post*, 24 July 1939, 2.
98 *Palestine Post*, 22 Apr. 1936, 1; cf. Balke, *Hakenkreuz im Heiligen Land*, 128–29.

in order to conduct propaganda among Germans and Arabs in Palestine.[99] The same month the *Palestine Post* announced, "English-German-Arabic Newspaper in Palestine. Dr. Reichert [the representative of the DNB] obtained permission to publish a two-page daily newspaper in English, German, and Arabic. The publication will address itself to Germans outside Palestine."[100] In May 1936, the *Palestine Post* reported that Dr. Paul Zobeck (or Zubak[101]), a converted Austrian Jew and alleged Nazi agent, was probably engaged in spreading Nazi propaganda in Palestine. He faced deportation on charges of illegal entry into the country.[102] In 1939, it was reported that a large number of copies of Hitler's *Mein Kampf* in Arabic had been imported from Egypt into Palestine. The translation was made in Egypt for a publisher who was said to be supported by the German Ministry for Propaganda. In this special edition, Hitler's assertion that Egyptians and Arabs were "non-Aryans" had been deleted.[103]

NS propaganda was conducted by ambitious, eager Nazis and supported by the AO in Germany, and mainly aimed at recruiting more Germans as members for the new branch in Palestine. As National Socialism was obsessed with the "Aryan race," Arabs and Jews were excluded from joining the party. The lectures, brochures, movies, and radio broadcasts brought significant results. Party membership grew from a mere six members in 1932 to more than four hundred in 1939.[104] Over the years, an NS network was established in Palestine mirroring the NS hierarchical and organizational system in Germany.

---

99 *Palestine Post*, 12 Mar. 1936, 2.

100 *Palestine Post*, 24 Mar. 1936, 5.

101 Bundesarchiv, Berlin (henceforth, BArch), R 58/6401, Bl. 298-304: Dr. Paul Zubak and his partner Margarete née Taumann were arrested in May 1936 by police officers in Tel Aviv. They confessed to being agents agitating among Arabs. They had been living in Palestine (Nazareth and Tel Aviv) since 1933.

102 *Palestine Post*, 17 May 1936, 2.

103 *Palestine Post*, 16 Jan. 1939, 2.

104 See appendix, list of names.

3 NS Groups and Events

Regular meetings and celebrations

Every dictatorial organization, regardless of its religious or political program, tries to infiltrate and control the daily life of its members. It keeps the member busy with regular meetings, new celebrations, and educational programs. It "occupies" existing national and religious holidays and gives them new meanings and thus did the NSDAP in Germany and in its country groups abroad.

In Palestine, regular meetings were introduced once or twice a month, including *Pflichtabende* (compulsory evenings), *Kameradschaftsabende* (social evenings), *Schulungsabende* (training programs), and *Gesangsabende* (singing evenings). The Pflichtabende were intended for members, but were occasionally opened to friends as well. The program presented lectures on topics such as "Das Neue Deutschland und die anderen" (The new Germany and the others) and "Rassenkunde des Deutschen Volkes" (Racial history of the German people). Patriotic National Socialist speeches were delivered, along with other specific topics, like first aid. In addition, there were, of course, discussions and decisions on party affairs.[105] In May 1934, a party applicant, Mrs. Walla, lectured in Jerusalem on the *Reichsarbeitsdienst* (State Labor Service) and its positive effects on the German economy and morality.[106] In October, Dr. Gmelin from the German Deaconesses' Hospital in Jerusalem lectured to about three hundred people on the "Gesetz zur Verhütung erbkranken Nachwuchses" (The law to prevent offspring that suffer from a hereditary disease).[107] In Haifa, Gottlieb Ruff, the Schulungswart (training officer), was responsible for the program of historical topics from the National Socialist viewpoint, such as "Austria in German History," "The Second Reich," and "International Jewry."[108] His sessions also included films. Compulsory and social meetings often took place at German schools and sports clubs.[109]

In Germany itself, new national holidays were introduced, and even Christian holidays were given an NS ideological slant as part of the effort to influence

---

105 Report of the NSDAP local group in Jerusalem on the events of Jan. 1934, and of the local group in Sarona-Jaffa on the events of Feb. 10, 1934, ISTA, 822/15-פ; Monthly Reports of the local NS group in Jerusalem 1933 to 1935; Report of Feb.–Apr. 1935, local NS group of Jerusalem and meeting of Jerusalem's NS officials on Jan. 31, 1935, ISTA, 821/5-פ.

106 Monthly report of May 1934, local NS group in Jerusalem, ISTA, 821/5-פ.

107 Special Report of the local NS group, Jerusalem, 23 Oct. 1934, ISTA, 821/5-פ.

108 G. Ruff, Education report, 28 Feb. 1939, ISTA, 821/9-פ.

109 Letter to Ruff, 3 Feb. 1934, ISTA, 822/15-פ; Monthly Reports, local NS group in Jerusalem, Nov. 1933–Dec. 1934, ISTA, 821/5-פ.

every aspect of German public and private life. Annual celebrations of the new National Socialist holidays stabilized this NS ideology.[110] German Nazis in Palestine observed these new holidays too, thus expressing and proving their loyalty to their fatherland.[111] According to archival material and community newsletters, they observed the following days:

- January 30: *Tag der Machtergreifung* (Day of Hitler's seizure of power)
- March 16: *Heldengedenktag* (Memorial day of heroes), formerly the *Volkstrauertag*, a national day of mourning
- April 20: *Führers Geburtstag* (Hitler's birthday)
- May 1: *Tag der deutschen Arbeit* (National labor day)
- June 21 (23): *Tag der Sommersonnenwende* (Summer solstice)
- September: *Reichsparteitag in Nürnberg* (Reich party rally in Nuremberg),
- Beginning of October: *Erntedankfest* (Harvest thanksgiving day)
- December 21: *Wintersonnenwende* (Winter solstice)
- December 24: *Volksweihnacht* (The people's Christmas)

The journal of the Temple Society described the festivities of May 1, 1934, celebrated as the *Fest aller Deutschen* (All-German celebration) in Jerusalem and Jaffa by the German community in Palestine. Masses of Germans attended the afternoon receptions of German representatives. Military marches were played at the German consulate in Jaffa. Consul Timotheus Wurst gave a speech praising Hitler's achievements for Germany and finished with *Sieg Heil!* Headmaster Hugo Ehmann took the floor and warned against Marxism and Socialism.[112] The day closed, as always with the singing of the *Deutschlandlied* and *Horst-Wessel-Lied*:

> Hold high the banner! Close the hard ranks serried!
> S.A. marches on with steady stride.
> Comrades, by Red Front and Reaction killed, are buried.
> But march with us in spirit at our side.
>
> Gangway! Gangway! Now for the Brown battalions!
> For the Storm Troopers clear roads o'er land!
> The Swastika gives hope to our entranced millions.
> The day of freedom and bread's at hand.
>
> The trumpet blows its shrill and final blast!
> Prepared for war and battle here we stand.

---

110 Cf. Hannes Kremer, "Neuwertung 'überlieferter' Brauchformen?" in *Die neue Gemeinschaft* 3 (1937).

111 *Die Warte des Tempels*, 15 Nov. 1936: 167; 30 Sep. 1938: 137–38; 31 May 1934: 77–78. *Neueste Nachrichten aus dem Morgenlande* (henceforth *NNM*) (Apr. 1936): 8.

112 *Die Warte des Tempels*, 31 May 1934: 77–78.

Soon Hitler's banners will wave unchecked at last.
The end of German slav'ry in our land![113]

Die Warte des Tempels reported that "the Jewish mob on the street" had gathered outside of the consulate, shouting "*Nieder! Nieder*!" (Down! Down!) to disrupt the singing.[114] The paper also reported on a field trip taken by German settlers from Haifa, Bethlehem, and Waldheim. The trip and reception were intended to strengthen Palestine-Germans' identity and to demonstrate their loyalty and closeness to their homeland.[115]

The following year, May 1 was observed in Jerusalem in a morning ceremony conducted by the Hitler Youth. In the afternoon, Germans from Jerusalem and the surrounding area gathered at the consulate to celebrate the national holiday with the representative of the Reich and the NSDAP. As with previous celebrations, there were speeches; *Sieg Heil!* was shouted; and the *Deutschlandlied* and *Horst-Wessel-Lied* were sung, followed by refreshments in the consulate garden.[116] A special police unit was sent to the German consulate on which the swastika flag had been hoisted.[117] The NSDAP in Palestine had suggested that German companies, shops, and schools should be closed on May 1; Cornelius Schwarz, the *Wirtschaftsstellenleiter* (economic adviser) reported to the Außenhandelsamt in Berlin that the Firm Aberle was the only German company open on May 1, 1935.[118]

In 1936, Cornelius Schwarz, then head of the NSDAP of Palestine, wrote to the German Consul General Doehle, proposing that May 1 could probably be celebrated in the courtyard of the Auguste Victoria Foundation on the Mount of Olives. Doehle forwarded invitations to Provost Rhein, Sister Theodore Barkhausen of the German Deaconesses' Hospital, Sister Bertha Harz of Talitha Kumi, and Dr. Franz Reichert of the German News Agency (Deutsches Nachrichtenbüro, DNB). In the end festivities took place in the afternoon at the sports club in the German Colony, because of the poor public transportation at that time to the Auguste Victoria site. Earlier that day, the Protestant minister and missionary Jentzsch had held a festive service at his church, to which the members of the NSDAP had been invited.[119]

113 Louis L. Snyder, *Encyclopedia of the Third Reich* (New York, 1976), 171, translated by Snyder.
114 *Die Warte des Tempels*, 31 May 1934: 77–78; Paul Sauer, *Uns rief das Heilige Land. Die Tempelgesellschaft im Wandel der Zeit* (Stuttgart, 1985), 236.
115 *Die Warte des Tempels*, 31 May 1934: 77–78.
116 Report of the local NS group in Jerusalem, May 1935, ISTA, 821/5-פ.
117 *Palestine Post*, 2 May 1935, 1.
118 Cornelius Schwarz to Außenhandelsamt, Berlin, 9 Mar. 1935, ISTA, 821/6-פ.
119 Correspondence, 13, 21, 23, and 28 Apr. 1936, ISTA, 497/1049-פ; Letter, 28 Apr. 1936, ISTA 530/1457B-פ; *Palestine Post*, 3 May 1936, 12.

In 1937, the Tag der Deutschen Arbeit (German labor day) was celebrated in the little forest near Bir-Salem, attended by six hundred persons. Consul General Doehle had sent invitations to Provost Rhein, Jakob Imberger of the Temple Society, Minister Schneller of the Syrian Orphanage, Minister Jentzsch, Deaconess Theodore Barkhausen, Margarete Ribbach, and Sister Constantina Herrmann. Germans interested in participating could register at the Lutheran Church of the Redeemer or the Syrian Orphanage in Jerusalem. The May 1 celebration of 1937 was a joint event of the Germans from Jerusalem, Jaffa-Sarona, and Wilhelma.[120] In 1938 and 1939, the May 1 activities took place in the community hall of the Temple Society or the German sports clubs in Jerusalem.[121]

January 30 commemorated Hitler's assumption of power, and among Palestine-Germas was considered the "birthday of the Third Reich."[122] The AO in December 1935 had ordered that this holiday also be observed by Germans abroad.[123] Germans in Palestine had observed this anniversary already in 1934 with a patriotic party at the Templers' community hall in Sarona, decorated with flags of the "new Germany" and NS banners. The hall was packed and included Germans and NSDAP members from Jerusalem. Cornelius Schwarz opened with the official greetings, followed by Headmaster Hugo Ehmann of the German School in Jaffa-Sarona, who gave an inspiring speech on the day's importance as the beginning of the new German nation. He reminded the audience of the great achievements of the Nazi party. Consul Wurst from Jaffa took the floor to praise the new order of the NSDAP. SA songs were sung and the meeting concluded with the singing of *Deutschland, Deutschland über alles* and the *Horst-Wessel-Lied*.[124]

The Frank family hosted the celebrations in Haifa, meant "to commemorate the national uprising of January 30, 1933."[125] Occasionally, the holiday was called the anniversary of "the national revolution" and "the national uprising of the German people."[126] A huge swastika, a picture of the Führer, and banners with NS slogans decorated the room.[127] In 1935, the anniversary of Hitler's ascent to power was celebrated at the sports club in the German Colony in Jerusalem, where the NS films *Unser Volkskanzler* and *Die Saar* were shown.[128] In the following year, the

---

120 Correspondence, 16 Apr. and 4 May 1937, ISTA, 497/1049-פ.

121 Consul General, Jerusalem, circular, 24 Apr. 1939, ISTA, 497/1049-פ.

122 *Die Warte des Tempels*, 28 Feb. 1934, 29–30.

123 Letter, 23 Dec. 1935, ISTA, 497/1049-פ.

124 *Die Warte des Tempels*, 28 Feb. 1934, 29–30; Report, NSDAP local group in Jerusalem, on events in Jan. 1934, ISTA, 822/15-פ.

125 Announcement, 19 Jan. 1934, ISTA, 822/15-פ.

126 Report to the press, NSDAP group Sarona-Jaffa, Jan. 1934, ISTA, 822/15-פ.

127 Ibid.

128 Monthly Report, local NS group, Jerusalem, 31 Jan. 1935, ISTA, 821/5-פ.

local NS group in Sarona met at the community hall of the Temple Society, which was filled with Hitler Youth members and the League of German Girls (Bund Deutscher Mädchen, BDM). As usual, the hall was decorated with flags and pictures of the Führer, and the evening began with a procession of flags and military music, followed by patriotic speeches and German national songs.[129] Likewise, the Nazis of Jerusalem gathered at the community hall of the Temple Society in the German Colony in Jerusalem. The invitation had called all fellow Germans (Volksgenossen) to come and participate.[130]

Hitler's birthday on April 20 was also observed in Palestine.[131] In 1936, party members in Jerusalem celebrated the Führer's birthday with songs performed by the choir of the Syrian Orphanage. Ludwig Buchhalter, the NS group leader in Jerusalem, gave the greeting, and read a few chapters of *Mit Hitler an die Macht* by Otto Dietrich. Following the official celebration, a casual meeting took place at the German sports club.[132] A week earlier, Cornelius Schwarz had written to Consul General Doehle in which he suggested giving all students a day off.[133] Another year, it was recommended to keep German shops, companies, and workshops closed in order to demonstrate solidarity with the German fatherland.[134] Hitler's fiftieth birthday in 1939 was given special attention in Palestine, as reported in the *Palestine Post*. Music and National Socialist speeches were part of the celebration in the German Colony neighborhood of Jerusalem. Local residents were reinforced by numerous visitors; some specially arrived from Germany. Ludwig Buchhalter observed that "The number attending the reception was probably equal to the number of able-bodied Germans living in the Jerusalem district, as it is scarcely thinkable that any could stay away from the Führer's birthday party."[135]

Harvest Thanksgiving Day in honor of German farmers was set in October. The Palestine-Germans observed this feast not only as their traditional Christian holiday but also as part of NS ideology. The Lutheran Church of the Redeemer newsletter, the *Evangelisches Gemeindeblatt*, notes that in 1936, its members joined the local NS group to celebrate the Harvest Thanksgiving Day at the com-

---

129 *Die Warte des Tempels*, 29 Feb. 1936, 31.

130 Note, 23 Jan. 1936, ISTA, 497/1049-פ.

131 *Die Warte des Tempels*, Stuttgart, 31 May 1934, 77–79; Correspondence, Apr. 1936 and Apr. 1939, ISTA, 497/1049-פ; Friedrich Wagner to Johannes Pross, Haifa, 15 Apr. 1939, ISTA, 1046/18-פ.

132 Special report on the celebration of Hitler's birthday, local NS group, Jerusalem, 2 May 1934, ISTA, 821/5-פ.

133 Cornelius Schwarz to Consul General Doehle, 13 Apr. 1936, ISTA, 497/1049-פ.

134 Correspondence, 17 Apr. 1939, ISTA, 497/1049-פ.

135 *Palestine Post*, 21 Apr. 1939, 2.

munity hall of the Temple Society in Jerusalem.[136] *Die Warte des Tempels* reported that the Harvest Festival celebration was an expression of the Templers' solidarity and ties with the entire German people. On this occasion, Cornelius Schwarz and Dr. Richard Hoffmann of the German consulate expressed their enthusiasm about the new German Reich.[137] In Sarona, too, the holiday led to expressions of togetherness with the entire German people. The day began with a religious service, followed by outdoor gatherings in the afternoon.[138]

In 1937, the Templers' journal called the Harvest Thanksgiving Day the "Feast of the German Ethnic Community" (Fest der deutschen Volksgemeinschaft). Gotthilf Wagner spoke at the community hall in Sarona, noting the importance of the NS slogan "*Gemeinnutz kommt vor Eigennutz*" (Public interest goes before self-interest), asserting that it should motivate everyone to practice their Christian faith very sincerely.[139] He drew a parallel between the traditional Templer Thanksgiving and the new NS national holiday by emphasizing their common grounds and thus harmoniously combining religion and nationalism. That year, the Temple community began with their traditional morning service. In the afternoon, there were speeches, music, *Sieg Heil!* exclamations, and singing the German anthem. In the evening, people listened to Hitler's speech on the radio.[140] According to a letter of Cornelius Schwarz, this event was a joint celebration of Nazi members and Templers, attended by representatives of the consulate, the NSDAP, and the Temple Society, who gave speeches.[141]

Memorial services for those killed in World War I, the Heldengedenktag, were also significant occasions for the German community in Palestine.[142] An article in *Die Warte des Tempels* explained that both the National Socialists and Temple Society members remembered those who had lived and died for a certain idea; neither Hitler nor the Templers were ungrateful to their pioneers.[143] Before 1933 this was called the National Day of Mourning and was linked to the maintenance of German war cemeteries. The National Socialists gave it a new name and fixed the date to March 16, instead of the customary fifth Sunday before Easter.[144] At the cemeteries in Jerusalem (Zionsfriedhof), Sarona, and Nazareth, Germans gath-

---

136 *EvGB* (Nov. 1936): 122.
137 *Die Warte des Tempels*, 15 Nov. 1936, 167.
138 *Die Warte des Tempels*, 15 Nov. 1936, 167; 30 Sept. 1938, 137–38.
139 *Die Warte des Tempels*, 30 Nov. 1937, 184.
140 Ibid., 185–86.
141 Cornelius Schwarz, correspondence, 9 Sept. 1937, ISTA, 497/1049-פ.
142 *Die Warte des Tempels*, 15 Dec. 1933, 180, 15 Apr. 1938, 54–55; Karl Ruff to all local NS groups, 10 Nov. 1933, ISTA, 823/8-פ.
143 *Die Warte des Tempels*, 15 July 1939, 97–98.
144 Snyder, *Encyclopedia*, 168.

ered to remember those who had been killed in action, invited by the local NS groups, including the uniformed Hitler Youth. Their leaders delivered speeches and the music group of the Syrian Orphanage performed songs such as *Vom treuen Kameraden* (About the loyal comrade).[145]

The opening of the German war cemetery in Nazareth on June 30, 1935 was a great patriotic event for Palestine-Germans. About five hundred of them, including Templers, Protestants, Catholics, and representatives of the local Nazi party attended, along with Turkish and British representatives, officials of the British troops and police (*die Oberbefehlshaber der Britischen Truppen, die Britische Polizei*), members of the Palestine and Transjordan Navy, and the German Consul General from Beirut. Karl Ruff, who had initiated the NS network in Palestine, spoke in the name of the German NSDAP. Other speakers included Provost Ernst Rhein of the Lutheran Church of the Redeemer in Jerusalem and Consul General Wolff. The *Horst-Wessel-Lied* was sung, and a message was sent to the Führer.[146] A detailed report was printed in the Catholic *Nachrichten-Blatt für die Teilnehmer und Foerderer des Deutschen Vereins vom Hl. Lande* informing its readers that the German military cemetery in Nazareth was created as an impressive monument to memorialize the heroes of World War I.[147] Six months earlier, Cornelius Schwarz had reported that the *Volksbund Deutscher Kriegsgräberfürsorge* (German league for the care of war graves) had contracted the German company Oppermann Brothers for the project, and the firm had sent a German architect to monitor the ongoing work. However, Schwarz had learned from Nazi members Rubitschung and Carl Wieland that the work itself was done by non-German sub-contractors, and he was angry to find that the cemetery was to be completed by foreigners.[148]

Political events and German flags

In 1935, the Templer colonies and the German Protestant communities in Jerusalem, Haifa, Jaffa, Waldheim, and the Acre region strongly sympathized with national events in Germany. The return of the Saar region and the re-establishment of the Wehrmacht were received with great joy and pride. There was not one Tem-

145 Report of 25 Feb. 1934, ISTA 822/15-פ; Report of the *Heldengedenktag*, no date, ISTA, 821/5-פ; Letter, HJ leader in Palestine, 15 Mar. 1935, ISTA, 822/3-פ; *Die Warte des Tempels*, 30 Apr. 1936, 63, and 15 Apr. 1938, 54–55.

146 *Die Warte des Tempels*, 31 July 1935, 105–7; *Palestine Post*, 1 July 1935, 5; Report, local NS group, Jerusalem, June 1935, local NS group in Jerusalem ISTA, 821/5-פ.

147 *Nachrichten-Blatt für die Teilnehmer und Foerderer des Deutschen Vereins vom Hl. Lande* (Oct. 1935): 121–25.

148 C. Schwarz, Report, Dec. 1934, ISTA, 821/6-פ.

pler colony that did not celebrate this event, reported *Die Warte des Tempels.*[149] On the pro-German result of the Saar plebiscite, the churches in Jerusalem, Sarona, Jaffa, and Haifa rang their bells for almost half an hour to express their delight.[150] Students of the German school in Sarona gathered around a radio to hear the results, followed by speeches from Hitler and Goebbels, and ending with the *Saarlied* and the German anthem. German students were given a day off on the occasion of this "victory." German shops and workshops closed early, and German consulates hoisted the German flag, as did many private houses.[151]

In honor of the successful outcome, the local NS group in Haifa in cooperation with the German sports club invited the Temple Society to a festive evening. Flags, banners with *Deutsch ist die Saar* (the Saar is German), torches, and Hitler's portrait decorated the room. Speeches were delivered by the head of the Temple Society, Philipp Wurst, and Minister Oertzen (Haifa). *Deutschland, Deutschland über alles* was sung along with the Christian hymn *Grosser Gott wir loben dich*. The evening ended with *Sieg Heil!* acclamations, the *Horst-Wessel-Lied*, and a speech by Karl Ruff.[152]

In Jerusalem, the local NS group also observed the occasion.[153] People listened tensely to the radio, awaiting the announcement. Afterwards, the "German victory" was met with happy faces, cheers, and congratulations.[154] About three hundred Germans attended the Jerusalem "victory party" that included the usual patriotic speeches, poems, the *Deutschlandlied* and the *Horst-Wessel-Lied.*[155]

March 12, 1938 was the day of the Anschluss, when Austria was "reunited" with Germany. On this occasion, the manager of German Short Wave Broadcasting (*Kurzwellensender*) lectured at the Templers' community hall in Jerusalem about the goals and program of the Kurzwellensender and Hitler's NS ideology. Speaking of Hitler in Christian religious terms, he pointed out that Hitler loved his people and was willing to die for them. God chose him to guide the German nation; Hitler's idea was alive and would spread all over the world.[156] As with the return of the Saarland, the Anschluss was positively received by Palestine-Germans. Students got a day off, and the journal *Evangelisches Gemeindeblatt*

149 *NNM* (Apr. 1936): 8; *Die Warte des Tempels*, 15 Feb. 1935, 19–20.
150 *EvGB* (Mar. 1935): 25–26; *Die Warte des Tempels*, 15 Feb. 1935, 19–20.
151 *Die Warte des Tempels*, 15 Feb. 1935, 19–20.
152 Ibid.; see also *Die Warte des Tempels*, 15 Apr. 1935, 54; Report on *Saarfeier*, Haifa, 15 Jan. 1935, ISTA, 821/5-פ.
153 *EvGB* (Jan. 1935): 17–18.
154 Monthly Report, local NS group in Jerusalem, 31 Jan. 1935, ISTA, 821/5-פ.
155 Monthly Report, local NS group, Jerusalem, 31 Jan. 1935, ISTA, 821/5-פ.
156 *Die Warte des Tempels*, 31 Mar. 1938, 45–46.

published the text of a telegram by Bishop D. Heckel welcoming the Austrian Anschluss and promising to pray for the German people and Hitler.[157]

Reaction to the dramatic events in the local non-German population was varied: Arabs exhibited great admiration for Hitler and his regime, while Jews were upset about the Anschluss. The Jewish Agency asked the British to increase immediately the number of immigrant visas for Austrian Jews.[158]

A few weeks later, on April 9, 1938, a plebiscite on the Austrian Anschluss took place in Palestine, combined with a vote on Hitler's party: "Do you agree to the reunion of Austria with the German Reich carried out on March 13 and do you vote for the (Reichstag) list of our Führer, Adolf Hitler?"[159] For the first time, the Germans of Palestine could participate in the ballot. German and Austrian voters were taken by cars, motorcycles, and busses to the steamship *Milwaukee* (*Touristendampfer*) at the port of Haifa, accompanied and protected by British military vehicles. The ship was flagged and the voters were welcomed aboard with music. Sailing away from the port for a few hours, the balloting began, with the overwhelming majority of the Germans and Austrians in Palestine voting in favor of Hitler. Six nays and one invalid voice were cast.[160] After announcing the results, the voters enthusiastically shouted "*Sieg Heil* to Germany and its creator Adolf Hitler!"[161]

On March 19, 1933, the swastika banner and the black-white-red flag had been hoisted at the German consulates for the first time.[162] The swastika, the most important symbol of the Nazis, was adopted by Hitler as the official emblem of his party. Although the symbol is one of the most ancient and popular ornamental forms, by 1910, the swastika was being used in Germany to denote "the superior Aryan race."[163] Hoisting the swastika banner and the black-white-red flag, the symbol of the Kaiser Reich, the Nazis in Palestine demonstrated their identity with their homeland under Hitler's rule. In general, they did not dare to show their flags in public outside the German colonies, the consulates openly displayed the swastika flag on every German national holiday, and marches with flags took place inside the colonies.[164]

157 *EvGB* (Apr. 1938): 47–48.

158 *Die Warte des Tempels*, 15 Apr. 1938, 55.

159 Snyder, *Encyclopedia* , 8.

160 *Die Warte des Tempels*, 31 May 1938, 77–78; cf. *Blumenthal's Neuste Nachrichten*, Tel Aviv, 10 Apr. 1938; Sauer, *Uns rief das Heilige Land*, 252–53.

161 Of 1,180 German voters, 1,173 cast their ballot in favor of Hitler; *Die Warte des Tempels*, 31 May 1938, 77-78).

162 *Die Warte des Tempels*, 15 Apr. 1933, 52; Sauer, *Uns rief das Heilige Land*, 231.

163 Snyder, *Encyclopedia*, 135.

164 Letter to the AO, Berlin, 24 Mar. 1936, ISTA, 821/4-פ; cf. correspondence of 14 and 17 July 1935,

The Jewish population responded variously to the German flags on display. Jews from Jaffa and Tel Aviv asked the consul in Jaffa to remove the flag. In Jerusalem, small groups came to the consulate to see the "Hitler flag." No riots erupted and no casualties were reported.[165] A few German businessmen felt uncomfortable with the idea of the swastika flown openly in Palestine, and therefore they asked Reichspräsident Hindenburg for permission not to hoist the flag in consideration of the Jews, and the desire to avoid a provocation. However, the Auswärtiges Amt (Foreign Office) rejected the request, and the German consulates in Jerusalem and Jaffa had to follow the order and hoist both flags.[166] But at that time, there were not enough black-white-red flags and swastika banners at hand. The necessary swastika flags were quickly produced at Cornelius Schwarz's home.[167] In 1935, the flag law was changed and the "German consulate in Jerusalem for the first time in its history hoisted the swastika flag alone...."[168]

In 1936 and 1938, there was a festive handover of the new German flags in Haifa.[169] The newspapers *Al Liva* and *Falastin* reported that a meeting of Nazi members had taken place in Haifa. A delegation of eighty Nazis had recently met with Hitler in Germany, and had received three swastika flags for the NS groups in Haifa, Sarona, and Jerusalem. Shouts of *Heil Hitler!* could be heard, and an honor guard was formed for the new flags.[170] Banners with a swastika were also ordered for the local NS groups in Wilhelma and Bethlehem-Waldheim.[171] The price for one flag was fifty Reichsmark.[172] In 1938, the local NS groups in Waldheim and Bethlehem/Galilee received their own German flags, which had been consecrated at the Reichsparteitag in Germany. To celebrate, all local NS groups and Consul General Doehle were invited to Haifa, where the festivities began with Nazi members marching in with flags. Cornelius Schwarz gave the greetings and a speech, followed by songs, and the swearing-in of new party members. As the flags were presented to the local group of Bethlehem-Waldheim, the song "We are going to pray" was played. The official part of the ceremony was followed by an informal meeting which concluded the consecration of the new flags.[173]

ISTA, 821/7-פ.

165 *Die Warte des Tempels*, 15 Apr. 1933, 52.

166 Ralf Balke, *Hakenkreuz im Heiligen Land. Die NSDAP-Landesgruppe Palästina* (Erfurt, 2001), 80–81.

167 Ibid., 81.

168 *Palestine Post*, 23 Sep. 1935, 5; *Die Warte des Tempels*, 15 Oct. 1935, 149.

169 Letter to the AO in Berlin, 24 Mar. 1936, ISTA, 821/4-פ.

170 *Private Correspondenz des Siegfried Blumenthal*, Tel Aviv, 5 Nov. 1936, 2.

171 Letter to the AO, Berlin, 24 Mar. 1936, ISTA, 821/4-פ.

172 Correspondence, K. Lange, Bethlehem-Waldheim, 14 July 1936, ISTA 821/7-פ.

173 Correspondence, OGL (Ortsgruppenleiter) Friedrich Wagner, Haifa, 14 Jan. 1938, ISTA, 821/9-פ.

The variety of the NS network in Palestine

With its local groups (Ortsgruppen), organizations, and affiliated associations (*Gliederungen und angeschlossene Verbände*), the NS country group in Palestine had a very similar organizational system to the NSDAP in Germany. Each local Nazi group and support point had its own leader. Group members met once or twice a month for lectures and social evenings. Children and teenagers were involved in the Hitler Youth program, which included groups for boys and girls from 10 to 18 years. Women became members of the Arbeitsgemeinschaft der Deutschen Frau im Ausland (AGdFA, Work Group of the German Woman Abroad). All German teachers and educators in Palestine joined the Nationalsozialistischer Lehrerbund (NSLB, the National Socialist Teachers' Alliance), workers and employees participated in the Deutsche Arbeitsfront (German Labor Front).[174] Winter Relief collections (Winterhilfe) supported needy Germans.[175] Political and ideological infiltration through social aid is very common in dictatorships. The Nazis in Germany set up various institutions to help low-income workers, support and honor mothers of large families, and entertain and train employees in various professions. Furthermore, they engaged the youth in sports and social paramilitary programs.

The Winter Relief Organization (Winterhilfswerk), established by Hitler in 1933, collected money from businesses and private individuals to aid unemployed and needy people. Hitler described the Winterhilfe as a means of educating the people in the direction of National Socialism. In March 1933 and November 1934, Provost Rhein, the head of the German Protestant community in Palestine, published a call in the *Evangelisches Gemeindeblatt* for church members to support this Nazi charitable project. Rhein's congregation responded joyfully in thus expressing their loyalty to Germany.[176] In November 1934, the Protestant newsletter announced that

> This year the *Winterhilfe* will be organized by the local group of the N.S.D.A.P. only. We will hold it [the donation] the same way as in our homeland. On the so-called Stew Sundays (as in Germany on Nov. 18, Dec. 16, Jan. 13, Feb. 17, March 17), the families and our German institutions will save some money for our *Volksgenossen* (ethnic comrades), who do not always have as much food as we do. All wage earners are supposed to give one portion of their salaries to the Winter Relief Organization. When the collectors come at the beginning

174 DAF and NSLB were legal entities affiliated with the NSDAP, having their own budgets.
175 YVA: R3/11, R3/18, R3/26; *EvGB* (May 1933): 38; *Palestine Post*, 2 May 1934, 7; 2 May 1935, 1; 23 Sept. 1935, 5; 3 May 1936, 12; *Die Warte des Tempels*, 15 Oct. 1935, 149; 31 May 1938, 76; Donald M. McKale, *The Swastika outside Germany* (Kent State, Ohio, 1977), 122–23; Ralf Balke, *Hakenkreuz im Heiligen Land*, 56–58.
176 *EvGB* (Mar. 1933): 21; and (Nov. 1934): 88.

of the month or the week after the Stew Sunday to collect the donations, they will notice that *Volksgemeinschaft* (ethnic community) and Christian brotherly love are not empty words to us. We are willing to make sacrifices.[177]

Similar sentiments had been expressed in the monthly report of the local NS group in Jerusalem in October 1934: "In contrast to previous years the Winter Relief Collection will be conducted in Jerusalem this year solely by the local group of the NSDAP. This is intended to emphasize the unity of this organization and our solidarity with our homeland."[178]

In 1935 and 1937–38, Walter Hoffmann (Jerusalem) was responsible for the Winter Relief campaign.[179] Ernst Seebass (Jerusalem) worked for the Winter Relief collection in 1937, and became its head administrator.[180]

The NSDAP took care not only of its needy members but also of workers and employees. The monolithic labor organization, Deutsche Arbeitsfront (DAF), was allied to the Nazi party and took the place of the labor union system of the Weimar Republic. It comprised the entire labor force of the Third Reich, including more than 20 million workers.[181] Employed Germans in Palestine also joined the DAF. New members were recruited at propaganda evenings or were "automatically added" to the organization after having moved from Germany to Palestine. Leaders and subleaders of the DAF in Palestine were Wilhelm Baumert (head of DAF), Abraham Dyck (Jerusalem), Alfred Hoenig (Wilhelma), Oskar Beck (Haifa), and Fritz Unger (Bethlehem/Waldheim).[182] According to archival material, the German Labor Front was very well organized, with such positions within it as treasurer,

177 *EvGB* (Nov. 1934): 88, "Die Organisation des Hilfswerkes ist in diesem Jahre einheitlich von der Ortsgruppe der N.S.D.A.P. aus geregelt. Wir wollen es so halten wie in der Heimat: an den Eintopf-Sonntagen (wie in Deutschland: am 18. Nov., 16. Dez., 13. Jan., 17. Febr., 17. März) soll in den Familien und unsern deutschen Anstalten am Essen etwas für die Volksgenossen abgespart werden, die sich nicht wie wir immer an den wohlgedeckten Tisch setzen können; alle Verdienenden sollen einmal monatlich einen Teil ihres Verdienstes für das Winterhilfswerk hingeben. Wenn dann am Anfang des Monats bezw. in der Woche nach dem Eintopf-Sonntag die Sammler kommen, um die Gaben abzuholen, sollen sie merken, daß uns Volksgemeinschaft und christliche Nächstenliebe nicht leere Worte sind, sondern daß wir willig sind, sie opfernd in die Tat umzusetzen."

178 Monthly Report, local NS group in Jerusalem, 31 Oct. 1934, ISTA, 821/5-פ: "Im Gegensatz zu früheren Jahren wird es [Winterhilfswerk] in Jerusalem heuer ganz und allein von der Ortsgruppe der NSDAP geleitet. Dies bezweckt in erster Linie das Einheitliche des Werkes zu betonen und unsere gemeinsame Verbundenheit mit der Heimat zu bekunden."

179 *Die Warte des Tempels*, Oct. 1935, 155; YVA: R 3/11.

180 Settlement of accounts, 4 Apr. 1937, YVA, R 3/11.

181 Snyder, *Encyclopedia*, 84.

182 DAF Palestine to DAF Germany, 11 Apr. 1939, ISTA, 823/6- פ.

librarian, administrator for press and news, training program conductor, and administrator of justice.[183] At the beginning of 1937, Wilhelm Baumert gave a speech in Haifa in order to recruit more members for the DAF.[184] In June of that year, the German Labor Front in Palestine consisted of sixty-four members.[185] By December 1938, Jaffa-Sarona counted 170 DAF members, including eighty-one NSDAP members.[186] Nevertheless, the head of Sarona's DAF group was not pleased with this figure. At the beginning of 1939, he complained that although the number of DAF members had increased in 1938, there were still fellow Germans, especially in farming, who continued to keep their distance from the Labor Front. In a letter to the *Gauwaltung* in Berlin he expressed his hope for an increase of DAF members for the year 1939.[187]

Affiliated to the DAF was the *Kraft durch Freude* (KdF — Strength through Joy) program.

> National Socialist recreational organization was designed to stimulate morale among workers.... It was the best-publicized program of industrial relations in the Third Reich. Participants in a new form of mass tourism, KdF holiday makers cruised on luxury liners and traveled by train to...Venice, Naples, and Lisbon. There were also many tourist trips to Norway.... The Kraft durch Freude organization received huge subsidies from the government. It became a big business itself.[188]

In Palestine, it was Wilhelm Doh who organized such KdF tours as a trip to the river Arnon (east of the Dead Sea) on October 16 and 17, 1937. Seventy-five people had registered to join the trip, but it was cancelled due to the political situation in Palestine.[189] On a weekend in September 1937, a boat tour was organized, with twenty-eight men and women; the boat was decorated with a swastika flag.[190] In July 1937, another cruise took place along the coast of the Mediterranean Sea to the river Rubin in the south, with the group spending a night on the beach.[191] In the following month of August, one hundred participants joined a visit to a mu-

183 DAF Palestine F[ritz] Imberger (*Kassenwalter*), Wilfried Imberger (*Pressewalter*), Dr. Richard Hoffmann (*Rechtswalter*) to DAF Germany, ISTA, 821/11-פ.
184 Wilhelm Baumert to Oskar Beck, 7 Jan. 1937, ISTA, 821/11-פ.
185 Letter, Wilhelm Doh, 25 June 1937, ISTA, 821/11-פ.
186 Letter, 12 Feb. 1939, ISTA, 823/4-פ.
187 Ibid.
188 Snyder, *Encyclopedia*, 199.
189 Correspondence, Wilhelm Doh, 22 Oct. 1937, ISTA, 821/11-פ.
190 Correspondence, Wilhelm Doh, 22 Sept. 1937, ISTA, 821/11-פ.
191 Correspondence, Wilhelm Doh, 20 Aug. 1937, ISTA, 821/11-פ.

seum in Jerusalem.[192] Letters and reports from these trips give the impression that the KdF participants really enjoyed the entertainment and relaxation provided by the NS regime.

Educators in Palestine, like their colleagues in Germany, joined the NS Lehrerbund (NSLB, National Socialist Teachers' Alliance). Founded in Germany in 1929, this organization was closely associated with the NSDAP; its purpose was to shape the teachers' political ideology (*Weltanschauung*) and further their education based on National Socialism.[193] In February 1934, the Auslands-Abteilung in Hamburg wrote to Karl Ruff that his request to introduce the National Socialist Teachers' Alliance in Palestine would be answered soon by the relevant offices, although we know that the Alliance's activities did not begin before 1935–36.[194] The aim was to turn German schools in Palestine into outposts of the German NSDAP.[195] Conferences and training programs for teachers were conducted by the AO in cooperation with the NSLB. In May 1937, teachers received a circular with an invitation to participate in further training meetings of the NSLB, called *Auslandslehrertagung* (meeting for teachers abroad) and *Schulungslehrertagung* (a training course for teachers).[196] In 1937 and 1938, a *Deutschlandlager der Auslandslehrer* (a camp in Germany for teachers abroad) took place. During ten days of intensive programs, teachers abroad were trained in NS ideology and education, after-school care and *Auslandsdeutschtum*.[197] A *Reichstagung* (national conference) of the NSLB in Germany was scheduled to take place in Cologne in August 1938, including an exhibit on the "Achievements in Art and Science by German Teachers," for which teachers from Palestine were invited to contribute.[198]

Dr. Kurt Hegele, the head of the teachers' organization in Palestine, received his instructions from the Office for Educators within the AO in Germany.[199] Mr. Kuhn from the Office for Educators required every teacher in Palestine to subscribe to the journal *Der Deutsche Erzieher im Ausland* (The German educator abroad), yet he complained in December 1938 that of the more than twenty mem-

192 Correspondence, Wilhelm Doh, 12 Aug. 1937, ISTA, 821/11-פ.

193 Wolfgang Benz, Hermann Graml, and Hermann Weiß, *Enzyklopädie des Nationalsozialismus* (Munich, 1997), 608.

194 Letter, *Auslands-Abteilung* in Hamburg, 8 Feb. 1934, ISTA, 822/15-פ.

195 Balke, *Hakenkreuz im Heiligen Land*, 56.

196 Letter, 12 May 1937, ISTA, 18/19-חח; cf. Sauer, *Uns rief das Heilige Land*, 255.

197 Kuhn, AO Office for Educators to Hegele, 27 May 1938, ISTA, 821/9-פ.

198 Letter, AO, 3 Feb. 1938, and Schwarz circular, 26 Feb. 1938, ISTA, 821/9-פ.

199 Roland Löffler, "Die Gemeinden des Jerusalemsvereins im Kontext des kirchlichen und politischen Zeitgeschehens in der Mandatszeit" in *Seht, wir gehen hinauf nach Jerusalem. Festschrift zum 150jährigen Jubiläum von Talitha Kumi und des Jerusalemsvereins*, edited by Almut Nothnagle, Hans-Jürgen Abromeit, and Frank Foerster (Leipzig, 2000), 185–212, 207.

bers of the Teachers' Alliance in Palestine, only five had ordered the journal.[200] Over time, all the local German teachers joined the NSLB.[201] This was certainly the case by June 1938.[202]

According to a letter and NSLB membership list of June 1938, there were six German schools in Palestine with 25 NSLB members.[203] In order to turn these schools into NSDAP outposts and control their policy, German schools were united under the guardianship of Nazi members. The curricula were changed, eliminating Christian values and ideas and introducing National Socialist education instead. School policy had to be freed "from the yoke of the Bible."[204] Furthermore, modern Jewry had to be fought and German culture protected from its "materialistic elements." Such were the declared goals of NS school policy in the Holy Land.[205] The German School Association (*Deutscher Schulverein*) drafted its statutes in the late 1930s, defining as its goal to provide a German education to German children and non-German students, except for Jews. Every German and everyone who knew Germans were accepted as members, except for Jews and *Judenmischlinge* (Jews of mixed race).[206]

The opening of the united German school in Jerusalem took place on October 18, 1937.[207] Members of the Lutheran Church of the Redeemer had opposed the unification of their school and the Lyceum Tempelstift (secondary school of the Temple Society), but without success.[208] The new institution was known as the Deutsche Schule, located in the German Colony in Jerusalem. The agreement of unification was signed by Consul General Doehle (named as president of the school board), with Philipp Wurst and Nikolai Schmidt as delegates of the Temple Society, and Hermann Schneller and Dr. Eberhard Gmelin representing the German Protestant community in Jerusalem.[209] All were members of the Nazi party or joined the following year. At the opening, Philipp Wurst of the Temple Society expressed his hope for fruitful cooperation between parents, teachers,

---

200 Letter, 14 Dec. 1938, ISTA, 821/9-פ.

201 Balke, *Hakenkreuz im Heiligen Land*, 57.

202 Letter, 30 June 1938, NSLB membership list of 1 June 1938 ISTA, 821/9-פ.

203 Ibid.

204 Löffler, "Die Gemeinden des Jerusalemsvereins," 208; Balke, *Hakenkreuz im Heiligen Land*, 87–88.

205 ISTA, 821/8-פ.

206 Draft of statutes, no date [end of 1937 to April 1939], ISTA, 821/9-פ.

207 The unification took place in 1937, not in 1938 (as stated by Balke, *Hakenkreuz im Heiligen Land*, 88–89).

208 ISTA, 821/8-פ. For more details on the dispute and ultimate unification, see Roland Löffler: *Protestanten in Palästina* (Stuttgart, 2008), 167–91.

209 ISTA, 821/8-פ; *Die Warte des Tempels*, 30 June 1937, 89–90.

and students, "in the spirit of Adolf Hitler."[210] The official constitution stipulated that the new school would run "on the educational basis of the Third Reich in accordance with Christian principles and respecting the freedom of religious conscience."[211] However, a clause provided for the total exclusion of all Jews and limited the number of Arabs to 25 percent, explained as necessary to preserve the German character of the school and to provide a German education.[212] The language of instruction was German, with Arabic as an elective.[213] The Reichsminister für Volksaufklärung insisted on having Arab students, in order to influence the potential Arab leaders of a future, independent state of Palestine.[214] The new German School accepted 89 students in 1937: 51 Germans, 27 Palestinians, 7 British, 2 Austrians, and 2 Americans.[215]

Hala Sakakini and her sister, daughters of the Arab educator Khalil Sakakini, attended the Templer school in Jerusalem. Hala wrote about the new Deutsche Schule in her memoir, *Jerusalem and I: A Personal Record*, published in English in 1990[216]:

> In 1937, our school and another German school in Jerusalem were united and formed from that year on.... I don't think any of us pupils liked the idea at first. We looked on the pupils of the other school as strangers whom we did not wish to have among us, but in a month or two we became used to the new arrangement as if it had been that way for years. Young teachers came over from Germany. They were full of fun and enthusiasm and we grew to like them very much. Dr. Hegele who taught us languages — German, English and French — became our class teacher. He was witty and charming, but also moody and unpredictable.... Herr Merz was another of those new arrivals. He had an M.A. degree and taught us mathematics, physics and chemistry. We girls thought him very attractive. Whenever he was dissatisfied with our work and had some criticism to make he would launch his attack by addressing the class with the word "Meine Herrschaften" in mock courtesy. A third new teacher was Herr Kunle who taught us drawing. He was an expert and we enjoyed his classes immensely.... With their arrival changes were brought about in school. We began for instance to have a school meeting every Monday morning before classes. Every week one of the teachers was in charge of this meeting. When it was the turn of one of the older teachers, the meeting would be more or less religious.... When it was the turn of one of those young teachers the meeting became more political in nature. The teacher would read to us a modern political poem, we would sing a few patriotic songs and then, invariably, we would wind up with

210 Balke *Hakenkreuz im Heiligen Land*, 89.
211 H. Schmidt, "The Nazi Party in Palestine and the Levant, 1932–9," *International Affairs* 28, no. 4 (1952): 460–69, 464.
212 Löffler, *Protestanten in Palästina*, 180.
213 ISTA, 821/8-פ, esp. report on the German School in Jerusalem, 1 Apr. 1939; Sauer, *Uns rief das Heilige Land*, 256; Schmidt, "Nazi Party in Palestine," 464.
214 Sauer, *Uns rief das Heilige Land*, 256.
215 *Die Warte des Tempels*, 15 Nov. 1937, 173–74.
216 Dalia Karpel, "Swastika in Jerusalem," *Haaretz* (Jerusalem), 28 Feb. 2008.

> "Deutschland, Deutschland über alles!" and "Die Fahnen hoch!" Of course, we enjoyed this latter kind of meeting much more than the other.[217]

The local NSDAP in Haifa also tried to influence school affairs in its area. A member of the NSLB was placed at the German school in Haifa, whose sole task was to inform the party about everything going on at the institution. In 1937, a "pure" *German Christmas* was celebrated there. The term *German Christmas* had been chosen to remind the members of the Protestant church "not to bring their Jewish or baptized Jewish friends with them."[218]

On July 20, 1937, the German school in Sarona celebrated the beginning of the summer vacation. The party began and ended with *Sieg Heil!* exclamations. The colorful program included plays, dances, competitive races, music, and German folk songs, concluding with the *Deutschlandlied* and *Horst-Wessel-Lied* in the evening.[219]

The German schools in Bethlehem and Waldheim were also united as the German School Bethlehem-Waldheim, with the goal of educating students in the spirit of National Socialism and the ideals of *Volksgemeinschaft* (ethnic community) and *Nationaler Geist* (nationalist spirit).[220]

The NS regime in Germany regarded sports as essential for a healthy national state. Hitler called for a physically hard youth to continue the racial struggle, so physical training was allotted two to three periods per week in the schools. In 1938 it was increased to five periods each week. All Germans, especially the youth, were supposed to demonstrate the superiority of the German-Aryan race to the world.[221] No wonder that sports also played an important role among German settlers and at the German schools in the Holy Land. According to a letter by Ludwig Buchhalter in Jerusalem, the NSLB head, Kurt Hegele, had to leave for Germany in October 1940 and his successor at the German School in Jerusalem was expected to be good at teaching sports.[222] German sports clubs had existed in the various German colonies long before the rise of National Socialism. Palestine's Nazis tried to win over their members. The monthly report of the local group in Jerusalem announced in 1934 that a new board, all of whose members belonged to the NSDAP, had been elected at the German sports clubs in Jerusalem. Ludwig Buchhalter expressed his hope that from now on the cooperation between the

217 Hala Sakakini, *Jerusalem and I. A Personal Record*, 2nd ed. (Amman, 1990), 55–56.
218 Balke *Hakenkreuz im Heiligen Land*, 89.
219 *Die Warte des Tempels*, 31 Aug. 1937, 136–38.
220 Protocol, no date [Dec. 1937 to Apr. 1939], ISTA, 821/9-פ.
221 Snyder, *Encyclopedia*, 328–29; Benz, *Enzyklopädie*, 251–56.
222 L. Buchhalter to Consulate, Jerusalem, 12 Apr. 1939, ISTA, 821/9-פ.

sports club and the party would improve "for the sake of *Deutschtum*."[223] In the following years, cooperation among NS groups, school authorities, and the sports clubs was good and successful, according to the archival material. In August 1934, the Hindenburg Sportfest took place in Sarona, the third of its kind. In the morning, representatives of the German sports clubs gathered at Sarona's cemetery to commemorate the death of Reichspräsident Hindenburg. At noon, telegrams were sent to the Führer. At 2:15 p.m., the athletes marched into the school yard in Sarona waving their flags and the competition began. The German consuls from Jerusalem and Jaffa attended the sports event, which began and ended with patriotic and nationalist speeches. The Hitler salute was given with raised arms. The flags of the German Reich were hoisted and the national anthem played.[224] In the following year (May 1935), Sarona hosted a joint sports event in which British and German athletes participated. At the opening, the leagues marched in with the Swastika flag and the Union Jack.[225]

At several meetings and celebrations, members of the Hitler Youth and League of German Girls took an active role by performing stage plays, reciting poems, marching and singing. The following chapter will describe the founding and activity of the Hitler Youth including its subgroups.

223 Monthly Report, local NS group, Jerusalem, 30 Nov. 1934, ISTA, 821/5-פ.
224 *Die Warte des Tempels*, Sept. 1934, 141–42; Monthly Report, local NS group, Jerusalem, Aug. 1934, ISTA, 821/5-פ.
225 Ibid.

Fig. 1. German Lutheran Church of the Redeemer, Jerusalem (between 1898 and 1914). Source: Library of Congress, Matson Collection.

Fig. 2. Schneller's House, Missionary Trade school, Jerusalem (between 1898 and 1946). Source: Library of Congress, Matson Collection.

Fig. 3. German Hospital, Prophets Street, Jerusalem, 9 August 1939. Source: Library of Congress, Matson Collection.

Fig. 4. Community Hall, Temple Society, German Colony, Jerusalem, 21 July 2006. Photo by H. Wawrzyn.

Fig. 5. Restored Templer house, Emek Refaim 16, German Colony, Jerusalem. Photo by H. Wawrzyn, 21 July 2006.

Fig. 6. Headstone: Christian Rohrer, head of the Temple Society, 20 March 1860–31 May 1934. Templer Cemetery, Jerusalem. Photo by H. Wawrzyn.

Fig. 7. Headstone: Philipp Wurst, head of the Temple Society, 16 June 1883–7 February 1941. Templer Cemetery, Jerusalem. Photo by H. Wawrzyn, 24 March 2006.

Fig. 8. German Protestant church, Waldheim. Courtesy of the Temple Society, Stuttgart, Germany.

Fig. 9. German Catholic guesthouse of the Borromean Sisters, Jerusalem. Photo by H. Wawrzyn, 14 June 2008.

Fig. 10. Nazi Party rally, Nazareth, prewar Mandatory Palestine. Used by permission, Yad Vashem Photo Archive, Jerusalem.

Fig. 11. Nazi and German flags, German Military Cemetery, Nazareth (June 1935). Used by permission, Yad Vashen Photo Archive, Jerusalem.

Die Warte des Tempels

Halbmonatsschrift zur Vertiefung in die Fragen und Aufgaben des Menschenlebens.

Jahrgang 91. 31. Januar 1934. Nr. 2.

Zum 30. Januar 1934.

Todes-Anzeige.

Gertrud Veronika

Fig. 12. Hitler portrait, *Die Warte des Tempels*, 31 January 1934. Photo by H. Wawrzyn.

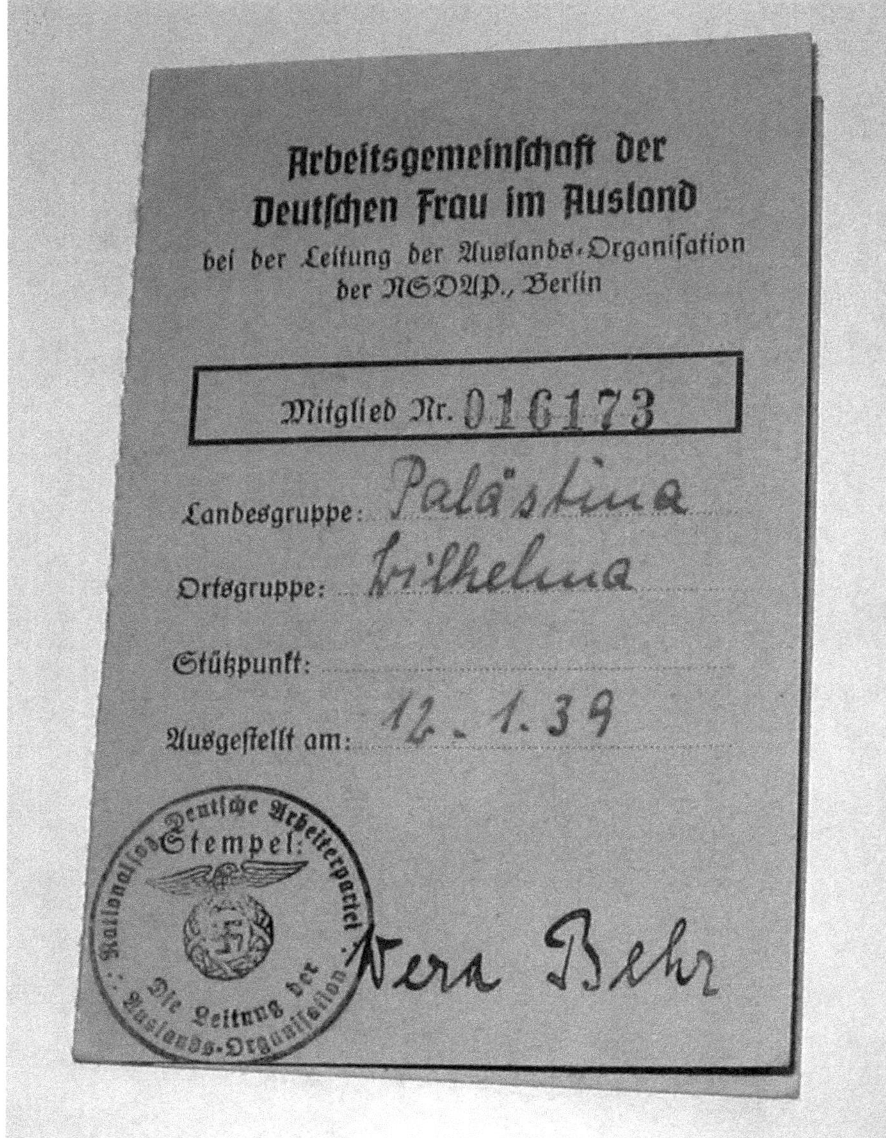

Arbeitsgemeinschaft der
Deutschen Frau im Ausland
bei der Leitung der Auslands-Organisation
der NSDAP., Berlin

Mitglied Nr. 016173

Landesgruppe: Palästina
Ortsgruppe: Wilhelma
Stützpunkt:
Ausgestellt am: 12. 1. 39

Nationalsozialistische Deutsche Arbeiterpartei
Stempel:
Die Leitung der Auslands-Organisation

Vera Behr

Fig. 13. Membership card, Arbeitsgemeinschaft der Deutschen Frau im Ausland. Photo by H. Wawrzyn.

Fig. 14. Boys School and Mufti of Jerusalem, Temple Mount (between 1921 and 1937). Library of Congress, Matson Collection.

Fig. 15. Bombing of King David Hotel, Jerusalem, 22 July 1946. Library of Congress, Matson Collection.

Fig. 16. British Government House, Jerusalem, 1932. Library of Congress, Matson Collection.

Fig. 17: Decorations on the occasion of the coronation of King George VI., Jerusalem, 12 May 1937. American Colony, Jerusalem, Photo Dept. (Library of Congress).

4 Hitler Youth

A branch of the National Socialist youth organization, Hitler Youth (*Hitler Jugend*, HJ) was founded in Palestine in 1934, a few years before membership became compulsory for every German boy and girl. At the beginning of 1934, the Auslands-Abteilung in Hamburg had promised Karl Ruff to help him establish both the NS Teachers' Alliance and the Hitler Youth in the Holy Land.[226] A few days later, Ruff started looking for potential leaders for the new youth organization.[227] The announcement of the foundation was published in the Temple Society journal, proclaiming its purpose: "To keep the German race and culture pure!"[228] Males of 14 to 18 years belonged to the actual HJ; while the association of *Deutsches Jungvolk* (DJ or JV, German Young People) accepted boys from age 10 to 14. The unit for *Jungmädels* (JM, Young Girls) was open to girls between 10 and 14 years, and the *Bund Deutscher Mädchen* (BDM, League of German Girls) was established for 14- to 18-year-old girls.[229]

On April 9, 1934, new members of the Hitler Youth were sworn in at the German consulate in Jaffa, vowing loyalty to Hitler, to fulfill his orders, hold his flag sacred, and prove themselves to be brave and loyal fighters of the National Socialist movement.[230] Each German colony in Palestine soon had its own HJ group. In 1935, Eugen Faber, born in Jerusalem in 1897 and not a member of the Temple Society, was appointed *HJ-Landesjugendführer* (country leader of the Hitler Youth) in Palestine. He willingly scheduled HJ meetings on Christian holidays, despite protests by the Temple Society and Protestant community, which saw the HJ in competition with their own Christian youth clubs and traditional Christian values.[231] Nevertheless, the HJ attracted many young people with their paramilitary training program and their strict and ritualized social life.[232] Recruiting and training the younger generation to National Socialist ideas meant shaping Germany's future – a goal as important to Nazi leaders in Palestine as it was to the party in Germany. The HJ in Nazi Germany proudly wore their uniforms and displayed

---

226 Auslands-Abteilung, Hamburg to Karl Ruff, Haifa, 8 Feb. 1934, ISTA, 822/15-פ.

227 Karl Ruff, correspondence, 19 Feb. 1934, ISTA, 822/15-פ.

228 *Die Warte des Tempels*, 31 July 1934, 111.

229 Carola Stern and Inge Brodersen, eds., *Eine Erdbeere für Hitler. Deutschland unterm Hakenkreuz*, 2nd ed. (Frankfurt am Main, 2005), 60–61; Wolfgang Benz, Hermann Graml, and Hermann Weiß, *Enzyklopädie des Nationalsozialismus* (Munich, 1997), 209–14.

230 Paul Sauer, *Uns rief das Heilige Land. Die Tempelgesellschaft im Wandel der Zeit* (Stuttgart, 1985), 247.

231 Provost Rhein to Eugen Faber, 5 and 12 Mar. 1935, EZA 5/3123; Ralf Balke, *Hakenkreuz im Heiligen Land. Die NSDAP-Landesgruppe Palästina* (Erfurt, 2001), 54.

232 Balke, *Hakenkreuz im Heiligen Land*, 54–56.

their flags in public, but in Palestine had to disguise their appearance in the non-German and Jewish environment. This gave the members a certain pleasingly conspiratorial character.[233]

Hala Sakakini wrote about the launching of HJ meetings at her school:

> One year, I think it was in 1935, our German classmates began to attend meetings after school. At first Dumia [Hala's sister] and I and our friend Zakieh, the only non-Germans in class, found it strange to be excluded. Our curiosity was naturally aroused, but our classmates would not tell us what the meetings were about. In a few months, however, the atmosphere of secrecy lifted. Everything was now done openly and with great enthusiasm. Our share of this new feeling was not less than that of our classmates. We soon learned the names of the different groups to which the children belonged (H.J. – Hitler Jugend; B.D.M. – Bund Deutscher Mädel). We were allowed to examine their badges and were always interested to know who was promoted from one group to another. Special uniforms had been ordered from Germany and these the children wore only for their meeting.[234]

Members met once a week at their *Heimabend* (home evening), at which NS lectures on race, genetics, comradeship, and German history were provided. They trained in hand-to-hand combat and sports, but also gathered for evenings of songs, folk dances, bonfires, paper chases, and other field games (*Geländespiele*). Arabic and Hebrew courses were offered along with practical skills like shorthand; and HJ members might even join a trip to Germany. In October 1934, an overnight field trip was planned for the HJ groups from Jaffa, Sarona, and Jerusalem.[235] In February 1938, the Hitler Youth opened its own youth hostel in Waldheim.

Every meeting ended by singing the official hymn of the Hitler Youth — "Prepare for your struggle." As the goal of all activities was to educate the youth and shape its character (*Charakterbildung*) in the spirit of National Socialism, the meetings included antisemitic indoctrination.[236] At an HJ meeting in Jaffa in April 1934, members were instructed to buy only at German shops and if possible only German products because Germans abroad had to stick together; otherwise, the Jews would dismember them and Germans abroad would be lost to their fatherland forever.[237] Another important goal was to convince the youth to use their influence on hesitant adults. The private diary of a Templer woman from the German Colony in Jaffa illustrates its success. In 1933 she described the Nazi party

---

233 Ibid.
234 Hala Sakakini, *Jerusalem and I. A Personal Record* (Amman, 1990), 54–55.
235 Letter, 10 Oct. 1934, ISTA, 822/3-פ.
236 Letters by Eugen Faber and Paula Hahn, 1937; and reports of 1937 and 1938, ISTA, 822/3-פ; Balke, *Hakenkreuz im Heiligen Land*, 56.
237 Sauer, *Uns rief das Heilige Land*, 247, quoted an HJ diary.

coldly, in the third person plural. The following year, her attitude had changed, when her son joined the HJ in Jaffa, went off to a youth camp in Germany, became a senior counselor there, and returned home a zealot. The mother's diary took on a different tone; she quoted from songs of the youth movement, and "they" became "we" in her writings. Within a few weeks of her son's return, she had joined the party.[238]

Palestine's Hitler Youth often played an active role in the observance of NS holidays. For example, ceremonies connected with the twice-yearly solstice (*Sonnenwende*) were conducted by members of the HJ. The first in Palestine took place on 21 June 1934.[239] In 1935, the local NS group in Jerusalem invited all German residents to the festivities taking place near Bethlehem. Hitler Youth members lit a bonfire, and HJ and BDM recited verses.[240] The Temple Society journal called the *Sonnenwendfest* the new-old German feast that recalled the Germanic ritual of sun worship and the beginning of a new season.[241] On the occasion of that summer solstice, a speaker noted:

> It is a privilege for us to celebrate the solstice in Palestine because this region, where lots of German blood has already been spilled, is our home. Furthermore, only at an outpost do you become very aware of the duty to your nation (*Volk und Vaterland*)! The celebration of the solstice shows us our tasks: We are called by the burning embers to do good deeds, to join the Ethnic Community. We are called to action.[242]

On July 7, 1934, a festive Pflichtabend (compulsory evening) was held by the local Nazi group in Jaffa-Sarona. In a decorated hall, a member of the HJ stood to the right side of the speaker's platform holding a flag. A young boy of the Jungvolk stood at the other side, also carrying a flag. Behind them, one could see the Führer's portrait. Eugen Faber gave the opening speech describing the goals of the HJ, whose weekly indoor and outdoor meetings were aimed at helping children

---

238 Moshe Temkin, "The History of the Hitler Youth in Jerusalem" (in Hebrew), *Yediot Achronot*, 1 Oct. 1999, 52–57; H. Schmidt, "The Nazi Party in Palestine and the Levant 1932–9," *International Affairs* 28, no. 4 (1952): 460–69, 463.

239 *Die Warte des Tempels*, 31 July 1934, 110; see also 15 July 1935, 101; HJ monthly reports, 1935–1939, ISTA, 822/4-פ; Balke, *Hakenkreuz im Heiligen Land*, 55.

240 Report of the local NS Group, Jerusalem, 1935, ISTA, 821/5-פ.

241 *Die Warte des Tempels*, 15 July 1935, 101.

242 Quoted by Balke, *Hakenkreuz im Heiligen Land*, 56: "Es ist ein Vorrecht, in Palästina Sonnenwendfeiern halten zu können: denn einmal ist dieses Land, auf dessen Erde schon soviel deutsches Blut geflossen ist, für alle ein Stück Heimat: und dann wird man sich seinen Aufgaben gegenüber Volk und Vaterland nirgends deutlich so bewußt, wie wenn man auf Vorposten steht! Die Sonnenwendfeier zeigt unsere Aufgaben. Es ruft uns auf mit seiner läuternden Glut zum Guten, es ruft uns zur Volksgemeinschaft, es ruft zur Tat!"

and teenagers become good Germans. Teaching and practicing the values of discipline, comradeship, obedience, and loyalty were essential. Cornelius Schwarz then spoke about National Socialism and its young members, who had to fight the battle between good and evil. As usual, the meeting closed with the anthem *Deutschland, Deutschland über alles*.[243]

Another meeting of HJ members and their parents took place at the Templers' community house in January 1935. It began with sixty-two members of HJ, JV, and BDM marching in.[244] On January 30, 1936 the same group gathered for the anniversary of Hitler's rise to power. Flags and pictures of the Führer decorated the crowded community hall. The evening began with a flag march and military music, followed by National Socialist speeches and songs.[245]

Beginning in 1935, members of the Hitler Youth and its subgroups, attended annual regional meetings (*Landesjugendtreffen*).[246] In that year, about two hundred boys and girls camped out in tents on the Mediterranean shore near Jaffa from April 17–20. The *Warte des Tempels* reported that the event's highlight was Hitler's birthday celebration on April 20.[247] The following year (April 8–11, 1936), the Landesjugendtreffen took place at a camp in the forest between Bethlehem in Galilee and Waldheim, near Haifa. Every morning, the flag was raised and given the Nazi salute. Flag marches, paramilitary field games, paper chases, bonfires, singing, stories about the Germanic people (*alte Germanen*), and soccer games made up the program.[248] Seventy boys traveled to Berlin in July 1935 to participate in the Reichsjugendtreffen in Germany; on their return, the Temple Society journal reported on their great pride and increased knowledge of Germany and National Socialism.[249]

Leaders of the Nazi party and the HJ emphasized several times in their correspondence that they wished to avoid drawing the attention of the local population. Of course, both Jews and Arabs could not help but notice their flags, marches, and gatherings, because many of their activities were held in the open. As early as 1932, young Germans had marched through the Jewish quarters of Haifa shouting "*Heil Hitler*!"[250] In 1936, Cornelius Schwarz, the Landeskreisleiter in Palestine, informed the consul general about a scheduled HJ roll call in Jan-

243 *Die Warte des Tempels*, 31 July 1934, 105.
244 *Die Warte des Tempels*, 15 Feb. 1935, 20.
245 *Die Warte des Tempels*, 29 Feb. 1936, 31.
246 Correspondence 1935, ISTA, 822/3-פ; Correspondence, bills, balances, 1937, ISTA, 821/4-פ; correspondence, Feb. and Mar. 1938, YVA, R 3/25.
247 *Die Warte des Tempels*, 15 June 1935, 83; Correspondence, spring 1935, ISTA, 822/3-פ.
248 HJ monthly report, Apr. 1936, ISTA, 822/6-פ.
249 *Die Warte des Tempels*, 15 June 1935, 84; 15 Oct. 1935, 148–49.
250 Balke, *Hakenkreuz im Heiligen Land*, 46.

uary. He wrote the roll call would take place in Sarona and would be open to the public.[251] In October 1934, the HJ group of Jaffa gathered on a Monday evening for its regular meeting at the German consulate in Jaffa. A rock was thrown through the window, and three unidentified boys fled the scene The rock was wrapped in paper with the written note "Rettet Thälmann!" (Rescue Thälmann!—a well-known Communist who was later murdered by the Nazis).[252]

A meeting with HJ members from Haifa and Bethlehem-Waldheim was planned in March 1939. Cornelius Schwarz advised canceling it because of the difficult situation and for security reasons.

> Since one is repeatedly trying to blame the members of Waldheim, I think we should refrain from everything that could attract attention there.... So far we have escaped unscathed. Therefore, we should be cautious and not tempt fate."[253]

Schwarz did not mention who was blaming the inhabitants of Waldheim, nor for what they were being blamed. Were they involved in the Arab uprising? Did they hide rebels and their weapons? Max Ulich, chairman of the Jerusalemsverein (Jerusalem Association), did note in his annual report for 1939–40 that the settlement in Waldheim had faced certain problems. The Jewish press accused the inhabitants of supporting Arab guerrillas by providing them a hiding place and an arms depot.[254] A year earlier, an HJ member in Haifa reported on September 6, 1938 that the members had to turn in their uniforms, emblems, and decorations for a time because Nazi officials had heard of a planned raid at their local NS group by the British police. The items were given back to them on November 1, 1938.[255]

The Palestine HJ was in contact with other NS country groups. In 1937, the Bulgarian Hitler Youth planned a trip to Egypt and Palestine, intending to meet HJ members in Haifa and Jerusalem.[256] By 1937, almost every German boy and girl in Palestine had joined the new youth movement. In 1938–39, its leaders were Eugen Faber (HJ head), Stephan Sickinger (Secretary of the HJ in Haifa), Walter Beck

---

251 Cornelius Schwarz to Consul General, 9 and 14 Jan. 1936, ISTA, 497/1049-פ.

252 C. Schwarz to Außenhandelsamt of the AO, 6 Nov. 1934, ISTA, 821/6-פ. Thälmann's murder took place in August 1944.

253 C. Schwarz to the local NS groups, 18 Mar. 1939, ISTA, 821/5-פ: "Nachdem immer wieder versucht wird Waldheim etwas anzuhängen, glaube ich auch, dass es besser wäre, dass wir alles unterließen, was jetzt dort auffallen könnte.... Wir sind bis jetzt ohne Schaden aus der Sache herausgekommen und wollen daher immer wieder vorsichtig sein und das Schicksal nicht herausfordern."

254 Cf. *NNM* (Apr. 1940): 8.

255 HJ, Haifa, protocols 1938–1939, ISTA, 822/9-פ.

256 Letter to the local NS groups Haifa and Jerusalem, 1 Apr. 1937, YVA, R 3/25.

(sports director), Gerhard Breisch, and Eberhard Scheerer (Heimabend organizer in Haifa).[257] By 1939, the Palestine Hitler Youth numbered more than 270 boys and girls between 10 and 18 years old.

257 List of names in appendix; and HJ Haifa, protocols 1938–1939, ISTA, 822/9-פ.

5 NS Women in Palestine

Like their male counterparts, many German women at home and abroad felt humiliated by the Treaty of Versailles. They disliked the democratic system of the Weimar Republic and longed for the former Kaiserreich. As the Führer and his party promised to strengthen the German Reich and improve Germany's reputation in the world, many women and men became members of the Nazi party for this particular reason. But it also happened very often that a woman decided to join the NSDAP because her husband or another male relative belonged to the party.[258] The idea of a large ethnic community especially attracted women who were politically active in right-wing parties. The majority of those in the German women's movement and the right-wing parties defined the woman's role as mother and guardian of the German culture and nation. This role entitled them to work outside of their home and family as nurses, teachers, and social workers. In the 1930s, the concept of "social motherhood" acquired a racial connotation, as the "social mother" came to be seen as the guardian and keeper of the race.[259] Women members of the NSDAP mainly belonged to the lower middle class and were tailors, teachers, secretaries, clerks, and saleswomen.[260]

National Socialists saw women as servants for their children, family, home, and nation, whose main task was to maintain the "Aryan race." Thus, their attitudes and goals regarding women were anti-feminist. Hitler once even suggested giving German citizenship only to married women. A woman was expected to work subservient to a man and to sacrifice everything for her family and fatherland.[261] Despite the anti-feminist program of the Nazi leadership, they sought to attract more women to the party. In order to unite all existing women's groups and to control their ideas about emancipation, the NS Women's League was founded on October 1, 1931, led initially by Elsbeth Zander. In 1934, it was reorganized under the leadership of Mrs. Gertrud Scholtz-Klink (1903–1978).[262] By spring 1933, the League had already established local groups in all the German cities; and at its peak it numbered 2.3 million women. Its goal was to engage women in the fields of charity (soup kitchens, sewing workshops), sanitation, National

258 Hans-Jürgen Arendt, Sabine Hering, and Leonie Wagner, eds., *Nationalsozialistische Frauenpolitik vor 1933. Dokumentation* (Frankfurt a.M., 1995), 33–36.

259 Raffael Scheck, "Zwischen Volksgemeinschaft und Frauenrechten: Das Verhältnis rechtsbürgerlicher Politikerinnen zur NSDAP 1930–1933," in *Nation, Politik und Geschlecht. Frauenbewegungen und Nationalismus in der Morderne*, edited by Ute Planert (New York and Frankfurt, 2000), 234–53; see 247–49.

260 Arendt, *Nationalsozialistische Frauenpolitik*, 33–36.

261 Ibid., 45–47, 51, 69.

262 Snyder, *Encyclopedia of the Third Reich* (New York, 1976), 250–51.

Socialist education, and training German housewives in home economics.[263] The principles of the NS Women's League were to fight the "Jewish Marxist spirit" and to keep up the Christian faith, giving common ground between National Socialism and the Christian religion. The badge of the League displayed a cross with a swastika and three letters — GLH for *Glaube, Liebe, Hoffnung* (faith, love, hope, a reference to Paul's famous passage on love in I Corinthians 13:1–13). NS propagandists pointed out that both National Socialists and Christians valued the woman's role as mother and wife, and fought against atheism. This party line was not very successful among Catholic women, but attracted many Protestant members.[264] This was also true in Palestine, where only one Catholic woman member is documented by name, while dozens of Protestant and Templer women joined the NS women's groups in the British Mandate.

Long before the existence of the NSDAP in Palestine, women of the German Protestant community in Jerusalem came together regularly to do needlework, organize charity bazaars, and pray for the Christian mission to the world. Women's prayer groups founded by the German Mission League for Women existed in Haifa, Waldheim, Jaffa, and Jerusalem.[265] Sarona and other Templer groups also sponsored ladies' auxiliaries which met at the Temple Society community houses to do needlework, knitting, and crocheting. In the 1920s and 1930s, the Ladies Auxiliary in Sarona organized an entertainment night at least once a year, at which a play would be performed, songs sung, and jokes told.[266]

With the political rise of the National Socialists, German women in Palestine became active in the new movement. In July 1932, the very first Nazi cell in Palestine numbered six people, of which two were women — Maria Wohlfarth from Jerusalem and her friend Gertrud Koch from Jaffa.[267] According to the correspondence of the NSDAP, Gertrud Koch worked at the Ottoman Bank, and joined not only the NSDAP but also the DAF (Deutsche Arbeitsfront, German Labor Front), volunteering as its treasurer. She left the party because of financial problems in December 1932.[268]

Luzie Weno, born in 1903, was an active and enthusiastic member of the NS group in Jerusalem from March 1934 on; officially entered as a party member in October 1934. She collected donations for the NS Winter Relief Program and oc-

263 Arendt, *Nationalsozialistische Frauenpolitik*, 49–50.

264 Ibid., 63.

265 Hans Wilhelm Hertzberg, ed., *Jerusalem. Geschichte einer Gemeinde* (Kassel, 1965), 70–71; *EvGB* (May 1925): 19; *EvGB* (July 1933): 54; *EvGB* (Aug. 1933): 63.

266 Helmut Glenk, *From Desert Sands to Golden Oranges. The History of the German Settlement of Sarona in Palestine, 1871–1947* (Victoria, 2005), 168–69.

267 Ernst Bohle to Karl Ruff, 16 July 1932, ISTA, 821/1-פ.

268 Correspondence, 1932, ISTA, 821/1-פ.

casionally helped lead the BDM in Jerusalem.[269] In September 1934, she lectured at a compulsory evening of the Nazi group in Jerusalem, speaking on "The German Woman and National Socialism." She pointed out that Hitler had helped the German woman find herself and follow her "natural" destiny. Women could now accept their responsibility for the family and the German nation and see their children as their most valued gift to the nation.[270]

A Catholic, Luzie Weno had come to Jerusalem sometime in 1932–33 to work as a teacher at Schmidt's Girls School.[271] She regularly joined the meetings of the Nazi party. Her superior, Father L. Sonnen, on the other hand, only participated in meetings organized by the consulate, and avoided those of the NSDAP. In October 1935, Luzie Weno joined a religious order, the Religious Cooperative of the Poor School Sisters (*Religiöse Genossenschaft der Armen Schulschwestern*), whereupon she cancelled her NSDAP membership. Ludwig Buchhalter, who headed the NS group in Jerusalem, and other party members were concerned and wondered whether Weno had left the party for religious reasons. In the correspondence preserved on the matter, we find that on January 19, 1936 she wrote to explain that she had left the party only because she could no longer afford the monthly membership fee for the NSDAP.[272]

Besides Luzie Weno, a few other women lectured on NS topics in Palestine and took an active role within the party and its various organizations. On May 10, 1934, Mrs. Walla, a party applicant, spoke in Jerusalem on the German Labor Service and its positive effect on the German economy and morality, based on the idea that all Germans were united through their work and nationality.[273] Ida Hahn, an active member of the Jaffa group, applied for membership in 1933 and was accepted in 1934. In February 1937, she presented a slide show on her trip to Germany to an audience of young girls, with whom she afterwards discussed the founding of a new group to teach needlework to girls and young women (*Zur Erlernung und Weiterbildung von weiblichen Handarbeiten*).[274] Helene Hornung

269 Character reference by Ludwig Buchhalter, Jerusalem, 10 Jan. 1939, ISTA, 821/9-פ.

270 Monthly Report, local NS group in Jerusalem, Sept. 1934, ISTA, 821/5-פ.

271 Cf. Valmar Cramer, *Ein Jahrhundert deutscher katholischer Palästinamission 1855–1955* (Cologne, 1956), 128. Schmidt Girls' School (now Schmidt's College) was founded in 1886 as a Catholic missionary school.

272 L. Buchhalter to AO (Office for Educators), 10 Jan. 1939; and Office for Educators to Ludwig Buchhalter, Jerusalem, 22 Dec. 1938, ISTA, 821/9-פ; Ludwig Buchhalter, Jerusalem, character reference for Luzie Weno, 10 Jan. 1939; Luzie Weno to Ludwig Buchhalter, Jerusalem, 18 Oct. 1935, BArch PK/T0026, pic. no. 1194-1223; Luzie Weno to NS official, 19 Jan. 1936, Barch PK/T0026, pic. no. 1194-1223; see also Barch-PK (ehem. BDC) 1200/0054/99.

273 Monthly Report, NS local group, Jerusalem, May 1934, ISTA, 821/5-פ.

274 ISTA, 822/15-פ; Report for the Gauwaltung in Berlin, 9 Mar. 1937, YVA, R 3/25.

belonged to the Arbeitsgemeinschaft der Deutschen Frau im Ausland.[275] In spring 1939, she spoke to the NS group in Wilhelma, asserting that German children in Palestine missed their homeland with its nature and landscape – the longing for the German soil would last forever from one generation to the next, she said.[276]

Several German women helped collect donations for the annual Winter Relief Program, which financed the NS People's Welfare Organization; among them were Meta Bauer, Hulda Beilharz, Hulda Frank, Irene Haar, Hulda Jung, Else Kruegler, and Erkentrud Schmidt, all from Haifa.[277]

A few young women held the position of a BDM leader; Anna Hornung, for example had been born in Wilhelma in 1906 and was a nursery school teacher.[278] Luise Bulach, also born in 1906 (in Jaffa) and trained as a kindergarten teacher, was in charge of the BDM group in Haifa.[279] Paula Hahn, a teacher in the NS Teachers' Alliance, held a leading position in the BDM in Jaffa-Sarona.[280] In this context, she wrote a character reference for a BDM member, Emma Baumert. Emma, born in Jaffa on September 10, 1922, belonged to the League of German Girls from May 1, 1934 to October 31, 1936. Paula Hahn described her as a good comrade who sometimes missed meetings because of a difficult situation at home.[281]

German women also helped establish new women's groups in Palestine in the 1930s. The Temple Society journal reported in May 1938 that Beate Wurst of the Temple Society had introduced a local branch of the NS Women's League (NS Frauenschaft) in Haifa. She visited the German Colony in March 1938 and explained the guidelines of the NS group to the women and young girls of the colony, encouraging them to become members. After a short hesitation, the response was so positive that only a few days later, the entire women's association of Haifa's Temple community had joined the new NS women's group. On April 24, 1938, the official foundation of the new association with some 150 invitees took place at the nicely decorated hall of the German sports club.[282]

---

275 Letter, 3 Jan. 1939, ISTA, 823/2-פ.
276 Helene Hornung, speech, spring 1939, ISTA, 823/2-פ.
277 See list of names in the appendix.
278 Membership records, United States Holocaust Memorial Museum (hereafter, USHMM); Yad Vashem, R 3/1.
279 Membership records, USHMM; List of March 9, 1937, YVA, R 3/1; NSLB membership list, 1 June 1938, ISTA, 821/9-פ.
280 NSLB membership list, 1 June 1938, ISTA, 821/9-פ; Letters, 16 Mar. 1935 and 6 Jan. 1938, ISTA, 822/3-פ; Circular, 25 Mar. 1939, ISTA, 823/2-פ; List, 9 Mar. 1937, YVA, R 3/1.
281 Paula Hahn, character reference, 7 Oct. 1936, YVA, R 3/20; ISTA, 822/15-פ.
282 *Die Warte des Tempels*, 31 May 1938, 76; Paul Sauer, *Uns rief das Heilige Land. Die Tempelgesellschaft im Wandel der Zeit* (Stuttgart, 1985), 252.

It should be noted that *Die Warte des Tempels* is the sole source to document the founding of a local branch of the NS Frauenschaft in Palestine. Further archival material, including correspondence, newsletters, and circulars from the AO in Berlin, and letters by Beate Wurst only show the activity of the local groups of the Arbeitsgemeinschaft der Deutschen Frau im Ausland in Haifa and other parts of Palestine, but make no mention of the NS Frauenschaft.[283] It can therefore be assumed that the Temple Society journal actually documented the beginnings of the AGdFA in Haifa, rather than the NS Frauenschaft (NSF) itself, which operated in Germany.

The Arbeitsgemeinschaft der Deutschen Frau im Ausland was established in Germany on 1 August 1933.[284] (Although McKale states that it was founded a year later.[285]) Its overseas work groups were directed by the Auslands-Organisation (AO) in Germany, which had formed several new departments in 1933–34.[286] The aim of the AGdFA was to gather together all National Socialist women abroad to support the ideology of the party, and to foster the German ethnic community (Volksgemeinschaft) in the fields of culture (teaching NS ideology, folk dance, German songs, etc.), social work (support for large families, collecting donations for the Winter Relief Program), and economy (training girls in household tasks, home economics).[287]

The Gau-Frauenschaftsleiterin (head of the NS women abroad), Wera Behr, was responsible for the overseas groups.[288] These associations were established in Guatemala, Chile, Brazil, and in other NS country groups.[289] In October 1936, Behr notified all German women abroad that they could join the NS Women's League after their return to Germany only if they had been members of the AGdFA. In early 1936, the League had changed its membership regulations. Only those who had provided outstanding service for National Socialism were wanted and accepted.[290] Leaders of the BDM, the Women's Labor Service, and the DAF Women's Office could still apply for membership because they had proven themselves as good and trustworthy NS leaders.[291]

---

283 Cf. ISTA 823/2-פ.

284 *Nachrichtendienst der NS-Frauenschaft*, 15 Nov. 1935, 430.

285 Donald M. McKale, *The Swastika outside Germany* (Kent State, 1977), 50.

286 *Nachrichtendienst der NS-Frauenschaft*, 1 Jan. 1935, 15; McKale, *Swastika outside Germany*, 50.

287 *Nachrichtendienst der NS-Frauenschaft*, 15 Nov. 1935, 430–32.

288 *Nachrichtendienst der NS-Frauenschaft*, 15 Oct. 1935, 379.

289 *DZ — Deutsche Zeitung für Guatemala und das übrige Mittelamerika. Deutsches Auslandsinstitut, Stuttgart. Wochenzeitung, Guatemala 1932 –1941*; *Mitteilungsblatt der Leitung der AO der NSDAP* (mid-Nov. 1936).

290 *Mitteilungsblatt der Leitung der AO der NSDAP*, no. 41 (beginning of Oct. 1936): 6.

291 Dorothee Klinksiek, *Die Frau im NS-Staat* (Stuttgart, 1982), 122.

In June 1938, Wera Behr notified leaders of the AGdFA about the official terms of admission: if a member of the NS Women's League or the German Women's Agency (*Deutsches Frauenwerk*) moved abroad, her personal data had to be collected before she could join the AGdFA.[292] In the following August, she pointed out that there was no membership ban or limitation for the AGdFA. Every woman National Socialist who applied for the AGdFA had to be accepted.[293]

By the beginning of 1939, local associations of the AGdFA were operating in Jaffa, Sarona, Wilhelma, Haifa, Waldheim-Bethlehem, and Jerusalem, and additional "Evening Groups" met in Jaffa-Sarona, Wilhelma, and Haifa. Beate Wurst of the Temple Society was nominated as country leader of the AGdFA in Palestine. She recruited women, wrote circulars to the local NS women's groups, forwarded official news from the Auslands-Organisation (AO) in Berlin, and organized meetings.[294] Hanna Dreher, born in 1876 in Stuttgart, was the head of the AGdFA in Wilhelma.[295] Johanna Decker was responsible for the quarterly reports of Wilhelma's NS women's work group.[296] Edeline Schmidt was assigned as NS women's leader in Haifa, and Lotte Beck headed the youth group of Haifa's AGdFA, formerly called Jungfrauenverein for women between 18 and 30 years old.[297] Leaders and active members of the AGdFA were allowed to wear the badges of the chief officers of the NS Women's League, but it was emphasized that only a woman of "Aryan" descent could do so. A woman suspected of possible Jewish origin had to produce her *Ariernachweis* (proof of "Aryan" descent).[298]

Members of the AGdFA paid a monthly membership fee.[299] Membership cards were printed in Germany and sent to the local groups of the AGdFA in Palestine in order to keep track of these fees.[300] The program of the AGdFA comprised lectures on education, reading the Führer's speeches and circulars from the NS Frauenschaft in Germany, singing songs, and celebrating special private events, such as the silver wedding anniversary of Beate Wurst and her husband.[301] Girls affiliated to the AGdFA youth groups sewed and wore their own uniform blouses.[302]

292 Wera Behr, circular, 1 June 1938, ISTA 823/2-פ.
293 Wera Behr, circular, 25 Aug. 1938, ISTA 823/2- פ.
294 ISTA, 823/2-פ (1938–1939). Beate Wurst sometimes referred to herself as "temporary country leader of the AGdFA" (in Feb., March, May, and Aug. 1939).
295 Luise Hoffman, correspondence, 30 Mar. 1939, ISTA, 823/2-פ.
296 Quarterly Report, Wilhelma, 30 June 1939, ISTA, 823/2-פ.
297 Cf. *Die Warte des Tempels*, 31 May 1938, 76.
298 *Mitteilungsblatt der Leitung der AO der NSDAP*, no. 32 (beginning of Nov. 1935): 6.
299 Letters and circulars, 1938–1939, ISTA 823/2-פ.
300 Beate Wurst, correspondence, 2 and 3 May 1939, ISTA 823/2-פ.
301 Quarterly Report, AGdFA, Wilhelma, 30 June 1939, ISTA 823/2- פ.
302 Wera Behr, circular, 25 July 1938, ISTA 823/2- פ.

The *Nachrichtendienst der NS-Frauenschaft* journal was circulated among the AGdFA members.[303] In addition, some members received the monthly *NS Frauenwarte*.[304] Members of the AGdFA members in Palestine were asked in January 1939 to provide short descriptions of their daily lives as housewives. Else Boger-Eichler, author and editor at the NS women's Department of Political and Home Economics, planned to publish a book called *Volksdeutsches Hausfrauentum* (Work of the ethnic German housewife), in which she would feature German housewives in Palestine. The following writers and topics were suggested by Beate Wurst and her assistant Charlotte Hiendlmayer: Maria Hardegg, "Stories of the Beginnings of the German Colonies"; Mrs. Dreher, "The Daily Life of a Teacher's Wife"; Anne Sawatzky, "The Daily Life of a Woman Farmer"; Helene Hornung, "Raising Children in an Agricultural Colony"; Anne Bulach, "The Day of a Woman Farmer and Orange Planter"; and Berta Hoenig, "Music and Social Life in a Swabian Colony in Palestine."[305]

Beate Wurst forwarded to members in August 1939 a circular asking them to recruit young "Aryan" women 18 to 32 years old for a nurses' training program in Germany because the fatherland and its NS groups abroad lacked nurses, and this would be a great opportunity to serve the ethnic community.[306]

In July 1939, Consul Timotheus Wurst asked his wife Beate to send forms and lists of names for the distribution of the Cross of Honor for the German Mother in Palestine.[307] From the local NS group in Wilhelma, the following mothers were to receive recognition: Kathrine Decker (11 children), Veronika Richter (9 children), Barbara Sawatzky (8), Anna Edelmaier (7), Hanna Dreher (7), Elise Loebert (7), Nane Kazenwadel (6), Anna Hornung (6), Maria Hahn (6), Lydia Vollmer (6), Karoline Reichert (6), Susanna Goerzen (6), Gottliebe Reichert (5), Helene Hornung (5), Anna Scheerle (5), Lydia Frank (5), Marta Sawatzky (5), Magda Scheerle (5), Dorothea Ottmar (5), Lina Decker (5), Frida Steller (4), Friederike Imberger (4), Katharina Dreher (4), Anna Sawatzky (4), Maria Hardegg (4), Anna Beilharz (4), Maria Klink (4), and Friederike Vollmer (6).[308]

The bronze, silver, or gold "mother's cross" had been introduced in Germany by the NSDAP in December 1938. It was meant as an analog to the soldier's Iron Cross, honoring women for strengthening the ethnic community, and only a few women rejected the award. The emblem consisted of a cross-shaped pendant with

303 *Mitteilungsblatt der Leitung der AO der NSDAP* (1934–1937).
304 Bill, 30 May 1939, ISTA 823/2-פ.
305 Correspondence, 3 Jan. 1939, ISTA, 823/2-פ.
306 Circular, 7 Aug. 1939, ISTA, 823/2-פ.
307 Beate Wurst to Hanna Dreher, 7 July, 1939, ISTA, 823/2-פ.
308 List, 6 Mar. 1939, ISTA 823/2-פ.

a swastika in the center. The bronze medal was awarded to mothers of at least four children, while the golden one was given to women with at least eight children. Only German women who could prove their "Aryan" descent, and whose children were likewise held to be pure members of the German ethnic community, were eligible.[309]

Friedrich Wagner, who headed the NS group in Haifa, had already developed the idea of honoring German mothers in Palestine in April 1939, and corresponded with NSDAP head Cornelius Schwarz on the subject.[310] The award was thus a component of the NS cult that worshipped the German ethnic mother of many children, stigmatized sick and childless women, and excluded "non-Aryan" mothers. Importing the idea to Palestine, where Germans lived as a Christian minority among Jews and Arabs, was an expression of their faith in, and support for, the superiority of the German race.

309 http://www.dhm.de/lemo/html/nazi/innenpolitik/mutterkreuz/; http://www.wikipedia.org/wiki/Mutterkreuz/ (Feb. 2006).

310 Friedrich Wagner to Cornelius Schwarz, 27 Apr. 1939, ISTA, 821/9-פ.

6 Outsiders and Opponents

Archival documents prove that a few Germans opposed the establishment of a NSDAP branch in Palestine, criticized its activities, or refused to join the party, its organizations, and affiliated associations. Hans Frank, who pictured himself as a true supporter of National Socialism, complained in October 1933 that only a few Germans in Palestine felt close to the Nazi movement while the rest remained hostile or indifferent.[311] Two years later in 1935, Cornelius Schwarz also mentioned the opposition to the goals and policies of National Socialism.[312]

Sister Theodore Barkhausen (1869–1959), a loyal member of the Rheinisch-Westfälischer Diakonissen-Verein in Kaiserswerth,[313] was asked to join the NS women's association in Palestine but she never accepted.[314] She had been in charge of the German Protestant guesthouse of the Auguste Victoria Foundation in Jerusalem from 1910 until World War I. From 1923 on, she headed the German Deaconesses' Hospital in Jerusalem and was the representative of the Kaiserswerth's work in the Orient.[315] Sister Theodore also was the spokeswoman of the Auguste Victoria Foundation, but she resigned in 1929 because she felt the way some Germans handled things in Palestine was embarrassing, arrogant, and improper. In her reports and letters to officials in Germany, she never showed any arrogance or pride in being German. It was very important to her to live according to the rules of the religious Order, serving the poor and helping the needy regard less their religion or nationality.[316] Her prominence and skills naturally brought her to the attention of the Nazi women's organization.

---

311 Hans Frank to Mr. Seiz, Mergentheim, 25 Oct. 1933, ISTA, 3160/9-פ.

312 Cornelius Schwarz, Jaffa to Außenhandelsamt, Berlin, 9 Mar. 1935, ISTA, 821/6-פ.

313 The Rhineland-Westfalian Society of Deaconesses (*Rheinisch-Westfälischer Diakonissen-Verein*) was founded in Kaiserswerth (Düsseldorf, Germany) in 1836. Its members were dedicated to the organization like Catholic nuns to their orders (uniforms, no salary, obedient to the Society's rules and Mother Superior). In order to point out this fact, it was decided to call this Society a Protestant order.

314 Ruth Felgentreff, "Diakonisse Theodore Barkhausen, 18. August 1869–1. November 1959," in *Mitteilungen aus Ökumene und Auslandsarbeit*, edited by Kirchenamt der Ev. Kirche in Deutschland (Breklum, 2002), 1–56, 54 mentions the NS Frauenschaft in Theodore Barkhausen's biography, but see chapter 5: NS Frauenschaft vs. Work Group of the German Woman Abroad in Palestine.

315 Felgentreff, "Diakonisse Theodore Barhausen, 53–54; see also Roland Löffler, "Die Gemeinden des Jerusalemsvereins in Palästina im Kontext des kirchlichen und politischen Zeitgeschehens in der Mandatszeit," in *Seht, wir gehen hinauf nach Jerusalem. Festschrift zum 150jährigen Jubiläum von Talitha Kumi und des Jerusalemsvereins*, edited by Almut Nothnagle, Hans-Jürgen Abromeit, and Frank Foerster (Leipzig, 2000): 185–212, 193.

316 Heidemarie Wawrzyn, *Ham and Eggs in Palestine. The Auguste Victoria Foundation 1898–1939* (Marburg, 2005), 39–46, 53, 125.

Her personal rejection of membership in the NS women's group is worth noting because the Kaiserswerth Order which had sent her to Jerusalem was loyal to Hitler and his new government. Hans von Cossel, the chief executive of the Rheinisch-Westfälischer Diakonissen-Verein, spoke at the institution's centennial in praise of the political changes of the previous three years in Germany, during which their compatriots in Germany and abroad had regained their national pride thanks to Hitler, "God's tool, the true Führer."[317] Officials of the Nazi regime appreciated the deaconesses' achievements in the Orient. Shortly before the outbreak of World War I, German settlements abroad bcame important to the German Reich as potential bastions of a peaceful imperialism. German values and power were brought to other countries through culture and language, social and missionary work. Women's groups operating abroad were seen as the ideal organizations to bring German culture and education into other regions. The woman as "mother of the culture" was able to introduce German values and ideas without raising suspicion in foreign countries.[318] This explains why the Nazi government welcomed the work of the Kaiserswerth deaconesses in the Orient; its director, Count Siegfried von Lüttichau,[319] could proudly announce that his organization had the very best of relations with the new regime in Germany.[320]

Provost Ernst Rhein, who headed the German Protestant community in Palestine, never joined the NSDAP. Among party members, he was considered a troublemaker because he occasionally criticized Nazi decisions, in particular their school policy and the dismissal of Consul General Wolff because his wife was Jewish.[321] In 1936–37, Rhein and a few other ministers opposed the establishment of

---

317 *Der Armen- und Krankenfreund* 10/12 (1936): 353–54.

318 Angelika Schaser, "Das Engagement des Bundes Deutscher Frauenvereine für das 'Auslandsdeutschtum': Weibliche 'Kuturaufgabe' und nationale Politik vom Ersten Weltkrieg bis 1933," in *Nation, Politik und Geschlecht. Frauenbewegungen und Nationalismus in der Moderne*, edited by Ute Planert (Frankfurt, 2000), 256–59.

319 In 1939, Count Siegfried von Lüttichau appointed the zealous Nazi member Auguste Mohrmann as Mother Superior. Cf. M. Berger, *Vorschulerziehung im Nationalsozialismus. Recherchen zur Situation des Kindergartenwesens 1933–1945* (Weinheim, 1986), and H.-M. Lauterer, *Liebestätigkeit für die Volks-gemeinschaft. Der Kaiserswerther Verband deutscher Diakonissenmutterhäuser in den ersten Jahren des NS-Regimes* (Göttingen, 1994).

320 *EvGB*, Nov. 1934: 87; *Der Armen- und Krankenfreund* 7/8 (1933): 7–12; 9/12 (1933): 212; 4/6 (1938): 88; Letter, 26 Nov. 1937, ISTA, 3160/9-פ; cf. Karl Klingemann, "Die Kaiserswerther Arbeit im Ausland und das Auslanddeutschtum," in *Auslanddeutschtum und evangelische Kirche. Jahrbuch 1934* (Munich, 1934), 126–142, 140–42.

321 *EvGB* (Oct. 1935): 106; *Palestine Post*, 25 July 1935, 1; *Die Warte des Tempels*, 15 Oct. 1935, 149; Roland Löffler, "Die Gemeinden des Jerusalemsvereins in Palästina im Kontext des kirchlichen und politischen Zeitgeschehens in der Mandatszeit," in *Seht, wir gehen hinauf nach Jerusalem. Festschrift zum 150jährigen Jubiläum von Talitha Kumi und des Jerusalemsvereins*, edited by Al-

a joint German school with a NS curriculum, being themselves in favor of a Protestant school that would promote German culture and language.[322] Nevertheless, at a discussion on the issue, Provost Rhein assured the NSLB Landesobmann and representatives of the Lyceum Tempelstift that the education of the Protestant School would always be aimed exclusively at the objectives of the Reich.[323] When Rhein applied for membership in the NS Teacher's Alliance (NS-Lehrerschaft), he was rejected because of his reputation.[324] Even so, he cooperated with the Nazis, since the majority of his parish council had joined the NSDAP.[325] Furthermore, one of his close friends was Dr. Franz Reichert of the DNB (German News Agency), an SD agent in Palestine who collaborated with the Nazi Security Service by providing the German government with information on Jewish companies and organizations, Arab rebels, and British military sites.[326] Provost Rhein's letters and activities show him to have been a strong German patriot with an anti-Jewish attitude. In August 1934, a memorial service for the President of the Third Reich, Paul von Hindenburg, was held at the Lutheran Church of the Redeemer attended by more than 500 people.[327] In his sermon, Provost Rhein praised Hindenburg as Germany's savior, sent by God to give the leadership to Adolf Hitler.[328] The following November, he wrote to the board of the Jerusalemsverein in Germany about a meeting at which the future of the Auguste Victoria Foundation guesthouse on the Mount of Olives was discussed. The possibility of reopening the guesthouse under Kaiserswerth management was considered, and he explained this would be the best way to maintain its Protestant character and restrict German Jews from using it. Rhein feared that Jews would "pour" into the hospice, pointing out that

---

mut Nothnagle, Hans-Jürgen Abromeit, and Frank Foerster (Leipzig, 2000): 185–212, 298; Ralf Balke, *Hakenkreuz im Heiligen Land. Die NSDAP-Landesgruppe Palästina* (Erfurt, 2001) 88–90, 110.

322 On the dispute, see the correspondence of the NSLB in Palestine, ISTA, 821/8-פ; Löffler, "Die Gemeinden des Jerusalemsvereins," 180, 190–91.

323 Roland Löffler, *Protestanten in Palästina* (Stuttgart, 2008), 176.

324 Letter, Cornelius Schwarz, 2 May 1937, ISTA, 525/1377-פ; Provost Ernst Rhein to C. Schwarz, 18 Feb. 1938, ISTA, 821/9-פ; Löffler, "Die Gemeinden des Jerusalemsvereins," 208; Balke, *Hakenkreuz im Heiligen Land*, 87–89.

325 Christoph Rhein, "Eine Kindheit in Jerusalem," in *Dem Erlöser der Welt zur Ehre. Festschrift zum hundertjährigen Jubiläum der Einweihung der evangelischen Erlöserkirche in Jerusalem*, edited by Karl-Heinz Ronecker (Leipzig, 1998), 222–28, 226–28; *EvGB* (May 1933): 21.

326 *Palestine Post*, 26 Sept. 1934: 2; *Die Warte des Tempels*, 31 July 1939, 110; Balke, *Hakenkreuz im Heiligen Land*, 113–14. For more details on Reichert's anti-Jewish and anti-British activities from 1934 until his deportation in June 1939, see ibid., 113–24.

327 YVA: R3/20; *Palestine Post*, 7 Aug. 1934, 1.

328 *EvGB* (Sept. 1934): 68–69.

the Catholic Emmaus guesthouse was already "flooded" by Jews from Germany.[329] Rhein's correspondence, reports, and remarks reveal him to be a proud German Protestant nationalist who welcomed the new Nazi era and was loyal to Hitler. In one of his annual reports he confessed that he had seriously thought of joining the Nazi party in order to publicly express his support for the German NS state, but ultimately decided against doing so because he thought that during difficult political times in Palestine he could serve the NS state more efficiently as an official non-Nazi who voluntarily served Hitler and Germany without any apparent pressure from the party. Furthermore, he was convinced that Christian ministers should not be officially involved in political activity.[330] Detwig von Oertzen, a minister in Haifa (1921–1937) advanced the same view.[331] In spite of all this, Nazi leaders in Palestine disliked Provost Rhein, calling him an "unpleasant clergyman."[332]

Another "unpleasant clergyman" was the Protestant minister, Heinz Kappes, who had left Germany because he disagreed with the new Reich Bishop Mueller and his church policy.[333] Kappes worked within the German Protestant community, giving sermons at the Protestant church in Jaffa and visiting church members in their homes. In January 1935, Cornelius Schwarz reported to the Außenhandelsamt (Foreign Trade Office) in Germany that Kappes opposed Germany's new NS policy and did not think highly of the NSDAP.[334]

Ilse Wolff, the wife of Consul General Heinrich Wolff, was a convert active in the German Protestant community, serving on the parish council of the Lutheran Church of the Redeemer in Jerusalem. From 1933 on, she and her husband were targeted in an antisemitic campaign because of her Jewish descent, with NS officials sometimes expressing the suspicion that Heinrich Wolff himself was "non-Aryan." The consul general served in Jerusalem from December 1932 to July 1935 but was not generally well-liked in the German community. In 1933, he supported the Haavara Agreement, a transfer pact between the Third Reich and the Zionist Federation of Germany to enable the transfer of capital of German Jews and promote their immigration to Palestine.[335] As German settlers feared the increas-

329 E. Rhein to Jerusalemsverein, Nov. 1934, EZA, 56/83. Emmaus-Kubebe was a German Catholic guesthouse, founded by the Deutscher Verein vom Heiligen Land; see *Das Heilige Land* (Jan. 1925): 33.

330 Ernst Rhein, Annual Report, Oct. 1932–Dec. 1933, EZA 56/188.

331 Detwig von Oertzen, correspondence, 20 June 1934, *Jerusalemsverein*, B 536.

332 Löffler, "Die Gemeinden des Jerusalemsvereins," 208.

333 C. Schwarz to Außenhandelsamt of the AO, 4 Jan. 1935, ISTA, 821/6-פ.

334 C. Schwarz to Außenhandelsamt of the AO, 13 Jan. 1935, ISTA, 821/6-פ.

335 The Haavara [transfer] Agreement was the sole contract negotiated between an official Third Reich authority and a Zionist organization. Germany benefitted in that German products were exported to Palestine, while the Zionist organizations were able to help resettle a large number

ing number of immigrant Jews and their competition as farmers, they therefore saw Consul Wolff as persona non grata.[336] In his correspondence with German NS officials, Wolff often criticized their antisemitic policy, but nevertheless applied for party membership in autumn 1933.[337] Shortly afterward, Karl Ruff, who had founded the Nazi branch in Palestine, began investigating Consul General Wolff and his wife, assisted by Ludwig Buchhalter and Cornelius Schwarz. Their report to the AO in Germany led to Wolff's dismissal in July 1935.[338] Jewish newspaper reports greatly deplored his dismissal, as did Provost Rhein, who published an article in the church newsletter honoring Ilse Wolff for her strong involvement in the Protestant community in Jerusalem; local Nazis angrily took note of it.[339]

At the beginning of the 1930s, doubts and objections were also voiced by some Temple Society members. Although the majority of Nazi party members were recruited from the Temple Society, a few Templers questioned the NSDAP program and its racist ideology. Older members of the Temple Society hesitated to join the new Nazi branch in Palestine because they were strongly concerned that a political party would split their community.[340] Georg Wagner, Sr. (born 1857), chairman of the Council of Elders and head of the Templer community in Jaffa, was never a member of the NSDAP although he believed that the Führer was sent by God.[341] Philipp Wurst (born 1882), head of the Temple Society from 1935 on, distrusted the local Nazi organization in Palestine because he disliked parvenus and arrogant people, as he considered the local NS leaders to be.[342] In December 1934, Cornelius Schwarz reported to the AO that Philipp Wurst's negative atti-

---

of German Jews, who otherwise would not have been able to leave Germany because of currency and other restrictions. For more details see Francis R. Nicosia, ed., "Central Zionist Archives, 1933–1939" in *Archives of the Holocaust* (New York, 1990): 3: 364–65, 51; idem, *The Third Reich and the Palestine Question* (London, 2000), 39–49; cf. Lenni Brenner, ed., *51 Documents: Zionist Collaboration with the Nazis* (Fort Lee, N.J., 2002); Joseph Paul Hoffmann, "The Price of Flight: German Jews, the Nazi Regime and the Finance of the Ha'avarah Agreement, 1933–1939" (Ph.D. diss., Columbian College of Arts and Sciences, George Washington University, Washington, D.C., 2002); Edwin Black, *The Transfer Agreement. The Dramatic Story of the Pact between the Third Reich and Jewish Palestine* (New York, 1999).

336 Balke, *Hakenkreuz im Heiligen Land*, 106.

337 Ludwig Buchhalter, correspondence, 28 Feb. 1934, ISTA, 822/15-פ.

338 ISTA, 3162/19-פ; Balke, *Hakenkreuz im Heiligen Land*, 106–11; Eckart Conze, Norbert Frei, Peter Hayes, and Moshe Zimmermann, *Das Amt und die Vergangenheit: Deutsche Diplomaten im Dritten Reich und in der Bundesrepublik* (Munich, 2010), 107–8.

339 *EvGB* (Oct. 1935): 106; *Palestine Post*, 25 July 1935, 1; Balke, *Hakenkreuz im Heiligen Land*, 109–10; cf. Buchholz, correspondence, 13 Dec. 1933, ISTA, 823/8-פ.

340 Cf. Report, meeting of NS officials, Jerusalem, 31 Jan. 1935, ISTA, 821/5-פ.

341 C. Schwarz, correspondence, 20 Dec. 1934, ISTA, 821/6-פ.

342 Balke, *Hakenkreuz im Heiligen Land*, 83–84.

tude towards the NSDAP was causing conflicts between the party and the Temple Society.[343] In 1934–35, Philipp Wurst, Ernst Baumert, and a few other Templers opposed the new German Faith Movement, which sought to abolish the Old Testament and "liberate" the Christian religion from its Jewish roots.[344] Some Templers even published flyers to protest the introduction of a "Germanic" religion.[345] All in all, however, Philipp Wurst's speeches and articles along with his willingness to cooperate with local Nazi leaders indicate that he was not a strong and determined opponent to National Socialism. In fact, his attitude gradually changed with the early foreign policy successes of the Third Reich, and in the autumn of 1938, he became a member of the NSDAP.[346]

The remaining Templers belonged to a "silent majority." They were either politically apathetic or didn't want to identify openly with one side or another. According to Alex Carmel, there were anti-Nazis within the Temple Society, such as Johannes Pross, a native of Haifa whose letters decried the infatuation of the youth with National Socialism. Like many other Templers, Pross was exiled to Australia in 1941 by the British as an enemy alien during wartime. In letters to his father, he wrote that many Templers in Australia continued to persecute and anathematize him until the 1950s because of his anti-Nazi views.[347]

Die Warte des Tempels published its first article by Dr. Alfred Weller and Richard Hofmann on the NSDAP in February 1932, focusing on Hitler, his program, and the development of the Nazi party. The essay continued in the March and June issues.[348] Weller and Hoffmann criticized the economic program of the new government and the antisemitism and racism of the NSDAP, among other issues. They pointed out that antisemitism played a major role within the party, although they did agree with the National Socialists that there was a racial difference between Jews and Germans. At the same time, the authors rejected the racial theories as arbitrary and refused to accept a racial ranking list. At the time of writing, in 1932, they called antisemitism an unjust prejudice that stigmatized Jews as capitalist, immoral, and greedy. Nevertheless, Weller and Hoffmann emphasized that National Socialism and the Temple Society had something in com-

343 C. Schwarz to Außenhandelsamt of the AO, Hamburg, 20 Dec. 1934, ISTA, 821/6-פ.

344 The German Faith Movement, founded in 1933 by Jakob W. Hauer (1881–1962), aimed to provide the Third Reich with a new, non-Jewish, religious basis. See Shaul Baumann, *Die Deutsche Glaubensbewegung und ihr Gründer Jakob Wilhelm Hauer (1881–1962)* (Marburg, 2005).

345 Balke, *Hakenkreuz im Heiligen Land*, 84–85.

346 Ibid., 83–84.

347 Alex Carmel, "What's this? Making fun of Nazis?," *Haaretz*, 29 Oct. 1999, 13.

348 Dr. Alfred Weller was an assistant physician at the German Deaconesses' Hospital in Jerusalem. Richard Hoffmann served in the German consulate.

mon — their patriotism.[349] Later on, in 1934, Hoffmann expressed doubt about the strength of the Nazi party; in several lectures, he pointed out that the success of the party was mainly based on Hitler's compelling and charismatic personality.[350]

German businessmen in Palestine also opposed the orders and decisions of local NS officials. On a number of occasions, they refused to follow orders, and even protested them for business reasons. Among other things, the antisemitic policy negatively affected their relations with local Jewish companies. Cornelius Schwarz informed the Foreign Trade Office in Berlin in May 1935 that German companies in Palestine cooperated with Jews and did business with them. The largest German enterprise in Palestine, Firm Paul Aberle, had branches in Jaffa, Jerusalem, and Haifa, and employed Germans, Jews, and Arabs. Its joint partner, Wilhelm Aberle, was the agent for the German Levant Shipping Line, the Hamburg-America Shipping Company, IG Farben, and several other German companies. He was on the board of directors of the Tempelbank, and was the mayor of the German Colony Jaffa-Sarona. Schwarz complained in his letters that German businessmen (citing Wilhelm Aberle in particular) did not welcome the establishment of the NSDAP in Palestine. These companies held that it would be better not to have any German party in Palestine; they feared that the Nazi party would split the German community and endanger business relations with Jews. In May 1935, Schwarz reported to the Foreign Trade Office in Berlin that the Firm Paul Aberle in Jaffa had been the only company that closed at 1 P.M. on the May 1 holiday. All other business owners had followed the Party's instruction to close their shops and businesses the whole day, highlighting the provocative character of celebrating German national holidays in the Holy Land.[351] Schwarz even accused Aberle of pressuring fellow Germans in Palestine *not* to join the Nazi party. He perceived Wilhelm Aberle as a ringleader in opposing the Nazi movement from the beginning and did not hesitate to inform the AO in Germany of this. When Wilhelm Aberle eventually applied for membership in the NSDAP, Schwarz thwarted his application.[352] Aberle's opposition towards NS directives is documented up to 1942.[353]

In spring 1933, protests by German businessmen had already occurred when the Auswärtiges Amt (Foreign Office) decided that on the Memorial Day of Heroes the new flags of the German Reich were to be raised at the German consulates

349 *Die Warte des Tempels*, 2 Feb. 1932, 25–27; 15 Mar. 1932, 33–35; 15 June 1932, 83–86.
350 *Die Warte des Tempels*, 28 Feb. 1934, 29.
351 Cornelius Schwarz, correspondence, 4 and 9 May 1935, ISTA, 821/6-פ.
352 Ibid.; Paul Sauer, *Uns rief das Heilige Land. Die Tempelgesellschaft im Wandel der Zeit* (Stuttgart, 1985), 271–72, 301–2.
353 Sauer, *Uns rief das Heilige Land*, 301.

in Jerusalem and Jaffa. German settlers welcomed the return of the black-white-red flag of the Kaiserreich, but many of them opposed the display of the second swastika banner. Businessmen sent a telegram to Reichspräsident Hindenburg asking for an exemption in consideration for the Jews in Palestine, but this was rejected by the Auslands-Abteilung. Businessmen in Palestine also attempted to oppose the anti-Jewish boycott, scheduled in Germany for April 1, 1933. Cornelius Schwarz reacted angrily to this protest, writing to his son in Egypt that such German groups had to be neutralized.[354]

Other objections were expressed by individuals. Heinrich Wagner refused to join the German Labor Front (DAF) in Jaffa-Sarona although his company was a NS Betriebszelle (business cell) of the local DAF. Johannes Weiss, the head of the DAF in Jaffa-Sarona, tried to recruit him in 1939, but without success.[355]

The daughter-in-law of Mr. K. Kaiser, who owned a bakery in Jaffa, delivered her baby in a Jewish hospital in Tel Aviv, a decision that angered Dr. O. Rubitschung and Cornelius Schwarz, party members who called it a scandal because Germans should support each other in times of hatred and boycott against the Palestine-Germans.[356]

Another curious case involved Egon Schultz, a NSDAP member who worked as a mechanic at the Syrian Orphanage in Jerusalem, and was engaged to Ms. Ottilie Thuma. His fiancée's father was from Syria and her mother (Friederike Thuma, née Wurst) from Germany. In July 1936, Egon Schultz sent a letter to the Ministry of Interior through the German consulate in Jerusalem asking to grant him permission to marry his fiancée.[357] On July 20, 1936, Ludwig Buchhalter, the local group leader in Jerusalem, wrote to Schultz pointing out that he could not remain a member of the Nazi party if he married a non-Aryan woman. A week later on July 28, 1936, he advised him not to marry Ottilie Thuma in consideration of his descendants and for the sake of the German people.[358] Later, Egon Schultz informed the local NS group in Jerusalem that he had received permission to marry from the German Ministry of the Interior, and was therefore handing in his resignation.[359]

Wilhelm Bender became a member of the NSDAP in Palestine on June 1, 1934. A teacher at the German school in Waldheim from October 1932 to December 1936, he joined the NS Teachers' Alliance, and was much engaged in party affairs, lecturing and volunteering for the Waldheim community, its families, and

354 Balke, *Hakenkreuz im Heiligen Land*, 80–81.
355 Correspondence, 24 Jan. 1939, ISTA, 823/4-פ.
356 C. Schwarz to Außenhandelsamt, 30 Dec. 1934, ISTA, 821/6-פ.
357 Egon Schultz to Ministry of Interior, 9 and 17 July, 1936, ISTA 6/19-תת.
358 Buchhalter, correspondence, 20 and 28 July 1936, ISTA, 6/19-תת.
359 Egon Schultz, correspondence, n.d., ISTA, 6/19-תת.

Nazi groups. Because of his interest in pedagogy Bender had been a member of the Anthroposophical Society until 1932. Nazi leaders such as Heinrich Himmler and Reinhard Heydrich blamed the Society for being internationally oriented and having close contacts with Jews and pacifists.[360] The society was prohibited in Germany from November 1935 on. Bender's former membership in the Anthroposophical Society led Nazi officials to question his loyalty and set him outside the profile of a "true Nazi." Furthermore, his character reference noted that he had never quit his membership in the Protestant Church. Wilhelm Bender left Palestine in December 1936.[361]

In August 1939, shortly before World War II broke out, a German settler in Jerusalem published an anonymous cry for help in the daily *Palestine Post*, declaring:

> We are constantly watched by a network of spies and Nazi officials who sow discord in our ranks so that no man can trust his neighbour. They compel us to become members of various Nazi organisations.[362]

In summary, it may be said that a few Protestants and Templers expressed disagreement with some elements of the NS ideology and their disapproval of certain local Nazis' directives. Among them, one can find NSDAP members, rejected applicants, and even those who believed that Hitler had been sent by God. Protest was never directed against National Socialism in its entirety and was not strong and determined enough to stop Nazi activity in the Holy Land. Most of the expressed disagreement arose out of religious, commercial, or private concerns. Opponents feared that Nazi policies would harm their business interests, split the local German communities, or water down their religious beliefs. According to the documented sources, antisemitism was not a great concern among Palestine-Germans. Objections decreased after 1935 when Cornelius Schwarz was appointed as Landeskreisleiter (regional Nazi leader) and Walter Doehle, a loyal Nazi party member, as consul general.[363] As no other objections are documented in archives and libraries, it can be assumed that the majority of Germans in Palestine either agreed with the NS ideology or kept silent and went on with their daily life.

It is noticeable and worth mentioning that the number of German Catholics within the Nazi organization was very low. Archival material refers to only two

360 http://www.waldorfanswers.org/AnthroposophyDuringNaziTimes.htm (10 Mar. 2006).
361 Character reference by Hans Sus, 20 Feb. 1938, ISTA, 821/9-פ.
362 *Palestine Post*, 21 Aug. 1939, quoted in Balke, *Hakenkreuz im Heiligen Land*, 70.
363 Balke, *Hakenkreuz im Heiligen Land*, 80 asserts that the opposition from the Templer side ceased completely after 1935. But documents at the Israel State Archives prove that a few protests continued until 1942.

Catholic Nazi members by name, Luzie Weno (mentioned in the previous chapter), and Father Hermann Keller, temporarily assigned to the Dormition Abbey in Jerusalem. Keller was a member of the Nazi party and the *Sicherheitsdienst*, the intelligence service under the command of SS leader Reinhard Heydrich.[364] A reporter from the *Jerusalem Post* speculates that Father Hermann Keller was actively involved in the failed attempt to rescue Edith Stein, a Jewish convert who was at that time a Carmelite nun. Her religious community in Germany had sent her to Echt in Holland for safety, but still fearful of the Nazis, she requested to be transferred to her order's house in Bethlehem. The Vatican rejected her request; according to contemporary accounts and interviews, the Mother Superior in Bethlehem expressed doubt that "the Jewish-born philosopher nun would fit in with the Arab Christian sisters in Bethlehem."[365] It is most likely – according to the reporter Douglas Davis – that Father Hermann Keller, who was close to the Vatican and fully aware of Edith Stein's case, would have been consulted. It is almost certain that he would have counseled against such a transfer because, after all, he was not only a member of the Nazi party, but also a star of the Sicherheitsdienst. Edith Stein was arrested by the Nazis in occupied Holland and died in Auschwitz on August 9, 1942.[366]

Besides Hermann Keller and Luzie Weno, one can find several names and addresses of Catholic clergymen and nuns who regularly received invitations to NS meetings and celebrations, but nothing is known or documented to prove they were ever involved in the party.[367] This is not surprising since the German Catholic community consisted of only 100–180 members in Palestine, and the Catholic Church generally proved more resistant to National Socialism than the German Protestant churches.[368] Numerous studies on the Catholic Church and its response to the Third Reich show that the pope, priests, and community in general reacted more defensively than offensively.[369] Therefore, the absence of German Catholics

---

364 Douglas Davis, *Jerusalem Post*, 9 Oct. 1998.

365 Ibid.; cf. Alec Israel, *The Monasteries and Convents of the Holy Land* (Jerusalem, 2002), 103–5.

366 Douglas Davis, *Jerusalem Post*, 9 Oct. 1998; Israel, *Monasteries and Convents*, 103–5; http://www.carmelite.com/saints/edith1.shtml (update: 7 Aug. 2007).

367 Invitation, Apr. 1939, ISTA, 497/1049-פ, with the names Bishop Fellinger, Sister Constantia, Abbot M. Kaufmann, Frater S. Kaufmann, Father P. Ostertag, Father J. Sonnen, and Sister Margarethe.

368 *Das Heilige Land* (Jan. 1925): 31–32; *Yediot Achronot*, 1 Oct. 1999, 54; Schmidt 1952: 461; Letter, Consul General of Spain, Jerusalem, 11 Dec. 1939, *Politisches Archiv des Auswärtigen Amts* (PA AA), R 41853; Report, 1940, PA AA, R 41854; Report, 1942, R 41855.

369 Peter Godman, *Hitler and the Vatican. Inside the Secret Archives taht Reveal the New Story of the Nazis and the Church* (New York, 2004), 171; Donald Niewyk and Francis Nicosia, *Columbia Guide to the Holocaust* (New York, 2000), 251–52; Rudolf Lill, "NS-Ideologie und katholische

from the Nazi groups in Palestine cannot be interpreted as strong resistance or outspoken objection. It was more likely silent protest or indifference.

Kirche," in *Die Katholiken und das Dritte Reich*, edited by Klaus Gotto and Konrad Repgen (Mainz, 1990), 144; Klaus Gotto, Hans Günter Hockerts, and Konrad Repgen, "Nationalsozialistische Herausforderung und kirchliche Antwort. Eine Bilanz," in ibid., 189; see also H. Schmidt, "The Nazi Party in Palestine and the Levant, 1932–9," *International Affairs* 28, no. 4 (1952): 466 (on Catholics in Palestine, 1932–1939).

7 Nazi Members

Figures, Religious Attitudes, and Political Background

In the late 1930s, approximately 2,000 to 2,500 non-Jewish Germans lived in Palestine.[370] Not all were Templers, as is sometimes mistakenly assumed. They came from several religious backgrounds and were living in Palestine for a variety of reasons. Generally speaking, they fell into three categories: Germans who had settled there permanently, such as the Pietist group of Templers; others who had come to serve in various Christian institutions for a longer period, such as the craftsmen-missionaries from St. Chrischona,[371] the Schneller family,[372] or the Deaconesses of Kaiserswerth[373]; and a third group of Germans on temporary duty, such as consuls, representatives of the Protestant and Catholic churches, and ministers and missionaries at churches and missionary outposts throughout Palestine.[374]

Nevertheless, the majority of the Germans in Palestine were part of the Temple Society, which consisted of 1,290 Templers in 1939.[375] The remaining Germans

370 Francis R. Nicosia, *The Third Reich and the Palestine Question* (London, 2000), 93, 253, n. 36: 1,800 Germans resided in Palestine in 1933, and 2,500 in 1937. YVA, R 3/11, 6 June 1937: 450 Germans in Jerusalem (345 adults, 105 children), 600 in Haifa, 607 in Sarona-Jaffa, 240 in Wilhelma, 89 in Bethlehem-Waldheim. Total: 1,986 Germans. The consulate's letters and files put the number of Germans in Palestine at 2,500 (letter, German consul general, Jerusalem, 1937; letter, German consul general, Jerusalem 1938, YVA, R 3/27; YVA, R 3/30; letter, Carl Lutz, 1939, YVA, P $19/2_3$). The average figure of 2,250 Palestine-Germans was taken for the calculations in this study.

371 For further information see Alex Carmel, *Christen als Pioniere im Heiligen Land. Ein Beitrag zur Geschichte der Pilgermission und des Wiederaufbaus Palästinas im 19. Jahrhundert* (Basel, 1981), 23–25; Martin Lückhoff, *Anglikaner und Protestanten im Heiligen Land. Das gemeinsame Bistum Jerusalem (1841–1886)* (Wiesbaden, 1998), 165–68; Mitri Raheb, *Das reformatorische Erbe unter den Palästinensern. Zur Entstehung der Evangelisch-Lutherischen Kirche in Jordanien* (Gütersloh, 1990), 62; and E. Jakob Eisler, *Peter Martin Metzler (1824–1907). Ein christlicher Missionar im Heiligen Land* (Haifa, 1999), 18–19.

372 Johann Ludwig Schneller founded the Syrian Orphanage in 1860. See Raheb, *Das reformatorische Erbe*, 66–77.

373 For more information on the Deaconesses of Kaiserswerth, see Heidemarie Wawrzyn, *Ham and Eggs in Palestine. The Auguste Victoria Foundation 1898–1939)* (Marburg, 2005), 37–51.

374 Erich Geldbach, "The German Protestant Network in the Holy Land," in *With Eyes toward Zion—III: Western Societies and the Holy Land*, edited by Moshe Davis and Yehoshua Ben-Arieh (New York, 1991), 150–69, 153.

375 Paul Sauer, *Uns rief das Heilige Land. Die Tempelgesellschaft im Wandel der Zeit* (Stuttgart, 1985), 268.

belonged to the German-speaking Protestant churches, with 420 to 500 members, and to the Catholic Church, with approximately 100 to 180 associates.[376] Between 1932 and 1939, approximately 740 Germans participated in the NS groups in Palestine.[377] This figure included more than 420 party members and party candidates (*Parteianwärter*), and almost 280 children and teens organized in the Hitler Youth program. The remaining forty or so people joined various NS groups and associations, such as the NSLB and DAF, without being officially party members. To get a general idea how many Germans in Palestine were under the influence of National Socialism with its racist and antisemitic ideas, it is important to count everybody who joined an NS group regardless of age and party membership status. In sum, approximately 33% of all Palestine-Germans participated in the NS network, and almost 19% of the Palestine-Germans were NSDAP members.[378]

The vast majority (approximately 75%) of the Nazi party members and NS participants came from the Temple Society. More than 42% of all Templers participated in Nazi party activities in Palestine, that is, every second or third Templer was involved in an NS group or belonged to the HJ organization.[379] Nevertheless, this figure opposes the assumption that *every* Templer was a Nazi, an idea that spread in Israel until the 1960s, mainly the result of a tendentious newspaper article by Haviv Knaan.[380] About 22% of the members affiliated with the NSDAP or an NS group in Palestine were Protestant or belonged to the Kirchlers.[381] Catholics with less than 1% were thus underrepresented. As we have seen, the German Catholic community was very small; and German Catholics, with their bitter memories of the *Kulturkampf* (cultural struggle, 1871–1878), tended to distance themselves from the German Protestants. Furthermore, Catholics generally proved themselves more resistant to National Socialism than the German Protestants.[382]

376 *Yediot Achronot*, 1 Oct. 1999, 54; *Das Heilige Land* (Jan. 1925): 31–32.
377 See Appendix: List of NS members.
378 Cf. Ralf Balke, *Hakenkreuz im Heiligen Land. Die NSDAP-Landesgruppe Palästina* (Erfurt, 2001), 69. 17% of Palestine-Germans belonged to the NSDAP in 1938.
379 Cf. Alex Carmel, *Haaretz*, 29 Oct. 1999, 13.
380 Ibid.
381 Kirchler were those who had joined the Temple Society but returned to the Protestant church in 1885–86.
382 Peter Godman, *Hitler and the Vatican. Inside the Secret Archives that Reveal the New Story of the Nazis and the Church* (New York, 2004), 171; Donald Niewyk and Francis Nicosia, *Columbia Guide to the Holocaust* (New York, 2000), 251–52; Rudolf Lill, "NS-Ideologie und katholische Kirche," in *Die Katholiken und das Dritte Reich*, edited by Klaus Gotto and Konrad Repgen (Mainz, 1990), 144; Klaus Gotto, Hans Günter, and Konrad Repgen, "Nationalsozialistische Herausforderung und kirchliche Antwort. Eine Bilanz," in ibid., 189; Jakob Eisler, Norbert Haag, and Sabine Holtz, *Kultureller Wandel in Palästina im frühen 20. Jahrhundert. Eine Bilddokumentation* (Epfendorf, 2003), 165.

Of approximately 420 party members, 26% were female and 74% male. This differs from the analysis of 1937 published by the AO, which claimed that 90% of all party members abroad were men.[383] When one focuses on everybody who joined the NS network regardless of their official membership status, the collected data show that approximately 37% were women and girls. The age profile of the NS movement indicates that many Germans belonged to the younger generation when they entered the party, HJ program, or one of its associations. Children and juveniles between ten and eighteen years made up more than one-third of all NS participants and party members. Middle-aged people between thirty and forty years were numerically very strongly represented. It is remarkable that according to the collection of several membership lists and records, those who joined NS groups at the age of nineteen or twenty were underrepresented. This was probably because they generally went to Germany for a certain period of time for studies, job training, or the Reich Labor Service. People sixty-one and older generally hesitated to join the NS groups or did not enter them at all. Professionally, the great majority belonged to the middle class. Teachers, including nursery and kindergarten teachers, were at the top of the professional groups, followed by farmers and engineers. There were also several clerks and bank officials, as well as craftsmen, businessmen, and merchants. A few architects, physicians, and clergymen joined the party organizations as well.[384]

Many German Protestants and Templers came from religious families; some were descendants of German pioneers who had lived in Palestine for more than sixty years. The Germans tended to live separately from the Arab and Jewish populations; and relations with these two groups centered mainly on economic matters.[385] Arabs worked in their colonies, and Jews were business partners and customers for their farm products.[386] Some German settlers consulted Jewish doctors for health problems.[387] Catholics generally lived within the walls of their in-

---

383 Donald M. McKale, *The Swastika Outside Germany* (Kent State, Ohio, 1977), 120, 233, note 2.

384 For detailed data and its sources see list of names in the appendix.

385 Balke, *Hakenkreuz im Heiligen Land*, 160; Roland Löffler, "Die Gemeinden des Jerusalemsvereins in Palästina im Kontext des kirchlichen und politischen Zeitgeschehens in der Mandatzeit," in *Seht, wir gehen hinauf nach Jerusalem. Festschrift zum 150jährigen von Talitha Kumi und des Jerusalemsvereins*, edited by Almut Nothnagle, Hans-Jürgen Abromeit, and Frank Foerster (Leipzig, 2000), 208–9; EZA 5/1947: Annual Report, Provost Rhein, 1931–1932; C. Schwarz, correspondence, 9 Mar. 1935, ISTA, 821/6-פ.

386 Helmut Glenk, *From Desert Sands to Golden Oranges. the History of the German Settlement of Sarona in Palestine 1871–1947* (Victoria, 2005), 155–60.

387 Ibid., 155–56.

stitutions, for most were monastics who had less contact with other Germans in general and local Nazi members in particular.[388]

As in many countries outside Europe, Germans tended to live together in close-knit colonies where they maintained their German culture, language, and heritage. They were proud of their private German schools, their sports groups, book clubs, and youth organizations.[389] In general, they felt like foreigners in foreign countries, no matter how long they had been living abroad. As foreigners and belonging to a minority, their sense of togetherness and German identity were extremely important to them.[390]

Culturally or religiously Christian, the Palestine-Germans shared a common faith and German national pride; their general political attitudes can be described as conservative, patriotic, and monarchic. They were proud of their achievements in Palestine such as the establishment of Christian institutions, the development of infrastructure, and several technological innovations.[391] In their letters and newsletters, they expressed fear of immigrant Jews, and showed sympathy for (Christian) Arabs as their affordable employees and fellow believers. Both German Protestants and Catholics emphasized their good connections with the Christian Arabs. Christianity was the strong bond that gave them a feeling of togetherness and a commitment to caring for their "brothers and sisters in Jesus Christ."[392]

It is remarkable that at least 30% of the NS participants and party members had been born in Palestine. More than twenty Palestine-born Germans were party members of the Nazi branches in Egypt, Turkey, Kenya, Mexico, and other places.[393] One might assume that the ties to Germany of that generation would not be

388 Balke, *Hakenkreuz im Heiligen Land,* 92; H. Schmidt, "The Nazi Party in the Levant 1932–9," *International Affairs* 28, no. 4 (1952): 460–69, 466.

389 Donald M. McKale, *Swastika outside Germany*, 4–5; Balke, *Hakenkreuz im Heiligen Land,* 92; Schmidt, "Nazi Party in the Levant," 466.

390 Cf. *Die Warte des Tempels*, 15 June 1932, 83–86.

391 Ruth Kark and Naftali Thalmann, "Technological Innovation in Palestine: The Role of the German Templers," in *Germany and the Middle East. Past, Present and Future*, edited by Haim Goren (Jerusalem, 2003), 201–24.

392 Article, Hermann Schneller, 23 Oct. 1934, ISTA, 821/5-פ; Response to DAF questionnaire, 1938, ISTA, 823/4-פ; *Das Heilige Land* (July 1906): 96; *NNM* (1914): 82–83; correspondence, esp. Nov. 1934, EZA, 56/83; sermon, E. Katz, 22 Apr. 1945, CZA, S25/4060; Paul Sauer, "Vom Land um den Asperg – im Namen Gottes nach Palästina und Australien," lecture, 20 Oct. 1995, Burgstetten.

393 *Nazi Party Membership Records*, submitted by the War Department to the Subcommittee on War Mobilization of the Committee on Military Affairs, United States Senate, United States Government Printing Office, Washington, D.C., 1947 (at the library and archives of the United States Holocasut Memorial Museum; henceforth, Membership Records, USHMM). See appendix, list of names and data.

very strong, especially among those whose families had already been living in Palestine for two generations. But most had grown up in a German idyll, which had been only sporadically disturbed by Jewish-Arab clashes.[394] Their parents preferred to live in close-knit units where they conserved their German language and culture, including German fashion and furniture.[395] Even German traditional folk dancing was cultivated with girls wearing appropriate costumes (*Trachten*).[396] In 1939, Helene Hornung of the AGdFA, pointed out that German children in Palestine missed their homeland, with its nature and landscape. She firmly believed that the longing for the German soil would last forever from one generation to the next.[397] Thus, while many Germans called Palestine their homeland, it seems they also missed the German homeland which their parents or grandparents had left many years ago. Many sent their children to Germany for higher education, other studies, or to learn a profession. Furthermore, in the 1930s young men of military service age were required to go to Germany to do compulsory military training. The Hitler Youth provided trips to Germany. A few Palestine-Germans even participated in the Nuremberg Rallies (Nürnberger Parteitage).[398]

Their ideological ties to Germany became stronger in the 1930s. It should be remembered that the Palestine-Germans had been deported to Egypt in August 1918, and allowed to return only in 1920.[399] The Weimar government in Germany had not sent support to them to rebuild and resume their work in Palestine, so there was a general sense of having been neglected. As a result, they were less critical and distant when it came to the new Nazi government. Most did not like the idea of having many political parties, which seemed to them to weaken Germany, and they opposed any democratic system, favoring the idea of a strong nation with one leader.[400] Thus, when the Nazis came to power, Germans in Palestine saw their hopes for a renewed, strong Germany being realized.[401] Many Christian believers saw the events of 1933 as a miracle which God had worked to save Germany. Listening to German broadcasts became an event capable of moving them to tears. Many Templers believed Hitler was destined to continue

---

394 Tempelgesellschaft Deutschland, *Damals in Palästina — Templer erzählen vom Leben in ihren Gemeinden* (Stuttgart, 1990).
395 Archives of the Temple Society, Stuttgart and Melbourne, photos of families, stage plays, rooms, and buildings.
396 Glenk, *From Desert Sands*, 181.
397 Helene Hornung, speech, spring 1939, ISTA, 823/2-פ.
398 Notes on Werner Frank, ISTA, 3162/10-פ.
399 Hans Wilhelm Hertzberg, ed., *Jerusalem. Geschichte einer Gemeinde* (Kassel, 1965), 59–61.
400 Cf. Löffler, "Die Gemeinden," 204; *Die Warte des Tempels*, 31 May 1933, 73.
401 Balke, *Hakenkreuz im Heiligen Land*, 69, 72, 224; letter, 2 Jan. 1946, Schumacher Institute, P-LK-01.

the national and religious work of Luther—to complete Luther's Reformation.[402] Käthe M. Pfänder, born in Haifa in 1922, described the new Nazi era and the reaction of the Germans:

> We noticed that Germany was gaining respect among other nations. For us, there was no difference between Germany and Nazi-Germany. After the war when we learned about the Nazi crimes, we could not believe them for a very long time. During the war, we thought it was bad-mouthing and hostile propaganda by Germany's enemies.[403]

402 Schmidt, *Nazi Party in Palestine*, 462.
403 Tempelgesellschaft Deutschland, *Damals in Palästina*, 389.

8 German Relations with the Jewish and Arab Population

Perception of Jews

While it might be true that several Germans had good relationships with their Jewish neighbors and customers, as Paul Sauer and Helmut Glenk claim, the perception of Jews in general was negative.[404] In various newsletters from the 1930s and even before, the Germans in Palestine pictured Jews as foreigners in the region and as enemies of the Arabs; European Jews had changed the country profoundly by bringing Western civilization to the region and destroying Arab culture. The German Protestants were foremost in claiming that the immigrant Jews had purchased all the Arab lands and dominated the local market so that many Arab families were reduced to poverty. The Jewish immigrants were seen as part of "World Jewry" — Zionists plotting with wealthy Americans and the British. Occasionally, Jews were seen as a danger to German youth. Jewish pubs and movie theaters in Tel Aviv were suspected of having a negative impact on the moral life of the young generation of the German settlers.[405] The young immigrant Jews were perceived as immoral, and as communists or atheists.[406]

In contrast, a survey of the Catholic journal *Das Heilige Land* (1931–1938) does not display a strong involvement in National Socialism or antisemitism. Articles on Palestine, Jewish immigration, Zionist activity, and the Arab riots do not reveal particularly pro-Arab and anti-Jewish tendencies, and seem very balanced. Terms like "Jewish communists," "Jewish capitalists," "World Jewry," "Jews were flooding the country," such as were found at that time throughout the writings of German Protestants, are absent. Only one advertisement for the NS Winter Relief Program appeared on the back of the 1937 edition (no. 1–2). In July 1937, Georg Mues wrote positively about Jews and Arab Muslims in the Holy Land, with no hostile remarks or sense of superiority. At the end of his article, he regretted that the holy sites were possessed by Muslims.[407] In April 1937, a fascist speech was

404 Paul Sauer, "Vom Land um den Asperg — im Namen Gottes nach Palästina und Australien," (lecture, Burgstetten, 20 Oct. 1995); Helmut Glenk, *From Desert Sands to Golden Oranges. The History of the German Settlement of Sarona in Palestine, 1871–1947* (Victoria, 2005), 198.

405 Correspondence, 20 June 1934, Jerusalemsverein, B536; Oertzen's annual report of the German Protestant communities Haifa-Waldheim (Jaffa, 1934).

406 *NNM* (1930): 46–50; *NNM* (1931): 126; *NNM* (1933): 26; *NNM* (Apr. 1940): 23; EZA 5/1947: Annual report of the German Protestant Community in Jerusalem, 1931/32; *EvGB* (Oct.–Nov. 1930): 77; *Das Heilige Land* 55 (1911): 48.

407 *Das Heilige Land* (July 1937): 127–30.

published expressing the opinion that patriotism was just and holy, but this article seems to have been exceptional.[408]

In the 1930s, German Catholic and Protestant institutions with a predominantly Arab clientele had to face increasing pressure caused by the regional hostilities between Jews and Arabs. With the increasing number of immigrant Jews to the Holy Land, Jewish houses and neighborhoods began to extend nearer to Christian building complexes, slowly turning their neighborhoods into a Jewish quarter. Altercations also erupted occasionally between Jewish neighbors and Arab pupils at the Christian schools.[409] In 1935, Consul General Wolff reported that the Syrian Orphanage buildings were for sale.[410] Hermann Schneller, who headed the institution, complained in 1937 to the German consul general in Jerusalem that the neighborhood had become a Jewish quarter, explaining that Arab workers and the parents of his Arab students were afraid to walk through the area. He planned to relocate from northwestern Jerusalem to the street which led to Bethlehem in the city's south, noting that "our institute as a German organization cannot remain in an environment of fanatical Jews."[411] Similar problems occurred at the German school for Arab girls, Talitha Kumi, located in the Jewish area near King George Street. Sister Bertha Harz, who headed the school, informed the consul general in Jerusalem that Jews from the neighborhood had several times thrown rocks at the pupils, had stolen fruit from the garden, attacked the deaconesses, and removed the entrance sign.[412] The journal *Der Armen- und Krankenfreund* reported in 1937 that the German Deaconesses' Hospital in central Jerusalem would transfer to the Auguste Victoria Foundation on the Mount of Olives because of the unbearable traffic noise and political disturbances. The hospital had been become "an island within a Jewish ocean."[413] The Catholic St. Paul's House and Schmidt's Girls College opposite the Damascus Gate were also to be sold. Transfer of the college seemed necessary because many Arab families did not dare to send their children to the school.[414]

---

408 *Das Heilige Land* nos. 1–2 (1937): back page; *Das Heilige Land* (Apr. 1937): 71.

409 Heinrich Wolff to the Foreign Office, Berlin, 11 July 1935, ISTA, 528/1426-פ; see also letter by Hermann Schneller, Jerusalem to Consulate General, Jerusalem, 16 Nov. 1937, ISTA 528/1426-פ; Frank Foerster, *Mission im Heiligen Land. Der Jerusalems-Verein zu Berlin 1852–1945* (Gütersloh, 1991), 179.

410 Report, 11 July 1935, ISTA, 528/1426-פ; cf. H. Schneller, letter, 22 July 1935, ISTA, 528/1426-פ.

411 Letter, 16 Nov. 1937 and telegram, 8 June 1935, ISTA, 528/1426-פ.

412 Letters of 10 Aug. 1936, 10 Oct. 1936, and 16 Apr. 1937, ISTA, 1063/14-פ.

413 "Eine Insel in einem jüdischen Meer," *Der Armen- und Krankenfreund*, no. 4/6 (1937):116–17; ibid., no. 4/6 (1933): 158.

414 Deutscher Verein vom Heiligen Lande to Consul General, 18 Dec. 1936, ISTA, 527/1429-פ; see also letters, 29 Dec. 1936 and 14 Mar. 1937.

German companies and businessmen continued to maintain ties with their Jewish counterparts, but with the disapproval of Nazi leaders in Palestine such as Cornelius Schwarz, who eagerly informed the Foreign Trade Office in Berlin about it.[415] Ludwig Buchhalter, who headed the NS group in Jerusalem, shared this attitude, and wrote in anger to Gottlob Bäuerle, who owned the Orient cinema, that he had learned that the theater had been rented to Jews. Concluding his letter, he added "Confidential, not for Jewish hands."[416] Hans Sus, who led the NS group in Bethlehem-Waldheim, noted in a letter to Cornelius Schwarz that he also opposed the idea of Jews working for a German enterprise.[417]

Meetings between the staff of the German consulates with Jews were quite different, not being based on business matters or neighborly relations. The consulates handled hundreds of denaturalizations of German immigrant Jews. Every month they received official notes with names and personal data from the Foreign Office, Gestapo, and Reichsführer-SS in Germany. Usually, the consul general merely confirmed the denaturalization procedure by noting "There are no objections to the denaturalization." If the new home address of the German emigrant was known, a letter was sent to inform them of their denaturalization with a request to return their German passports for good.[418] In 1935, the consulate general informed German Jews bearing Reich passports that should they return to Germany, they would be immediately interned in camps for the purpose of "correction," to adjust them to the new civil life there.[419] Overall, the official letters and notes give the impression that the consulate staff dutifully conducted the denaturalization procedure without being aware of the cruel and central role of antisemitism within the National Socialist system.[420]

At the same time, a German Jew testified that Consul Timotheus Wurst in Jaffa and his staff member Dr. Richard O. Hoffmann went to great lengths to help immigrant Jews settle in Palestine.[421] One might question whether their action was based on humanitarian or financial reasons, considering that Timotheus Wurst was not only consul but also director general of the Tempelbank, which earned huge profits from the "immigration of capitalist Jewish elements," and

415 C. Schwarz to Foreign Trade Office, Berlin, 9 Mar. 1935, ISTA, 821/6-פ.
416 Ludwig Buchhalter to Gottlob Bäuerle, 31 Jan. 1936, YVA, R 3/17; David Kroyanker, *The German Colony and Emek Refaim Street* (Jerusalem, 2008), 59.
417 Hans Sus to C. Schwarz, 16 Mar. 1936, ISTA, 821/7-פ.
418 Correspondence, German Consulate, Jerusalem, various items, ISTA, 1036/4-פ.
419 *Palestine Post*, 20 June 1935, 1.
420 Correspondence, German Consulate, Jerusalem, various items, ISTA, 1036/4-פ; Ralf Balke, *Hakenkreuz im Heiligen Land. Die NSDAP-Landesgruppe Palästina.* (Erfurt, 2001), 107.
421 Paul Sauer, *Uns rief das Heilige Land. Die Tempelgesellschaft im Wandel der Zeit* (Stuttgart, 1985), 260–61.

in addition the bank played an important and profitable role in implementing the Haavara agreement. According to bank reports of 1935, Temple Society members benefited enormously from the increasing economic development in Palestine.[422]

With the beginning of the Arab uprising in 1936, the Germans in Palestine were often confronted with both Jewish and British suspicion that they supported the Arab cause financially and by providing weapons. German officials always rejected such charges by pointing out their neutrality. Officially, they declared more than once that they did not intend to side with any faction in Palestine since their well-being depended on both Arab workers *and* Jewish customers. Nevertheless, their political stance against the establishment of a Jewish National Home and their passive behavior in certain situations did not exonerate them. In 1936, German Consul General Walter Doehle reported to the Foreign Office in Berlin that the Jewish press suspected the Germans in Palestine of siding with the Arab rebels. Only once, he claimed, an Arab from Lydda [Lod] had asked at the consulate in Jerusalem for a delivery of weapons, but his letter had never been answered.[423] Referring to a later incident in 1938, Doehle confirmed that Arab fighters were using the German settlements as hiding places and accommodations. Doehle, who was called to a meeting with the Chief Secretary, explained that the settlers in Waldheim and Bethlehem were passive and simply did nothing to prevent such "visits." They were trying to avoid provocation and difficulties with the Arab population, which actually meant they were unwilling to oppose or resist the Arab incursion. Doehle insisted this was the only way to survive and remain neutral.[424] The consul and other Nazi officials emphasized that the official strategy was neutrality, siding with neither Arabs nor Jews. Still, they thought that a successful outcome for the Arab uprising would be in their own interest as well, making a Jewish National Home less likely.[425]

Apart from two consuls (Heinrich Wolff and Timotheus Wurst), Reich and Nazi officials in Palestine opposed the German-Zionist transfer agreement (Haavara) and the possible founding of a Jewish state because it would endanger their relationship with the Arabs, which was mostly perceived and described as positive. In 1937, they realized that the policy of the Third Reich towards Jews was actually supportive of the establishment of a Jewish state. The continuation of the Haavara agreement "encouraged" Jews to leave Germany and move to Palestine.

---

422 *Die Warte des Tempels*, 15 Apr. 1935, 50–51; 30 June 1935, 93–94; 31 Aug. 1935, 125; Sauer, *Uns rief das Heilige Land*, 260–61.
423 Consul General to Foreign Office, Berlin, 7 July 1936, YVA, R 3/27.
424 CG Walter Doehle to Dr. Melchers, Haifa , 3 Dec. 1938, YVA, R3/30.
425 Consul General to the Foreign Office, Berlin, 7 July 1936, YVA, R 3/27.

Germans in Palestine were thus afraid of losing the Arabs' sympathy and getting blamed by Arabs worldwide for having inadvertently supported the demise of Arabs in Palestine. Consul General Walter Doehle explained to the Foreign Office in Berlin that a Jewish state would fight the German settlers economically and politically, forcing them to give up their colonies and return to Germany. Doehle believed that only an Arab state would enable the various elements of the Palestine population to live peacefully together. He also understood that an Arab state would mean losing Palestine as the main site for emigration for the German Jews, at odds with the important Nazi desire for a "*judenrein*" Germany. Doehle therefore suggested continuing the status quo.[426]

When the British discussed dividing British Mandatory Palestine into three regions (British, Arab, Jewish) in 1937–38, many Palestine-Germans reacted with shock. In the Peel Commission plan, the German colonies Wilhelma, Bethlehem/Galilee, Waldheim, and Haifa would have been assigned to the Jewish segment. Only the German colony in Jerusalem would have remained under a British Mandate. In 1938, a delegation of German settlers, nominated by the representatives of the Reich and the Nazi branch in Palestine, informed the Woodhead Commission that they wished to remain under British rule; it was unthinkable for Nazis to live under Jewish rule.[427] This request was rejected, and the delegation's spokesman, Philipp Wurst, agreed to the option of living under Arab authority.[428]

Relations with the Arab population

Towards the Arab population, Protestant Germans especially, often emphasized the good and untroubled German-Arab relations. Despite the official German neutrality, letters and articles clearly pictured them as siding with the Arabs of Palestine long before the Arab uprising in 1936. From the German point of view, the Arabs were the real inhabitants, the "natives" (*die Eingeborenen*) of the region. In 1934, Cornelius Schwarz called the Arabs in Palestine the host people, furiously opposing the Jews because the Arabs were being driven into the background. Germans believed the Arabs had earned the right to live in Palestine because they had been living there for about 1,300 years. They had brought Arab culture and language to the region and had "Arabized" it. Arab demonstrations against Jew-

426 Consul General to the Foreign Office, Berlin, 22 Mar. 1937, YVA, R 3/27.

427 Correspondence, German consulates, 1937–1938 YVA, R 3/27; Balke, *Hakenkreuz im Heiligen Land*, 103, 132–34; Sauer, *Uns rief das Heilige Land*, 266–67.

428 Balke, *Hakenkreuz im Heiligen Land*, 133.

ish immigration was understood as a defence of their national rights and a struggle for their own *Lebensraum* – a term used by the Nazis to justify the extension of German "living space" into neighboring zones.[429]

For many decades, Germans seemed to have been well liked among Arabs.[430] Speaking German and displaying swastika pennants and party badges sometimes enabled German drivers and motorcyclists to go through Arab villages without harm. When the German shouted Heil Hitler!, the Arab fighters became friendly and responded with "Heil Hitler."[431]

During the Arab revolt (1936–1939), such good relations changed. Palestine-Germans felt increasingly insecure because they were threatened and sometimes blackmailed by the Arab rebels; there were attacks, and even the murder of a few Germans (mainly from the Temple Society).[432] Numerous documents from the German consulate in Jerusalem contain reports about the risks and danger the Germans in Palestine faced during and after the uprising. Arabs tried to force the German colonists not to sell land or their products to Jews. Attacks were not only conducted by Arabs, but also by Jewish groups.[433] By the end of 1938, Germans recognized that the former Arab sympathy for them had decreased.[434]

Nevertheless, in 1939 Gerhard Jentzsch, the Protestant minister at the missionary station in Bethlehem, commented that

> We Germans love the Arabs and therefore we are happy to see changes within the Arab people. The desperate Arab people has formed a combat group which pursues the same goals as the ones of our missionary work, i.e., waking up the Arab people and turning the Holy Land into a land where a holy people could live and serve God.[435]

---

429 Annual reports of the German Protestant Community in Jerusalem, 1921/22, 1922/23, 1923/24, and 1924/25, EZA 5/1989; *NNM* (1911): 193; NNM (1913): 221; *NNM* (1931): 68; *NNM* (1933): 23f; *NNM* (1934): 52; *NNM* (1936): 62–70; *EvGB*, (Oct.–Nov. 1930): 77–78; G. Kampffmeyer, "Die Stellung der Araber zu den Gegenwartsproblemen Palästinas," in *Zeitschrift des Deutschen Palästina-Vereins*, edited by Martin Noth (1930): 248–259, 252; Letter, Cornelius Schwarz, 13 Nov. 1934, ISTA, 821/6-פ.
430 Annual report of the German Protestant Community in Jerusalem 1926/27, EZA 56/83; Annual report of the German Protestant Community in Jerusalem 1922/23, EZA 5/1989; *EvGB* (Oct.–Nov. 1930): 77.
431 German Consul General to Auswärtiges Amt, Berlin, 22 Mar. 1937, YVA, R 3/27; see also Sauer, *Uns rief das Heilige Land*, 264; Helmut Glenk, *From Desert Sands to Golden Oranges. The History of the German Settlement of Sarona in Palestine, 1871–1947* (Victoria, 2005), 200.
432 Balke, *Hakenkreuz im Heiligen Land*, 146; Glenk, *From Desert Sands*, 200; Moshe Temkin, "The History of the Hitler Youth in Jerusalem," *Yediot Achronot*, 1 Oct. 1999, 57.
433 Correspondence, 1938, mainly Consul General Doehle to Foreign Office, Berlin, YVA, R 3/30.
434 Melchers to Foreign Office, Berlin, 23 Nov. 1938, YVA, R 3/30.
435 *NNM* (Dec. 1939): 99.

Jentzsch's wife also emphasized the Germans' love for the Arab population, but in a conversation with Cornelius Schwarz in 1938, she noted the differences between Arabs and Germans, and said she could never approve of mixed marriage. In 1937, she had welcomed the opening of the new German School in Jerusalem, an initiative of the Nazis in Palestine. She had decided to send her children there because the number of Arab students was strictly limited, which helped reduce what she saw as their bad and immoral influence, favoring a clear separation between German and Arab children. Cornelius Schwarz happily praised this missionary family's attitude in his correspondence with the Foreign Office.[436]

The anti-Jewish and pro-Arab attitude of the Germans in general and among the Nazis in particular was intensively observed by the British in the late 1930s.[437] From documents at the Public Record Office in London, one learns that German missionaries in Palestine in particular had raised British suspicion that they were spreading propaganda among the Arabs under cover of missionary work.[438] On November 14, 1938, it was noted that a sheikh had forwarded a letter to Hitler by way of missionaries in Haifa.[439] Statements by Consul General Doehle prove the British observations correct. Doehle, known as a very loyal Nazi party member, wrote to the Foreign Office that the German missionary organizations were doing excellent propaganda work for the German culture and nation among the Arabs. Doehle praised the work of the Syrian Orphanage – calling it a patron of German culture among Arabs.[440] In the context of the NS ideology, German language and culture were important characteristics of the German ethnic community. It can be assumed that Doehle praised the "excellent work for the German culture" because it helped propagate the ideas of National Socialism; as we saw in the second chapter, the staff of the orphanage, especially the Schneller family, were very active in distributing NS literature throughout the country.[441] The Jerusalemsverein, which supported German and Arab Protestant communities in Palestine, declared that one of its important tasks was to bring the idea of ethnic community (Volksgemeinschaft) to the Arab people.[442] It is therefore unsurprising that the Nazis distributed Hitler's *Mein Kampf* among Arabs, and it is also very likely that they brought the *Protocols of the Elders of Zion* into Arab countries, as Simon

436 Cornelius Schwarz to AO Germany, 2 Mar. 1938, ISTA, 821/9-פ.
437 Balke, *Hakenkreuz im Heiligen Land*, 138.
438 British Public Record Office London (BPRO), Foreign Office (FO) 371/21887, 29 Nov. 1938.
439 BPRO, FO 371/21887, 14 Nov. 1938.
440 Walter Doehle to German Foreign Office, 11 July 1938, 12 May 1939, ISTA, 528/1426-פ.
441 YVA, R 3/18, R 3/25, R 3/26.
442 Flyer, 1939, ISTA, 528/1426-פ.

Wiesenthal recalled after World War II.[443] Several German consulates, especially those in the Middle East, asked the German government to adjust the "scale of races" in favor of the Arabs, who were excited about the Führer and welcomed NS literature and propaganda but strongly objected to ranking the Arab "race" at fourteenth place on the NS racial list. The diplomats suggested declaring Arabs to be Aryans, but although the matter was discussed at the Reichskabinett in Germany, it was ultimately rejected because such an exception would undermine the German people's consciousness of being a member of the superior race (*Herrscherrasse*).[444] Ernst Bohle from the Auslands-Organisation pointed out that Nazi party membership was for German citizens only.[445]

In July 1938, the British Foreign Office received information on a delivery of arms from Germany to Palestine.[446] Merchandise in transit had been discovered in the Romanian port of Constanţa, when a crate had dropped "from the top of the crane onto the quay with the result that the case broke open and revealed its contents to be dismounted machine guns."[447] The daily *Palestine Post* reported in 1939 that firearms and munitions were to be smuggled into Palestine through Ras el-Nakura on the Lebanese border, but French authorities there had seized more than a hundred German Mauser rifles and several thousand rounds of ammunition.[448] Even earlier, in July 1936, *Tirgumim* had reported that German cartridges had been found on Arabs.[449] Simon Wiesenthal presumed that the German colonies had secret arsenals for the "Mufti's followers," as he put it.[450]

At the end of 1938, the Chief Secretary William Battershill, learned that Arab rebels were very active in the region of Waldheim and Bethlehem in the Galilee, where two of the German settlements were used as hiding places. Consul General Doehle, called to meet with the Chief Secretary, told him that the Germans of Waldheim and Bethlehem would do nothing to prevent such "visits," which meant in practice that they were unwilling to oppose or resist the Arab incursion. Doehle argued that this was the only way to survive and stay neutral.[451] In January 1939, Doehle reported to the Foreign Office in Germany that the British had raided

---

443 *Palestine Post*, 16 Jan. 1939, 2; Simon Wiesenthal, *Großmufti—Großagent der Achse* (Salzburg and Vienna, [1946]), 12.

444 *Blumenthal's Neuste Nachrichten* (Tel Aviv), 20 Jan. 1938.

445 Francis R. Nicosia, *The Third Reich and the Palestine Question* (London, 2000) 91–92.

446 BPRO, FO 371/21888 (5 July 1938).

447 BPRO, FO 371/21888 (23 July 1938).

448 *Palestine Post*, 29 May 1939, 2.

449 *Tirgumim*, 14, 20, and 24 July 1936.

450 Wiesenthal, *Großmufti—Großagent der Achse*, 12.

451 Walter Doehle to Dr. Melchers, Haifa, 3 Dec. 1938, YVA, R 3/30.

the Waldheim Colony, but no evidence had been found.[452] In March of that year another raid was conducted in Waldheim. This time, shell casings were found which belonged to the blacksmith Staib. Both Arabs and Jews sought out and used metal items in order to produce bombs. Finds such as the shell casings of course increased British suspicion of the Germans.[453]

In sum, it could not be proved that the Nazis in Palestine were actively involved in the 1936–1938 Arab uprising, as the British and the Jewish Yishuv suspected, but German officials always denied. Officially, the Templers and Protestants emphasized their neutrality towards Jews and Arabs, pointing out their known good intentions and many achievements in improving infrastructure and agriculture, and introducing new technology to the region. Nevertheless, their anti-Jewish and pro-Arab attitude is quite evident in articles in their communal newsletters, and in the correspondence of the German consulate, making it difficult to believe their declared neutrality. Evidence was sometimes hidden from the British and documents destroyed.[454] Archival files clearly reveal that Arab rebels used the German settlements as hiding places and accommodation while the inhabitants did nothing to prevent them from doing so.[455] Maintaining their daily life depended on their Jewish customers and Arab workers, and they could not risk openly siding with the one party or the other. The Templers were eager to assure the economic survival of their colonies, threatened by the constant suspicions they faced from both the British and the Jews.[456] They were caught between conflicting frontlines: the Jews accused them of training and arming Arab rebels; the British suspected them of smuggling weapons into the country; and Arab rebels pressured them for financial and military support through threats and blackmail, while Reich and Nazi officials simply wanted to maintain the status quo

452 Walter Doehle to Foreign Office, 10 Jan. 1939, and idem to Dr. Melchers, 5 Dec. 1938, YVA, R 3/30.

453 Dr. Melchers to Walter Doehle, 14 Mar. 1939, YVA, R 3/30.

454 HJ, Haifa, Protocols, 1938–1939, ISTA, 822/9-פ. H. Schmidt, "The Nazi Party in Palestine and the Levant, 1932–9," *International Affairs* 28, no. 4 (1952): 460–69: "The condition in which I found the documents clearly indicated...that some documents had been torn out of even well preserved files.... [T]his was done by the Germans in the autumn of 1939 prior to handing over their papers to the Spanish Consulate.... Some screening of material must have taken place in 1938, because subsequent correspondence mentions missing documents. For this reason no valid conclusions can be drawn from any *argumentum ex silentio*. This applies especially to fifth column activities...." (p. 460).

455 Walter Doehle to Dr. Melchers, Haifa, 3 Dec. 1938, YVA, R 3/30; cf. German Consulate, Jerusalem to Foreign Office, Berlin, 20 July and 14 Sept. 1938, PA AA, R 104790.

456 Correspondence, 1938 and 1939, YVA, R 3/30; Glenk, *From Desert Sands*, 197; Nicosia, *Third Reich and the Palestine Question*, 107–8.

in Palestine.[457] Despite contradictory statements in the sources available, it still remains likely that some Nazis in Palestine did support the Arab uprising. First, German settlers were directly or indirectly in contact with the rebels through their Arab workers.[458] Second, there must have been some NS individuals involved in handling the smuggled weapons which have been documented. Third, since relevant documents were destroyed by the Germans in 1938 and 1939, "no valid conclusions can be drawn from any *argumentum ex silentio*."[459] Hence, it can be concluded that a number of Nazis in Palestine tried to bring about National Socialism not only by establishing a strong ethnic (racial) community but also by supporting the Arab cause.

457 Consul General to Foreign Office, Berlin, 7 July 1936 and 22 Mar. 1937, YVA, R 3/27.
458 Correspondence, German Consulate, Jerusalem, 11 July and 28 Oct. 1938, PA AA, R 104790.
459 Schmidt, "Nazi Party in Palestine," 460.

9 Reaction of the Local Population

Jewish reactions

Jews anxiously followed events in Germany and Palestine.[460] The increasing number of Nazi activities in the region was noted, including the observance of the German National Labor Day,[461] celebration of Hitler's birthday,[462] and the 1935 dedication of the German War Cemetery at Nazareth, which attracted five hundred people, including Germans from the local Nazi party.[463] The spread of NS propaganda (journals, posters, pamphlets, and other forms) caused concern among Jewish residents in the country.[464] Anti-Jewish posters urging Arabs to boycott Jewish cinema houses infiltrated the Arab quarter in Haifa: "Keep away from Jewish cinema houses, which are contemptible!"[465] The screening of German movies at Jewish-owned cinemas led to confrontations. In Tel Aviv, one Jewish audience protested so strongly that a German movie was removed from the program.[466] When the passage of the anti-Jewish Nuremberg Laws was announced in 1935, more than two thousand Jewish youth from all over Palestine filled the Edison Theater in Jerusalem to protest.[467]

In 1932–33, Jewish newspapers in Palestine had devoted little space to the development of the Nazi party branch in the region. From January 1933, when Hitler became chancellor, however, political events in Germany were given a central place in such publications, with almost daily coverage. In the spring of that year, a few newspapers published detailed reports about the German persecution of Jews, giving readers a strong sense of the grave threat from the new Nazi regime in Germany. Coverage of events and the changes in Germany was seen mainly through the prism of Zionist interests focused on Palestine and the question of how those events would affect the Zionist movement. The *Palestine Post* generally concentrated on the European and global significance of Hitler's installation as chancellor and Führer of the German people.[468]

---

460 *Die Warte des Tempels*, 30 Apr. 1933, 62.
461 *Palestine Post* 2 May 1934, 7; 3 May 1936, 12.
462 *Palestine Post*, 21 Apr. 1939, 2; *Die Warte des Tempels*, 31 May 1934, 77.
463 *Palestine Post*, 1 July 1935, 5.
464 *Palestine Post*, 2 Feb. 1936, 10; 13 Aug. 1934, 5; 28 Sept. 1934, 5; 26 Sept. 1934, 2; 1 Jan. 1935, 3; 24 Mar. 1936, 5; 17 May 1936, 2; 24 July 1939, 1–2.
465 *Palestine Post*, 13 Aug. 1934, 5.
466 Schumacher Institute, P-LK-01.
467 *Palestine Post*, 8 Dec. 1935, 1.
468 Benny Morris, *Righteous Victims. a History of the Zionist-Arab Conflict, 1881–2001* (New York, 2001), 372–78. 405–7.

Jews in Palestine protested German National Socialism and its anti-Jewish policy, which gravely concerned them and created tension and animosity toward the local Germans. Mass meetings were held in Jerusalem and Tel Aviv.[469] In May 1933, when books by Jewish authors were burnt in Germany, Jews responded by burning NS brochures and pictures of Hitler in Palestine.[470] From 1933 to 1935, Jews called for boycotts on German products and companies, and banned German films from Jewish-owned cinemas. Although Jewish boycotts were partial and came in "waves," as Cornelius Schwarz put it, the German settlements were still affected to a certain extent. In Wilhelma, Bethlehem-Galilee, and Sarona the Jewish boycott had a direct impact on the sale of milk and vegetables. German bakers had to reduce their bread production as well.[471] The anti-German boycott in Palestine weakened in the autumn of 1933, but resumed in the following spring. In 1935, an anti-German boycott was in response to the passing of the Nuremberg Laws. Jews affixed posters on shops and stores, announcing "German goods are sold here!" In general, the strength of the boycott varied with the sale of oranges to Germany – the second-largest importer of Palestinian oranges in the 1930s. Jewish leaders had to take into account the need to sustain this market and not jeopardize the orange export; thus the anti-German boycott slacked off during the export season, although it resumed as soon as the oranges were sold.[472] Overall, the boycott of German goods was much weaker in Palestine than in countries such as Poland, France, England, and the United States. Franz Reichert, who represented the German News Agency in Palestine, concluded that the boycott did not serve the Zionists' interest in creating a Jewish National Home, which relied on the import and purchase of German goods through the Haavara agreement, as well as the economic goals of Palestine's orange planters.[473]

When the swastika flag was raised for the first time at the German consulate in Jerusalem in 1933, small groups approached the consulate but no casualties were reported.[474] Occasionally, the Jerusalem consulate walls were covered with

469 *Die Warte des Tempels*, 31 May 1933, 79.

470 Schumacher Institute, P-LK-01.

471 *Die Warte des Tempels*, 30 Apr. 1933, 62; Helmut Glenk, *From Desert Sands to Golden Oranges. The History of the German Settlement of Sarona in Palestine 1871–1947* (Victoria, 2005), 198; Morris, *Righteous Victims*, 392–93, 395; Schumacher Institute, P-LK-01. Cornelius Schwarz, Jaffa to AO Germany, 9 Mar. 1935, ISTA, 821/6-פ.

472 Cornelius Schwarz, Jaffa to AO, Germany, 29 Apr. 1934, and 9 Mar. 1935, ISTA, 821/6-פ; Glenk, *From Desert Sands*, 400.

473 Franz Reichert, "Report on the Jewish Boycott in Palestine," *Industrie & Handel* (Berlin), no. 164, 19 July 1933, ISTA, 3160/9-פ; cf. Morris, *Righteous Victims*, 391–401.

474 *Die Warte des Tempels*, 15 Apr. 1933, 52.

anti-Hitler graffiti.[475] In Jerusalem, Tel Aviv, and many other parts of the country swastika flags were burnt in the traditional bonfires lit on the occasion of Lag ba'Omer.[476] In Jaffa, a few Jews entered the garden of the consulate, where they removed the German flags, tearing them and taking the swastika banner with them.[477]

Ron Lahav, who lived in Palestine in the 1930s, reported:

> With the beginning of large scale immigration from Germany in 1933 the German consulates were very much involved in dealing with legal and personal affairs for the refugees, as well as rapidly becoming centers of German political intrigue and espionage. The Germans built a big modern consular building at the entrance of Rehavia, that part of Jerusalem which became the center of German Jewish life.... There were many pictures of the swastika flag, which after 1933 became the official flag of Germany, flying from this building.[478]

The swastika flag caused anger and fear among the Jewish population, especially among those who had just escaped the Nazi terror. Lola Blonder, born in Vienna in 1894, fled Austria in 1938, emigrating with her son and daughter to Palestine.[479] She described her experience at the German consulate in Haifa:

> Again, I am standing in an office shaking from head to foot. Again, I am standing on German ground. Again, portraits of Hitler are fixed on the wall. The officials salute with "Heil Hitler!" I am at the German consulate in Haifa where I have to present my passport with the tourist visa. My stay [in Palestine] has to be approved by the German consul. I have to wait. Will they search me here? Will they find me here? My knees become shaky. When the officer finally gave me back my passport approved with a swastika stamp, I left the consulate as a broken woman. Never again I will set foot on German soil! The German consulate in Haifa is Nazi ground. It monitors us all.[480]

---

475 *Die Warte des Tempels*, 31 May 1933, 79.

476 *Palestine Post*, 21 May 1935, 5; *Palestine Post*, 7 May 1939, 2. Lag ba'Omer (literally, the 33rd day of counting the Omer), is a minor Jewish holiday that falls between Passover and Pentecost.

477 Schumacher Institute, P-LK-01.

478 Ron Lahav to Heidemarie Wawrzyn, personal communication by email, 2 Oct. 2006.

479 Anna Rattner and Lola Blonder, *Zuflucht Palästina. Zwei Frauen berichten* (Vienna, 1989), 16–17.

480 Ibid., 126: "Wieder stehe ich zitternd vor einem Schalter. Wieder stehe ich auf deutschem Boden, wieder hängen Hitlerbilder an den Wänden, die Beamten grüßen mit dem Hitlergruß: 'Heil Hitler!' Ich bin auf dem Deutschen Konsulat in Haifa, wo ich meinen Paß mit dem Touristenvisum vorzulegen habe. Mein Aufenthalt muß vom deutschen Konsul bestätigt werden. Ich habe zu warten. Werden sie mich hier suchen? Werden sie mich hier finden? Meine Knie beginnen zu wanken. Als man mir den Paß mit dem Hakenkreuzstempel zurückgibt, wanke ich gebrochen zum Tor hinaus. Nie wieder, nie wieder will ich deutschen Boden betreten! Das Deutsche Konsulat in Haifa ist Nazi-Boden. Es überwacht uns alle."

Similar reactions occurred when Jews saw a German in a Nazi uniform. Dr. Segal recounted the story of a young man who was visiting friends in Tel Aviv for Passover. As he wanted to eat leavened bread, which is not readily available during the week of the holiday, his friends advised him to go to the German Colony in Sarona to buy it. There he encountered some SA members, and was so upset that he decided to leave Palestine and go to Spain to fight the fascists.[481]

In 1933, the *Brown Book of the Hitler Terror and the Burning of the Reichstag* was published and translated into 17 languages. Millions of copies were distributed blaming the Nazis themselves for setting the *Reichstag* on fire. A year later in 1934, the *Brown Book* was banned in Palestine, angering and upsetting the Jewish population, while the distribution of Hitler's *Mein Kampf* was still allowed. The ban was perceived as unjust, and Zionist journals thoroughly reported on these protests.[482]

A very alarming incident– a massacre of 19 Jews, including 9 women and 3 children – took place on 2 October 1938 in Tiberias.[483] The following January, the *Palestine Post* reported that

> Mr. Stuart Emeny who was in Palestine recently as a special correspondent of the *News Chronicle*...says there is evidence in Palestine which suggests active German intervention on the behalf of the Rebels, and a German, it is alleged, helped to organize the massacre of the 19 Jews in Tiberias at the beginning of October last.... Mr. Emeny recapitulates the details of the Tiberias incident, adding that a German ex-officer resident in Palestine is suspected to have had a hand in many Arab acts of sabotage on high-tension pylons....[484]

Although Germans in Palestine often complained that all Jews hated them and suspected them all of being Nazis, the press seemed to distinguish between "good" and "bad" Germans. When the leader of the Temple Society, Christian Rohrer, died in an accident in 1934, the *Palestine Post* honored his work, writing: "He had always preached the gospel of peace. He declared himself to be against the doctrine of the superiority of given races, and for that reason had not favoured the Nazi race theory."[485] Christian Rohrer did not join the NSDAP but the Nazis in Palestine saw him as a man who had followed the latest events in Germany with great interest and had always tried to understand the NS ideas.[486]

481 Dr. [first name unknown] Segal, conversation with Heidemarie Wawrzyn, Jerusalem, autumn 2005.

482 See *Die Warte des Tempels*, 31 Mar. 1934, 47.

483 *Palestine Post*, 4 Oct. 1938, 1.

484 *Palestine Post*, 10 Jan. 1939, 3.

485 *Palestine Post*, 1 June 1934.

486 Monthly report, June 1934, local NS group in Jerusalem, ISTA, 821/5-פ.

German Consul General Wolff never took a clear stand for or against the new Nazi regime and its antisemitic policy in Germany. When he had to leave his position because of his wife's Jewish origins, the *Palestine Post* wrote:

> Dr. H. Wolff Dismissed. German Consul's Wife's Jewish Grandmother the Cause. Wolff was a popular consular officer. He came to Palestine in 1932. He has carried out his duties to his Government in a loyal manner but he managed...to retain respect and the confidence of many who had been wronged by his Government and who had come in contact with him.[487]

All in all, the Jewish reaction to German National Socialism and antisemitism in Palestine in the 1930s was mild and moderate. Historian Ralf Balke assumes that, for the sake of the Haavara treaty, the majority of the Jewish leaders did not react very strongly.[488] It should also be considered that the Germans were a minority in the region, thus many Jews paid little attention to them, concentrating rather on their own troubles including the Arab uprising, problems associated with settling down in Palestine, and the ongoing persecution of Jews in Europe, which many of them had just escaped. Later on, at the end of World War II, Jewish leaders reacted much more strongly. Following the German capitulation in May 1945, the Jewish Agency wrote a letter of complaint to the British focusing on Nazi activities in Palestine in previous years:

> The German community in this country was comprised before the war of four rural settlements and three urban or suburban quarters, apart from a number of individual residents, firms and institutions. The political frame of mind of this community was for years before the war a source of profound concern and anxiety to the Jews of Palestine and, it is believed, to the British authorities. With the advent of Hitler, the vast majority of the Germans of Palestine embraced the Nazi doctrines with enthusiasm and gave every tangible indication of their political and ideological allegiance to the Third Reich. In the disturbances of 1936–1939 their sympathies were avowedly with the terrorist bands and their supreme leader, Amin el-Husseini. German settlements were known to be harboring terrorists and assisting them with information, shelter and technical means. German workshops were used for the manufacture of land mines and other means of destruction and for the instruction of Arab terrorists in their handling. At the outbreak of war some of the younger members of this colony left Palestine in time to join the German army. Some were subsequently sent back to Palestine as spies or agents. One Palestinian German is reported to have achieved great notoriety as a principal commissioner in charge of the extermination of Jews; he showed a thorough knowledge of Palestinian-Jewish affairs and even boasted knowledge of Hebrew. Authentic reports which reached us indicate that with very few exceptions, the interned inmates of the German colonies Sarona, Wilhelma, Waldheim and Bethlehem were throughout the war

487 *Palestine Post*, 25 July 1935, 1.

488 Ralf Balke, *Hakenkreuz im Heiligen Land. Die NSDAP-Landesgruppe Palästina* (Erfurt, 2001), 165.

> and are to this day fervent Nazis. On the day of the German capitulation the entire youth of Bethlehem marched through the colony singing Nazi songs, while the memorial service for Hitler held in that colony on V-Day was essentially a re-dedication to the locals of the lost Führer. The Jewish Agency, however, feels it its duty to give emphatic expression to Jewish feeling on this subject. Jews in Palestine feel utterly unable to contemplate the return to their country or the resumption of free residence in it of this community of Jew-haters. It appears to them inconceivable after millions of their brethren were exterminated by the Nazis and their henchmen with the tacit approval of the mass of the German people, that here in the very land of the Jewish National Home, Nazi Germans as fanatical as any of those who perpetrated the horror in Europe, should be allowed to re-establish themselves in so close and revolting proximity to Jewish settlements and quarters and outrage the feelings of every Jew who meets them.[489]

At the end of the letter, the executive of the Jewish Agency asked the British government to deport all Germans from Palestine.

Arab reactions

The Temple Society journal and the Jerusalem Church of the Redeemer newsletter reported that Palestine's Arabs strongly sympathized with German National Socialism. They had rallies shouting, "Three cheers to Germany! Three cheers to Hitler!"[490] Arabs admired the "awakened Germany" and its Führer. Arab employees of the German Christian organizations noted with great joy the changes of 1933 which inspired them to hope and struggle for their own national independence. They saw Germany as the only country that had freely expressed its sympathy for the Arab struggle against hopelessness.[491] When the German consul general passed through northern Palestine, the Arabs shouted "*Heil Hitler!*" and saluted the consul with raised hands.[492] Some Arabs in Palestine even founded their own National Socialist groups, although these never lasted long.[493] In 1932 and 1933, Arabs sent a petition to Hitler asking not to allow German Jews to settle in Palestine any longer.[494] The petition was unsuccessful because German politics up to the beginning of the war supported Jewish emigration to Palestine in order

---

489 Executive of the Jewish Agency to Field Marshal John Vereker, Jerusalem, 4 June 1945, CZA, S25/4060.

490 *Die Warte des Tempels*, 30 June 1936, 92.

491 "Aus der Arbeit des Jerusalem-Vereins," ISTA 528/1426-פ; German consul general to Auswärtiges Amt, Berlin, 22 Mar. 1937, YVA, R 3/27.

492 BPRO, FO 371/21887 (14 Nov. 1938).

493 *Die Warte des Tempels*, 15 Mar. 1935, 37.

494 *NNM* (Apr. 1932): 12–13; *NNM* (April 1933): 24.

to solve the *Judenfrage* ("Jewish Question") in the homeland.[495] Arab youth also expressed sympathy with Nazi Germany. When in 1935 delegates returned from an Arab youth conference in Haifa, their train to Afula bore a swastika chalked on one of the coaches with an Arabic inscription beneath it reading "Germany over All."[496] On March 15, 1935, *Die Warte des Tempels* wrote that many Arabs saw Hitler as the most important man of the 20th century and almost every Arab knew his name. Fascism and National Socialism with its anti-Jewish attitude were accepted positively by many Arabs.[497] The Arab newspaper *Falastin* described Hitler as the most powerful head of state whose orders could not be stopped by any party or law; Germany would be turned into a huge, terrifying arms cache which would terrify the rest of Europe.[498] Representatives of the Reich and the NSDAP in Palestine described the Arabs' hope for a great Arab state:

> Arabs in Palestine were waiting for Hitler to come to Palestine and expel all the Jews. They hoped for a German intervention to solve their conflict with consideration of their needs. Rommel was their legendary hero. Many Arabs truly believed in the Germans' victory. Some of them even listened to the short-wave German broadcast, the *Kurzwellensender*.[499]

But as more Arabs in Palestine came to recognize that the German government and its representatives in Palestine were not actually willing to openly support their cause, they had less sympathy for the Germans. In 1938, Consul Melchers from Haifa wrote to the Foreign Office in Germany that the positive Arab attitude towards the Germans was decreasing.[500] One can find many consulate documents from 1936 to 1939, reporting the risks and dangers the Germans in Palestine had to face since the Arab uprising.[501] Germans in Palestine felt increasingly insecure as Arab rebels threatened and blackmailed them in hopes of obtaining German support for their cause. German colonists were pressured to join the Arab strike, and were forcefully urged not to sell land and goods to Jews.[502] An Arab gang,

495 Isaiah Friedman, "Germany and Zionism, 1897–1918," in *Germany and the Middle East: Past, Present and Future*, edited by Haim Goren (Jerusalem, 2003), 61–68.
496 *Palestine Post*, 13 May 1935, 7.
497 *Die Warte des Tempels*, 15 Mar. 1935, 39.
498 *Falastin*, 9 Dec. 1935, ISTA, 3136/11-פ.
499 Letter and special report, Chef der Sicherheitspolizei to Reichsführer SS, 21 Dec. 1942, BArch, NS 19/186.
500 Consul Wilhelm Melchers, Haifa to Auswärtiges Amt, Berlin, 23 Nov. 1938, YVA, R 3/30.
501 Correspondence, 1938, mainly Consul General Walter Doehle to Auswärtiges Amt, Berlin, YVA, R 3/30.
502 Ibid.

equipped with German carbines, threatened German settlers near Acre.[503] Arabs also carried out attacks against the Germans, including a murder.[504]

The Templer colony in Bethlehem-Galilee experienced some unpleasant incidents in May and June 1936. Two Arabs from Nazareth, members of the strike committee, asked the Templers there to give money to support their strike against the British government. The Templers rejected the request, explaining that they intended to remain neutral toward the ongoing Jewish-Arab conflict, one of them mentioning that they had fewer problems with their Jewish neighbors than with their Arab neighbors. This was overheard by the Templers' Arab workers, who were angry and went on strike. After several talks with the strike committee, it was brought to an end. A month later, on 9 June 1936, another incident occurred. An Arab worker, employed by Johannes Herrmann, became offensive and provocative. Herrmann told him to leave, but he refused to go, so Herrmann pushed him out of his house or farm, whereupon the worker attacked his boss's son Theodor with a knife. The whole incident was reported to the British, and when the Arab workers in Bethlehem heard about it, they went on strike again. The district official and his assistant in Haifa tried to calm the situation and mediate, but without success. The situation became very tense and the Templers even considered firing all their Arab workers. Johannes Herrmann had refrained from pressing charges against his son's attacker, and members of the strike committee and the sheikh of the workers' home village continued their efforts to restore calm; on June 13, 1936, the Arabs returned to work at the Templer colony.[505]

As noted above, the attitude among Arabs towards the Germans worsened as they realized the German government was unlikely to provide financial and military support for their fight for independence against the British and the Jews.[506] Ralf Balke's research suggests that few Arabs really liked and supported the Palestine-Germans and he calls the supposedly good Arab-German relationship a complete fiction.[507]

Without having access to Arabic newspapers and documents, it is difficult to discern what the Arabs in Palestine themselves thought about their relationship with the Germans. All sources of which we are currently aware on this particular matter are based either on translations from Arabic to English or on perceptions

---

503 Consul Wilhelm Melchers to Auswärtiges Amt, Berlin, 23 Nov. 1938, YVA, R 3/30.

504 Paul Sauer, *Uns rief das Heilige Land. Die Tempelgesellschaft im Wandel der Zeit* (Stuttgart, 1985), 263–65; Balke, *Hakenkreuz im Heiligen Land*, 147–52.

505 Albert Blaich, report addressed to the German consulate in Jerusalem, 14 June 1936, ISTA, 821/7-פ.

506 Consul General Walter Doehle to Auswärtiges Amt, Berlin, 14 Jan. 1938, YVA, R 3/27.

507 Balke, *Hakendreuz im Heiligen Land*, 152.

of the Arab population given by Germans, British, and Jews in Palestine. A further study on the Arab-German relationship by an Arabic-speaking historian would probably shed new light on this topic. However, it seems that the relations between Arabs and Germans were ambiguous. On the one hand, many Germans in Palestine hired Arab workers and helped them to make a living. Almost every Templer family had one or two Arab employees. On the other hand, it was well known that Arab workers were cheap laborers and they were probably aware that their German "bread givers" exploited them. Furthermore, the Germans in Palestine remained foreigners from the viewpoint of the local population because they generally cultivated their specific German culture and lifestyle and refused to acculturate. It is very likely that the so-called good Arab-German relationship was wishful thinking but did not reflect the reality, especially after 1936.

10 The Official End of the NSDAP Branch

Internment of Palestine-Germans in 1939

On September 1, 1939, Germany invaded Poland and two days later Great Britain declared war on Germany. In August, the Reich had sent the coded message, "the chauffeur has arrived," to its consular officials. Vice-Consul Otto Ernst Eckert was charged with ordering all German males of draft age or who had done military training in Germany to report to the armed forces there. According to British records, 413 Germans officially left Palestine between August 1 and September 2, 1939.[508] On the night of August 31, the Greek steamer *Paris* departed Haifa with 232 German draftees and 88 family members on board.

With the outbreak of the war, the British ordered the closure of virtually all German companies and businesses in Palestine, including the Temple Society Bank.[509] The *Palestine Post* reported at the beginning of September that Germans had been arrested in Jerusalem, the consulate searched, and the swastika flag hauled down as a large crowd of Jews gathered in front of the building. German Colony and Schneller Orphanage residents were also detained, along with other Temple Society members in Sarona and Jaffa.[510] The Schneller family's Syrian Orphanage and all its workshops were shut down.[511] The arrest of German businessmen and home owners made it necessary to put all German property, including empty shops and homes, under police protection immediately, and a Custodian of Enemy Property was assigned to administer the properties of Germans who had already left the country. As the German companies and farms were known to be flourishing enterprises, there was much interest in buying or leasing them. The High Commissioner decreed that the remaining Germans could continue to manage their own property, while church property was to be supervised by neutral clergymen.[512]

Although more than 200 German draftees had managed to leave Palestine on the eve of World War II, more than 110 of them from Jaffa, Sarona, and Wilhelma

---

508 Ralf Balke, *Hakenkreuz im Heiligen Land. Die NSDAP-Landesgruppe Palästina* (Erfurt, 2001), 74–76; Paul Sauer, *Uns rief das Heilige Land. Die Tempelgesellschaft im Wandel der Zeit* (Stuttgart, 1985), 273 (Haifa, 70 draftees; Bethlehem, 18; Waldheim, 12; Jaffa/Sarona, 41; Wilhelma, 16; and Jerusalem, 75).

509 Sauer, *Uns rief das Heilige Land*, 274.

510 *Palestine Post*, 4 Sept. 1939, 2.

511 *Palestine Post*, 7 Sept. 1939, 2.

512 *Die Wahrnehmung der Deutschen Interessen in Palästina im Zweiten Weltkrieg 1939* (10 Dec. 1939), YVA, P 19/2_3.

missed the departure of the Greek steamer on August 31 because they were unwilling to depart. German draftees who remained were interned immediately and taken to a former prison camp in Acre.[513] The German journal of the Jerusalemsverein, *Neueste Nachrichten aus dem Morgenlande* (*NNM*, Latest News from the Orient), informed its readers that all German men under the age of fifty were interned in a "concentration camp" at Acre.[514] Swiss Kanzlei-Sekretär (chancellery secretary) Carl Lutz, who had been placed in charge of safeguarding German interests in Palestine in September and October 1939, reported that the German men had been arrested by the C.I.D (Criminal Investigation Department) beginning at 1 p.m. on the day the war was declared. Almost every German man in Jerusalem and Haifa was detained and taken to Acre, while the arrests in Jaffa was limited to men under the age of fifty.[515] The Templers Gotthilf Wagner, Philipp Wurst, and Johannes Pross remained free in order to deal with the numerous problems caused by the detainment and internment.[516]

Approximately two hundred male detainees were taken to the prison camp in Acre. Besides the "Aryan" Germans, Jews with German wives were also held there. Arabs who had friendly connections to the Germans were also detained, among them the teacher Elias Haddat and Dr. Taufik Canaan from the German Deaconesses' Hospital in Jerusalem. Wooden barracks housing approximately thirty men each were added to the former jail. Inmates themselves organized the cleaning, cooking, and catering.[517] Conditions were harsh at the beginning, but soon the bakery and kitchen operations were handed over to trained detainees. Wilhelm Stoll, an elder of the German-speaking Protestant congregation in Haifa, took it upon himself to bake bread for all the inmates in the camp. Gradually, the situation changed for the better.[518]

As the men were often bored, they occasionally took excursions to the nearby beach, collecting wood and shells. Using their pocketknives or eating utensils, they made brooches and other ornaments. For Christmas 1939, the milk car from

513 *NNM* (Dec. 1939): 111–12; Balke, *Hakenkreuz im Heiligen Land*, 74–76; Nikolai Schmidt, Report, Tempelgesellschaft-Archiv (TGA), T-576b$_1$; Gania Dolev, *Chronicle of a Utopia. The Templers in the Holy Land 1868–1948* Exhibition catalogue, Eretz Israel Museum, Tel Aviv, 2006, 29.
514 *NNM* (Apr. 1940): 9, 18.
515 YVA, P 19/2$_3$: *Die Interessen in Palästina im Zweiten Weltkrieg 1939* (Dec. 10, 1939); *NNM* (Dec. 1939): 111–12; Sauer, *Uns rief das Heilige Land*, 273–74; see also http://onlinearchives.ethz.ch/xylix/.
516 *Die Wahrnehmung der Deutschen Interessen in Palästina im Zweiten Weltkrieg 1939* (10 Dec. 1939), YVA, P 19/2$_3$; *NNM* (Dec. 1939): 111–12; Sauer, *Uns rief das Heilige Land*, 273–74.
517 *Die Wahrnehmung der Deutschen Interessen in Palästina im Zweiten Weltkrieg 1939* (10 Dec. 1939), YVA, P 19/2$_3$; *NNM* (Dec. 1939): 111–12.
518 *NNM* (Apr. 1940): 18–19.

Bethlehem-Waldheim brought presents and eight Christmas trees to the detainees. The milk deliveries enabled the detainees to keep in contact with the inhabitants of Bethlehem-Galilee and Waldheim; sometimes even secret letters could be exchanged, since officially, they were allowed to send only one letter per week to their families. Family members were permitted to send much-appreciated food parcels.

In October–November 1939, a few detainees were released from Acre and returned to their settlements in Waldheim, Bethlehem-Galilee, Wilhelma, and Sarona to help run the farms. Cornelius Schwarz, the NSDAP head in Palestine, and two other men were exchanged for British officers, and allowed to leave for Germany.[519]

In September 1939, the British Mandate government turned the German farming settlements of Sarona, Wilhelma, Bethlehem-Galilee, and Waldheim into large internment camps, while women and children from the German colonies in Jerusalem, Jaffa, and Haifa were temporarily permitted to remain in their homes under British and Jewish police surveillance.[520] The four farming settlements were surrounded by barbed wire and watchtowers, guarded by Jewish and Arab auxiliary police (*Hilfspolizisten*) under a British commandant with a small staff. German women, children, and elderly men lived in these camps.[521] It was also suggested that the Auguste Victoria Foundation on the Mount of Olives be converted to an internment camp, but this plan was never carried out.[522] Within the internment camps, the Germans could move freely and were allowed to produce their own food, and could sell their products through Arab agents.[523] There were plenty of vegetables and fruit in the German gardens, but less milk was produced than before the beginning of the war. Many cows had been slaughtered because the German women were unable to do all the heavy labor of dairy farming by themselves. Nevertheless, they tried to maintain their farms while their husbands were in custody in Acre. They were helped to some extent by Italians, Hungarians, and other illegal aliens who had been sent to the internment camps at the beginning of the war. Arabs were also hired to work in the fields, vineyards, and orchards, and some of the German men were given permits to leave the camp to

519 Sauer, *Uns rief das Heilige Land*, 277.

520 *Die Wahrnehmung der Deutschen Interessen in Palästina im Zweiten Weltkrieg 1939* (10 Dec. 1939), YVA, P 19/2_3; *NNM* (Dec. 1939): 111–12; Sauer, *Uns rief das Heilige Land*, 273–74.

521 *NNM* (Dec. 1939): 111–12; Balke, *Hakenkreuz im Heiligen Land*, 74–76; Dolev, *Chronicle*, 29.

522 Erika Arndt, report, 5 Mar. 5, 1943, PA AA, R 41531.

523 *Die Wahrnehmung der Deutschen Interessen in Palästina im Zweiten Weltkrieg 1939*, YVA, P 19/2_3; http://www.teachers.ash.org.au/dnutting/germanaustralia /e/palestine3.htm; *NNM* (Apr. 1940): 9, 18.

supervise their Arab employees.[524] As we saw, in October–November 1939, a few detainees had been released from Acre to return to their settlements in order to maintain and repair equipment and help run the farms, especially the dairy production. In February 1940, sixty-eight additional men were permitted to return to their homes to work in agriculture.[525]

Women and children from the German colonies in Jerusalem, Jaffa, and Haifa initially were allowed to remain in their homes; later on being transferred to the rural internment camps.[526] Peter Gewitsch, eleven years old at the beginning of World War II, recalled the following story: two police officers, one British and the other Jewish, went to the home of the watchmaker Muenzenmay in the German Colony in Haifa in order to question or deport him as an enemy alien. During the interrogation, Muenzenmay's son, a well-known Nazi party member, called the Jewish policeman "*Saujude!*" The British officer noticed his comrade's angry reaction and asked what the word meant. When he learned it meant "dirty Jew," the British officer hit Muenzenmay's son with his rifle butt, causing his death. No investigation followed this incident.[527]

The German school and kindergarten in Haifa were reopened at the beginning of October 1939. Since all the male teachers were in Germany, the teaching was done by assistants (*Hilfskräften*).[528] Christian Sunday services in Waldheim and Haifa were regularly held by Mr. Henrici, the head of the Carmel Mission, who had not been interned, and was given a permit to go to Haifa twice a month, accompanied by an Arab friend and driver.[529] A few days before Christmas 1939, the Haifa German Colony inhabitants received the order to move into one of the four German internment camps. After December 27, 1939, members of the Carmel Mission (*Karmel-Mission*) also had to move into an internment camp.[530] On May 13, 1940, ninety-four German citizens living in Jaffa were ordered to report to the Waldheim camp.[531]

---

524 Paul Sauer, "Vom Land um den Asperg – im Namen Gottes nach Palästina und Australien," lecture, 20 Oct. 1995, Burgstetten; Nikolai Schmidt, Report, TGA, T-576b_1.

525 Helmut Glenk, *From Desert Sands to Golden Oranges. The History of the German Settlement in Palestine 1871–1947* (Victoria, 2005), 201–4; *NNM* (Apr. 1940): 19; Spanish Consul General Manuel del Moral, Jerusalem to Politische Abteilung, Auswärtiges Amt, Berlin, 13 Feb. 1940, PA AA, R 41854.

526 Theodora Wieland, report, Dec. 1942, PA AA, R 41530; Erika Arndt, report, 5 Mar. 1943, PA AA, R 41531.

527 Peter F. M. Gewitsch, Haifa to Heidemarie Wawrzyn, Jerusalem, email correspondence, 27 Dec. 2005.

528 *NNM* (Apr. 1940): 18.

529 Ibid.

530 Ibid., 19.

531 For further details on the internment camps and the situation of the Palestine-Germans during the war, see *Zweites Merkblatt über die Lage der Deutschen in Palästina* (Dec. 1940), EZA 5/3123.

Internees at the four camps had to line up once a month for inspection by a C.I.D. officer. Nikolai Schmidt, who headed the Temple Society from 1941 on, complained that the C.I.D. had collected a huge file of evidence of hostile activities allegedly committed by the Palestine-Germans – such as weapons smuggling, munitions production, training of Arab rebels, and financial support for the Arab cause. Schmidt called such accusations a "fairy tale" and emphasized the good will and intentions of the Templer community.[532]

The secretary of the Spanish consulate general in Jerusalem visited the internment camps once the month as well. At the beginning of the war, the Swiss consulate had looked after German interests, but later on, the Spanish consulate continued the relief work. Women from a British welfare organization also came to the camps from time to time, but the Germans did not ask for or accept their support, because the German government was sending them a sufficient sum by way of the Spanish consulate. Twice a year, representatives of the Red Cross visited the internment camps, and the internees were encouraged to collect money for German prisoners of war in Africa.[533]

In cases of serious illness, a special pass would be issued to allow internees to obtain medical care outside the camp. A physician and a dentist visited the camps of Waldheim and Bethlehem-Galilee at least once a week.[534] Direct communication with the world outside the camp was difficult: only one letter per month, of twenty-five words or less, was allowed to be mailed overseas via the Red Cross. These letters were censored and could take months to reach their destinations. Even mail from one internment camp to another could take up to three weeks to arrive. At first, the Germans still kept their short wave radios, on which they listened to the news from Germany. Their outspoken delight with German victories in Western Europe led the British Police to confiscate all the radio receivers on May 24, 1940, after which they were no longer allowed to use radios and telephones, although they could still get the local newspapers.[535] That same month, the British raided Sarona. All the men were assembled on the sports field; while the women and children were ordered to go to the community hall. Several police groups then conducted thorough house searches.

532 Nikolai Schmidt, report, TGA, T-576b_1; Glenk, *From Desert Sands* 2005: 214.

533 Schmidt, report, TGA, T-576b_1.

534 Spanish Consul General Manuel de Moral, report, 4 April 1944, PA AA, R 41855; Red Cross, report, Nov. 1940, PA AA, R 41854.

535 Glenk, *From Desert Sands* 2005: 204–6, 214; Red Cross, report, Nov. 1940; and leaflet by the Auswärtiges Amt, Dec. 1940, PA AA, R 41854; Theodora Wieland, report, Dec. 1942, PA AA, R 41530.

> Cupboards and drawers were emptied and bed linen pulled up as each house was searched from top to bottom. The authorities were looking for any weapons or radios/transmitters. All cameras, many books and all maps were confiscated. The search took several hours. During this time, the women and children at the hall were body searched. Children's prams and pushers [*sic*] were stripped and also searched. After the house searches, many residents came home to a very messy home – goods and belongings were strewn over the floor and pictures and wall hangings torn off the walls.[536]

Swiss Kanzlei-Sekretär Carl Lutz petitioned for improved living conditions in September 1939 and tried to secure the release of the prisoners and those facing deportation. He applied to the Mandatory government, for example, on behalf of Nazi party members Hermann Schneller and Cornelius Schwarz in Acre. Schneller's release was approved sometime before September 13, 1939, and although Schwarz's request was rejected, a month later he was able to leave Acre and was required to return to Germany.[537] Lutz also visited Wilhelm Weigold, a Nazi party member interned at Waldheim, in support of his efforts to continue cultivation of the fields and the release of internees. Lutz, it should be noted, also oversaw the interests of German Jews in 1939; two years later when he served at the Swiss consulate in Budapest, he aided the rescue of Jews from Hungary.[538]

All in all, the German internees saw their living conditions in the camps as unpleasant, cramped, and hard. Food rations were received from the military, supplemented by products from the internees' property. Since each camp had to accept German settlers from Jerusalem, Jaffa, and Haifa, as well as some non-German illegal aliens, the sites became crowded and nearly unbearable, especially in summer. The German internees found it difficult to get along with other nationalities – sometimes one could encounter as many as fourteen different nationalities in one camp, and complaints arose about the "foreign, non-Aryan people," as well as the dirt, noise, and fights, allegedly caused by those "aliens."[539] The internment ended with the Allied victory in 1945, but the security barriers were kept, this time to protect the Germans from Jewish extremists who sought revenge for the murder of millions of Jews by the Nazi regime.[540]

---

536 Glenk, *From Desert Sands*, 206.

537 C. Schwarz, report on the months of September, October, and November 1939, PA AA, R 41853.

538 *Die Wahrnehmung der Deutschen Interessen in Palästina im Zweiten Weltkrieg 1939*, YVA, P 19/2_3; Nikolai Schmidt, Report, TGA, T-576b_1. Carl Lutz and his wife Gertrud were recognized as Righteous among the Nations by Yad Vashem in 1964.

539 Nikolai Schmidt, Report, TGA, T-576b_1; Glenk, *From Desert Sands* 2005: 206; Theodora Wieland, Report, Dec. 1942, PA AA, R 41530.

540 Paul Sauer, "Vom Land um den Asperg – im Namen Gottes nach Palästina und Australien," lecture, 20 Oct. 1995, Burgstettin.

With World War II and the internment by the British, Nazi party activities in Palestine were drastically decreased. The NS groups were officially banned at the beginning of the war, although members continued their activity in secret. Naturally, nothing had changed the Germans' patriotic and nationalist attitudes, for their admiration for the Führer was almost unlimited and they continued to mark the National Socialist holidays such as Hitler's birthday and the solstice.[541] Wilhelm Fugmann, a German Lutheran missionary, recalled that even after their 1941 deportation to Australia, the German Templers maintained their faith in the Third Reich and proudly called themselves "Deutschländer."[542]

According to British records, 288 men and 1,107 persons including women, children, elderly men, and a few of the Catholic and Protestant clergy were interned on September 21, 1939.[543] In 1941, before the deportation of more than six hundred Germans to Australia, the Auslands-Organisation counted 1,752 German internees in Palestine.[544] The Spanish consul general in Jerusalem, Manuel del Moral, reported in December 1939 that members of the Catholic orders were interned at different locations in Jerusalem and Haifa. He listed 151 Catholics, including twenty-six nuns of the St. Borromaeus Order at their convent on Bethlehem Road in Jerusalem; sixteen nuns of the same order at the Schmidt School opposite the Damascus Gate; twenty-five Benedictine monks at the Dormition Abbey on Mount Zion; thirty-six monks and nuns of various Catholic orders (Franciscans, Lazarists, etc.) at the Austrian Hospice; and forty-eight German sisters of the St. Borromaeus Order at the hospice of the German Colony in Haifa and the Eliasruhe rest house on Mount Carmel.[545] In 1942, the number of sisters interned at the Borromean convent in Jerusalem had increased to 134 because nuns of German nationality from the whole of Palestine and Syria were then living there.[546]

The deportation to Australia in 1941

In the summer of 1941, General Erwin Rommel won a series of important battles in the North African desert and was advancing from the western desert towards

541 Special Report, 21 Dec. 1942, BArch, NS 19/186; Balke, *Hakenkreuz im Heiligen Land*, 77; Paul Sauer 1985, *Uns rief das Heilige Land. Die Tempelgesellscaft im Wandel der Zeit* (Stuttgart 1985), 276–77.

542 Thomas Greif, "Interniert am Ende der Welt," http://www.sonntagsblatt-bayern.de/archiv01/17/woche2.htm.

543 Balke, *Hakenkreuz im Heiligen Land*, 76; Sauer, *Uns rief das Heilige Land*, 276.

544 Auslands Organisation, Berlin to Auswärtiges Amt, Berlin, 17 Sept. 1941, PA AA, R 41527.

545 Spanish consul general correspondence, Jerusalem, 11 Dec. 1939, PA AA, R 41853.

546 Annual report, 1942, PA AA, R 41855.

Egypt and Palestine. The British authorities decided to deport more than 600 persons from the younger German families to Australia. Sailing on the *Queen Elizabeth* were 536 Templers, 84 Protestants, 32 Roman Catholics, and 13 Jews who had German "Aryan" spouses.[547] The German Foreign Office listed 661 persons: 255 men, 292 women and young girls, and 114 children under the age of fourteen.[548] They were imprisoned as enemy citizens in detention camps at Tatura in Australia's Victoria state, where they remained until 1946–47.[549]

The deportation took place on July 31, 1941. Settlers from Bethlehem-Galilee and Waldheim were taken by bus to a train east of Haifa, which left at 1 p.m. for Lydda [Lod], where they were joined by internees from Jaffa, Wilhelma, and Sarona.[550]

> All the people of Sarona were summoned to the community hall. It was announced that a number of people would be deported to an unnamed destination. The British Police had prepared a list of those who had to leave. The selected internees were given 72 hours to pack. Each adult was allowed 40 kilograms and each child 30 kilograms of luggage plus what they could carry as personal hand luggage and a specified amount of money per person. The selected internees were advised that if their luggage was overweight it would be left behind. They did not know where their journey would take them except that they would be going to a place where it would be springtime and to take some summer clothing and a few woolen (warmer) garments. From this the settlers deduced that it was likely to be somewhere in the southern hemisphere. The authorities permitted some personal sewing machines and a few kerosene heaters to be taken. In addition, some educational material and books from the school were taken to allow the children's education to be continued.[551]

From Lydda, the train, guarded by Jewish police under British command, brought them to Kantara in Egypt. Ferried across the Suez Canal, they continued by train through Ismailia to Suez, and thence into the Red Sea where the liner *Queen Elizabeth* lay at anchor out of range of the German Luftwaffe. They departed on August 2, arriving in Sydney, Australia on August 23, 1941; a day later, they were transferred by train to the camps at Tatura.[552] Four internment camps had been set up, each holding 1,000 people. The Germans from Palestine were interned in Tatura camp III, subdivided into four compounds, A, B, C, and D. The latter was already occupied mainly by German and Austrian Jews who had escaped from Nazi

---

547 Sauer, *Uns rief das Heilige Land*, 278. See also YVA, P 19/2_3: *Die Wahrnehmung der Deutschen Interessen in Palästina im Zweiten Weltkrieg 1939* (10 Dec. 1939).

548 Records of Sept. 1939–Dec. 1941, PA AA, R 41527.

549 Dolev, *Chronicle*, 29; Sauer, "Vom Land um den Asperg,"; idem, *Uns rief das Heilige Land*, 278.

550 Sauer, *Uns rief das Heilige Land*, 278–79.

551 Glenk, *From Desert Sands*, 206–8.

552 Ibid., 208; Sauer, *Uns rief das Heilige Land*, 278–80.

Germany, so the arriving Palestine-Germans were sent to the remaining compounds.

German Lutheran missionaries who had served in Papua New Guinea were also interned in Tatura. They reported that the Templers introduced a strongly organized party network in camp III, with NS social evenings, roll calls in uniform, and the formation of Hitler Youth groups for boys and girls. The camp leader was a loyal NSDAP member. The Australian guards observed the activities, but did not interfere since it was up to the Germans to organize themselves. Anyone critical of National Socialism had a hard time in Tatura. Theodor Fast, a teacher, for example, was not well-liked for that reason.[553] Johannes Pross was another whose anti-Nazi attitude was met with hostility.[554] Quarrels sometimes broke out between the Jews of Compound D and the German Nazis of the other compounds. Several times the Jews asked the Australian officials to remove the Nazis and fascists from their part of the camp, but their complaints were ignored. On the evening of September 28, 1941, German youth in the C Compound began singing German songs at the fence of the D Compound. Jewish women from the D section became enraged, calling them "Nazi-Schweine," and a riot broke out. A man from C Compound attempted to cross into D; a guard fired warning shots, and the D inmates were ordered to return to their barracks and remain there until order was restored. The Jewish inmates petitioned for a ban on Nazi songs within the camp. The Australian commander tried to play down the incident, but the only measure taken to avoid similar problems in the future was to transfer the non-Jewish inmates from D Compound to the B Compound.[555]

Up to the end of the war, the Germans in Tatura were torn between their hope for an end to the war and their loyalty to the Third Reich. After Hitler's death was announced, internees gathered in Compound C for a memorial service on May 6, 1945. Director Hermann Schneller, formerly head of the Syrian Orphanage in Jerusalem, focussed in his sermon on the New Testament passage, "Greater love has no man than this that a man lay down his life for his friends" (John 15: 13). On May 8, 1945, the official end of the war and surrender of the Third Reich was announced. A few days later, on May 16, the Australians replaced the former Nazi camp leader Gottlieb Ruff with Wilhelm Fugmann, a non-Nazi who was democratically elected.[556] Nationalist demonstrations and the dissemination of

---

553 Sauer, *Uns rief das Heilige Land*, 283.

554 Alex Carmel, "What's this? Making fun of Nazis?" (in Hebrew), *Haaretz*, 29 Oct. 1999, 13.

555 Sauer, *Uns rief das Heilige Land*, 284.

556 Sauer names Fritz Lippmann as the new camp leader (Sauer, *Uns rief das Heilige Land*, 291), but Thomas Greif, "Interniert am Ende der Welt," http://www.sonntagsblatt-bayern.de/archiv01/17/woche2.htm states it was Wilhelm Fugmann.

National Socialist ideas were forbidden. German flags, standards, and symbols of the Third Reich, pictures of Hitler, and NS pamphlets had to be handed in. Schoolbooks containing the National Socialist ideology were banned. Marches and exercises of the Hitler Youth had to cease immediately. The German Nazis did not, in the end, hand in the NS literature, standards, and flags. Instead, they held a ceremony at which everything was burned. Gottlieb Ruff spoke, and the youth performed songs praising German courage, loyalty, and faith. The Third Reich had come to an end.[557]

557 Greif, "Interniert am Ende der Welt"; Sauer, *Uns rief das Heilige Land*, 290–91.

11 Exchange Operations between Palestine-Germans and Jews from Europe

Gania Dolev recounts that

> A fascinating episode...took place during the War when hundreds of Palestinian Germans, most of them Templers, were exchanged for Jews imprisoned in Europe. Under pressure from the families of Jews – who were citizens of Palestine that happened to find themselves in Germany [and Poland] at the beginning of the war – and the demands of Templer families who had managed to leave the country prior to the outbreak of hostilities, three complex exchange agreements were devised [in December 1941, November 1942, and July 1944].[558]

National and international organizations and offices, such as the Jewish Agency in Geneva, the American consulate in Berlin, the Swiss Delegation (*Schweizerische Gesandtschaft*) in Berlin, the Red Cross, and others, were engaged to affect the exchanges.[559]

The first exchange in December 1941

A large number of Jews from Palestine who had traveled to Germany and Poland on the eve of World War II were trapped there and soon found themselves interned in camps. Their families in Palestine formed committees that sought to rescue their relatives from the Nazis.[560] While the German government did express interest in an exchange of internees, especially after the deportations of Palestine-Germans to Australia in July 1941, the British hesitated.[561] They objected to

---

558 Gania Dolev, *Chronicle of a Utopia. The Templers in the Holy Land 1868–1948*. Exhibition catalogue. Tel Aviv: Eretz Israel Museum, 2006, 29.

559 Francis R. Nicosia, ed. *Central Zionist Archives, Jerusalem 1933–1939*, Archives of the Holocaust. An International Series, vol. 3, edited by Sybil Milton and Henry Friedlander (New York, 1990); and idem, *Central Zionist Archives, Jerusalem 1939–1945,* Archives of the Holocaust. An International Series, vol. 4, edited by Sybil Milton and Henry Friedlander (New York, 1990), 145–248; Helmut Glenk, *From Desert Sands to Golden Oranges. The History of the German Settlement of Sarona 1871–1947* (Victoria, 2005), 215; Ralf Balke, *Hakenkreuz im Heiligen Land. Die NSDAP-Landesgruppe Palästina* (Erfurt, 2001), 77; n.a., *From Bergen Belsen to Freedom. The story of the exchange of Jewish inmates of Bergen-Belsen with German Templers from Palestine. A symposium in memory of Dr. Haim Pazner*. Jerusalem: Yad Vashem, 1986.

560 *From Bergen Belsen to Freedom,* 14–15.

561 *From Bergen Belsen to Freedom*, 15.

returning people to Germany who could contribute to the German war effort.[562] Talks for the first exchange transport lasted two years.

Employees of the German consulates in Palestine, the Deaconesses of Kaiserswerth, and those Germans who had immediate family in Germany were chosen for the initial exchange. Those selected were brought to the transit camp at Athlit near Haifa. After a few nights there, they were taken via Syria and Turkey to Vienna and from there to Germany.[563] Anna Rohrer's granddaughter Brigitte, nine years old at the time, recalled the following details:

> We arrived in Vienna in December [1941]. It was very cold. It was the horrible winter of 1941/42 which was a plague for the soldiers in Russia. At the arrival in Vienna, my mother's toes suffered from frostbite because we did not have appropriate winter clothes and shoes. Before we departed from Sarona, my grandmother gave me a little enamel bowl because she knew that I got easily seasick. During our trip I had to use this bowl several times. This gift is my last memory of my grandmother Anna Rohrer who left Jerusalem only in 1950. She immigrated to Australia via Cyprus. She went together with her daughter Edith Imberger, her son-in-law and three grandchildren.
>
> On our way from Palestine to Germany, we spent a few nights in the barracks in Athlit [transit camp near Haifa]. I recently visited this place in spring 2006. These days the place looks very clean and sterile. It does not fit my memories at all.... I remember beds built out of orange boxes which broke easily. Our toilets consisted of empty oil canisters posted in the middle of the room. It was very embarrassing to use these utilities because it was not possible to use them without making a noise.
>
> Near Aleppo, Syria, Australian soldiers guarded us for one or two nights. They were warmhearted and supportive, very different from the British officers and Jewish guards.... In Adana, Waldemar Fast, Von Papen's ambassador, welcomed us. Every child received two bags of candies, a real treat for us. I was very disappointed because a few of us got only one bag.[564]

Waldemar Fast was posted in Ankara in 1941, as the assistant of Ludwig Moyzich, the "actual head of the Gestapo in Turkey."[565] Fast had been born in Jerusalem in 1911 and was a member of the Temple Society who joined the NSDAP in 1934. Suspected of being a spy, he managed on the eve of World War II to flee and join the Reichssicherheitshauptamt (Reich Central Security Office) in Germany.[566] Ac-

562 *From Bergen Belsen to Freedom*, 1986: 15–16; *Palestine Post*, 4 May 1941, 3; 25 July 1941, 3.
563 Brigitte Kneher, Temple Society Germany to Heidemarie Wawrzyn, email, 3 Nov. 2006; Glenk, *From Desert Sands*, 216; Memorandum, U.S. Embassy, Berlin, Oct. 1941, PA AA, R 41527.
564 Brigitte Kneher (née Rohrer, born 1932) to Heidemarie Wawrzyn, email, 12 Nov. 2006.
565 Quoted in Klaus-Micahel Mallmann and Martin Cüppers, *Halbmord und Hakenkreuz. Das Dritte Reich, die Araber und Palästina* (Darmstadt, 2006), 98.
566 Ibid., 98.

cording to Balke, Fast served in the SS and participated in a killing unit in Russia before being posted to the German embassy in Ankara.[567] He was assigned to accompany the German exchange groups of 1941, 1943, and 1944 from the Syrian border, through Turkey to Vienna.[568]

The first transport from Palestine to Germany consisted of approximately sixty-five people, mainly women and children, a few elderly men, and fourteen deaconesses of Kaiserswerth.[569]

In this first exchange, forty-six to forty-nine Jews with British Mandate passports were allowed to return to their homeland.[570] The *Palestine Post* reported their arrival on December 21, 1941: "Palestinians back from Berlin. Many Touching Scenes at Bat Galim":

> Released from Berlin less than a fortnight ago, 29 Palestinian women, 16 children and one elderly man, exchanged for a similar number of German women and children detained in Palestine..., arrived back home yesterday afternoon after having been separated from their families since the summer of 1939. When they were trapped in Poland after the invasion, they were taken to Berlin and the adults imprisoned at the beginning of 1941 when the R.A.F. raids became severe. The children were sent to a home and were permitted to visit their mothers every four to six weeks. There were many touching reunions between the women and their husbands and other relatives, who had given up all hope of seeing them again until the end of the war.... Every emotion, from happy smiles to tears of relief, was seen on the faces on either side.[571]

The second exchange in November 1942

Germans who had left Palestine to join the Wehrmacht in 1939 applied to the German Foreign Office (Auswärtiges Amt) in Berlin in the fall of 1941 for an exchange

567 Balke, *Hakenkreuz im Heiligen Land*, 123.
568 *From Bergen Belsen to Freedom*, 58–59; Brigitte Kneher, Temple Society Germany to Heidemarie Wawrzyn, email, 3 Nov. 2006.
569 Records on the 1941 exchange, PA AA, R 41527 and R 41528; Paul Sauer, *Uns rief das Heilige Land. Die Tempelgesellschaft im Wandel der Zeit* (Stuttgart, 1985), 292. The deaconesses listed at the archives of the Foreign Office in Berlin: Charlotte Daum, Terese Gundrum, Käthe Joeckel, Ida Kamrau, Dora Kuhncke, Gertrude Kuhncke, Hilda Kueppers, Anneline Majert, Johanna Meierbert, Clara Roentgen, Annelise Stoehr, Wilhelme Schönwald, Margarete Woennmann, Lina Zinn.
570 Itinerary of 1941, PA AA, R 41528: from Berlin: 18 Jews, including 6 children; Ilag-Liebenau: 6 Jews; Kattowitz: 7 Jews, including 4 children; Frankfurt/Oder: 3 Jews, including 1 child; Amsterdam: 2 Jews; Warsaw: 5 Jews, including 1 child; Radom: 5 Jews, including 2 children.
571 *Palestine Post*, 21 Dec. 1941, 3.

of their interned wives and children in Palestine.[572] But at that time, few Germans were willing to leave because they did not want to abandon their property in Palestine. The Foreign Office, in correspondence with the Auslands-Organisation and the Reichskommissariat für die Festigung des deutschen Volkstums (Reich Office for the Consolidation of German Nationhood) suggested promising the Palestine-Germans property for a new colony within German territory after the end of the war.[573] This plan and the persistence of their husbands in Germany led more Palestine-German wives to register for the second exchange transport.

In April 1942, Germany and Britain began to negotiate a second exchange. Six months later, in October 1942, in the final stage of the talks, there were about 300 Germans to be exchanged for some 200 Palestinian Jews. The unequal number led to a British demand that Jews from Warsaw and Radom who had relatives in Palestine would also be included. The Nazis could not locate these additional Jews listed by the British. The listed Jews had probably already been transported to extermination camps or murdered by the SS and its collaborators.[574] The British government did not cancel the exchange agreement, but asked the German government to keep looking for the missing Jews and guarantee their departure to Palestine as soon as they were found. The second exchange was scheduled for November 1942.[575]

Already a month before, on October 2, German internees in Palestine were taken from different internment camps to the transit camp in Athlit. Departing from the camps, they sang the German anthem *Deutschland, Deutschland über alles*.[576] At Athlit they waited for the negotiations to be finalized. Conditions in the camp were very poor, as they had been the year before. The barracks were infested by bedbugs, and many mattresses had to be burnt, with kerosene used to clean the barracks. The food was of poor quality and with winter approaching many of the inmates became ill.[577] Several women sent detailed reports to the Auslands-Organisation in Berlin describing the difficult situation. Among the writers were Theodora Wieland, Erika Arndt, and Paula Kuebler, whose poem shows a strong nationalist and anti-Jewish attitude[578]:

---

572 Sauer, *Uns rief das Heilige Land*, 292; cf. *From Bergen Belsen to Freedom*, 55–56; Rudolf Weller to Auswärtiges Amt, Berlin, 19 Sept. 1941 and Hermann Lauer to Auswärtiges Amt, Berlin, 6 Oct. 1941, PA AA, R 41527.

573 Sauer, *Uns rief das Heilige Land*, 292–93; Balke, *Hakenkreuz im Heiligen Land*, 78.

574 Chaya Brasz, *Transport 222: Bergen-Belsen – July 1944* (Jerusalem, 1994) 17; Records on the Nov. 1942 exchange, PA AA, R 41529.

575 Sauer, *Uns rief das Heilige Land*, 293–94; see also Klaus Hillenbrand, *Der Ausgetauschte.* (Frankfurt a.M., 2010).

576 Theodora Wieland, report, Dec. 1942, PA AA, R 41530.

577 Glenk, *From Desert Sands*, 216–17.

578 Records on the Nov. 1942 exchange, PA AA, R 41530 and R 41531.

Eine Jüdin kontrolliert in Segeantenhüllen,
Sie spricht ein Deutsch – es ist zum Brüllen.

Des Morgens früh beim Kontrollieren
Tut sich die Jüdin kein bissel genieren
Das grelle Licht rasch anzudrehn
Mit lautem Schritt durch die Bude zu gehen.
Sie zählt und zählt, oh welch ein Graus,
Kriegt selten die richtige Zahl heraus.
Um zwölf Uhr steigt die zweite Kontroll';
Sie kommen zu Dritt, es ist doch toll!
Zwanzig sie zählen, acht Kinder, zwölf Frauen –
Ne halbe Stund' drauf, soll man noch trauen,
Sind sie schon wieder da und zählen,
Es sollen schon wieder welche fehlen!
Gefehlt hat von uns sicher keins,
Doch fehlts wohl bei ihnen am Einmaleins.
Am Abend steigt die dritte Kontroll';
Mit Gottes Hilfe und Vater Knoll
Bringen die richtige Zahl sie zurecht,
Das war eine Arbeit, wahrlich nicht schlecht!

Wenn dann abends alles bei Tische sitzt,
Kommt die Jüdin abermahls angeflitzt.
Zwanzig sie zählt, die Zahl, sie stimmt
Und niemand mehr es tragisch nimmt,
Wenn sie abermals fängt zu zählen an,
Weil sie immer noch nicht trauen kann.
So stellen sie die Kontrolle an!
Wahrlich eine Gaude für jedermann!

In Sofia und Belgrad begrüsst man uns mit Musik,
Kein Auge bleibt trocken vor innerem Glück!
Unter Deutschen sind wir endlich wieder,
Gesungen werden Heimatlieder.
Allmählich fühlen wir uns frei,
Dem Vaterland gehört man aufs neu'!
Treue in Sturm, Not und Gefahr!
Sei unser Gelübde immerdar!
Gott steh uns bei in diesem Krieg,
Damit uns werde ein deutscher Sieg![579]

On November 6, 1942, the second exchange transport from Athlit to Germany began, first by bus and then by train via Syria and Turkey. A few days later, in mid-

579 Paula Kuebler, poem, Dec. 1942. PA AA, R 51531.

November, the returnees were festively welcomed by representatives of the Vienna municipality and the NSDAP, with greetings from the former German consul in Jerusalem, Walter Doehle. According to his report, 160 women, 130 children, and a few elderly men were with this transport. From Vienna, they continued to various destinations in Germany.[580]

Gertrud Deininger recounted the following:

> On November 5 [*sic*], 1942, we were taken by busses from Athlit to Afula. There, from far away, we saw the settlement Waldheim for the last time. In the evening, a train brought us from Afula via Damascus to Aleppo where we boarded the *Orient Express*. The British handed us over to the Turkish authorities. Our journey continued. We reached Haidar Pasha where the exchange took place. We noticed almost nothing about the exchange because we saw our exchange partners only from afar. German officials took over now. We crossed the Bosporus, then boarded a chartered train and traveled through the Balkans. In Greece, we saw many hungry children. In Sofia and Belgrade, members of the German colonies came to the train stations to greet us. They gave us tooth brushes and other useful things explaining that such things could not longer be bought in Germany. We were shocked about this news. The train took us through Hungary and then, on November 11, 1942, we reached Vienna. In Vienna, a reception at the city hall was held for us. We toured the city and spent two nights in a hotel. The weather was cloudy and everything seemed very old and grey to me. After two days, we left Vienna by train and on November 14, we finally reached Stuttgart in Germany where an aunt of mine took me in.[581]

On November 19, 1942, the *Times* reported that

> forty-five British and sixty-nine Jewish residents of Palestine, released from internment in Germany in exchange for German internees in Palestine, arrived at the Afula railway station on Monday. Thirty children were among them.... Only seventeen of them had been interned in Germany, the rest having been interned in Poland.[582]

The unequal ratio of those exchanged (301:114) provoked considerable anger among the Jews. In addition to the second exchange, a small transport of fifteen Jews from Sosnowitz, Tscheslau, and Berlin took place in January–February 1943.[583]

---

580 Records on Nov. 1942 exchange, PA AA, R 41530; *Wiener Neueste Nachrichten*, 14 Nov. 1942; *Wiener Mittag*, 14 Nov. 1942; Sauer, *Uns rief das Heilige Land*, 294.

581 Gertrud Wassermann-Deiniger, *Wir haven hier keine bleibende Statt. Geschichte der Familie Deininger in Palästina 1868–1948* (self-published, n.p., 1983), 60–61 (English summary by the author). The dates in this memoir for the departure from Athlit, arrival in Vienna and Stuttgart differ slightly from the dates given by Sauer, *Uns rief das Heilige Land* and the PA AA in Berlin.

582 *Times* (London), 19 Nov. 1942.

583 Records on the exchange of Nov. 1942, PA AA, R 41529 and R 41530; Glenk, *From Desert Sands*, 216; *From Bergen Belsen to Freedom*, 17; Eberhard Kolb, *Bergen-Belsen. Vom "Aufenthalts-*

The arrival of the earlier group of Jews exchanged in December 1941 had received limited press coverage, but the second group's appearance had a remarkable impact. Their testimonies were recorded and some were published in the newspapers. Even children were interviewed, among them Eliyahu Ben-Eliesar.[584] Some had left Poland after having witnessed the large-scale actions in the ghettos of Warsaw, Radom, Kielce, and other places. There was now no doubt about the destruction of the Jewish people and their communities in central Europe.[585]

The third exchange in July 1944

The implementation and the publicity surrounding the second exchange raised great hopes among the Jews. Could it be possible to save hundreds or even thousands of Jews through such exchanges? Jews in Palestine and Switzerland, as well activists in Holland, Belgium, and other countries were eager to explore this possibility.[586] From mid-1942 on, the German Foreign Office and Himmler were developing a plan to exchange a great number of prisoners for German citizens in Palestine, South America, and the British Empire. They planned a huge reservoir of thousands of exchange candidates from the Bergen-Belsen camp, and began in July 1943 to concentrate Jews for this purpose.[587] Negotiations between the British and the German governments, however, proceeded very slowly and with difficulty. While the British and Germans were mainly concerned with obtaining equal numbers of those to be exchanged, the Jews waiting in the Bergen-Belsen camp suffered nerve-wracking anxiety.[588] On June 29, 1944, 222 men, women, and children were told to prepare for their departure.[589] The next day, on June 30, they were transferred by train to Vienna, where they were joined by approximately sixty-one survivors from the Vittel and Laufen camps. From Vienna those in the

lager" zum Konzentrationslager 1943–1945 (Göttingen, 1996), 22; *Times* (London), 19 Nov. 1942; see also Hillenbrand, *Der Ausgetauschte*, 177–78, 190–97.

584 *From Bergen Belsen to Freedom*, 17.

585 Ibid., 17; *Palestine Post*, 22 Nov. 1942, 3; see also Nicosia 1990: 168 (telegram of 20 Nov. 1942), and Hillenbrand, "Der Ausgetauschte."

586 *From Bergen Belsen to Freedom*, 18; Brasz, *Transport 222*, 11.

587 *From Bergen Belsen to Freedom*, 22–24; Ben Flanagan and Donald Bloxham, *Remembering Belsen. Eyewitnesses Record the Liberation* (London, 2005), 133–36: Kolb, *Bergen-Belsen*, 21–34.

588 *From Bergen Belsen to Freedom*, 25; Francis R. Nicosia, ed. *Central Zionist Archives, Jerusalem 1939–1945*, Archives of the Holocaust. An International Series, vol. 4, edited by Sybil Milton and Henry Friedlander (New York, 1990), 227, 248; cf. Rainer Schulze, "Keeping very clear of any 'Kuh-Handel.' The British Foreign Office and the Rescue of Jews from Bergen-Belsen," *Holocaust and Genocide Studies* 19, no. 2(2005): 226–51.

589 *From Bergen Belsen to Freedom*, 25–26.

exchange transport continued to Turkey and from there to Palestine, arriving safely in Haifa on July 10, 1944, and were warmly greeted by their relatives.[590] "Refugees tell tale of horror," the *Palestine Post* informed its readers. The 281 Nazi victims had arrived from Europe to Athlit, where they described the situation of thousands of Dutch and German Jews who had kept hidden until the Gestapo tracked them down.[591]

They had been exchanged for forty-one or forty-two Germans from Palestine and approximately seventy from South Africa.[592] A German witness from the Temple Society, described their situation and departure from Palestine:

> In Athlit we were totally cut off. There were no newspapers for us and this at the time of the invasion and the assassination attempt on the *Führer's* life. We did not know anything about the situation in Germany. All internees were very happy to leave, to escape the barbed wire and the hostility that surrounded us. We were looking forward to our return and reunion in Germany. We never saw our exchange partners. On the Bulgarian border we noticed the first German soldier. My God, we were so happy to see the German soldiers.[593]

Most of the third transport were Templers, whose journey took them eventually from Vienna to Stuttgart, arriving on July 13, 1944. Only a few days afterward, on July 26, 1944, ten of them were killed in an air raid.[594]

590 Ibid.; Simon H. Herrmann, *Austauschlager Bergen-Belsen. Geschichte eines Austauschtransports* (Tel Aviv, 1944), 82, 88, 95–96.

591 *Palestine Post*, 14 July 1944: 3. The *Post* gave the number as 281 persons, but other sources put it between 280 and 283.

592 Correspondence on the third exchange, 1943–1944, PA AA, R 41532 and R 41533; Sauer, *Uns rief das Heilige Land*, 206; cf. *From Bergen Belsen to Freedom*, 25–26, 55–56.

593 N. Ben Nathan, interview with Templer Helena Heynold-Wagner, *Transport 222*, documentary by N. Ben Nathan (Washington D.C.: United States Holocaust Memorial Museum, c. 1990).

594 Among the Templers killed were Dieter, Johanna, and Roswitha Baldenhofer; Katharina Decker; Jakob Goerzen; Cornelia, Hans, Katharina, and Olga Heselschwerdt; and Sophie Kuebler. Glenk, *From Desert Sands*, 217; Sauer, *Uns rief das Heilige Land*, 296.

12 Planned Hostilities against Palestinian Jews 1941–1944

An SS killing unit for Palestine?

While the exchange negotiations were underway, absorbing the attention of the Germans in Palestine, World War II progressed, affecting the various local populations in Palestine very differently. The German Armed Forces High Command had decided to send an expeditionary force to Libya to support the Italian army; the Afrika Korps was formed under the command of General Erwin Rommel (1891–1944). In the following months, the Libyan cities of Cyrenaika, Benghazi, and Tobruk fell to the Germans. The British began a strong offensive in November 1941, forcing Rommel and his Panzer Group Africa to retreat. Rommel reinforced his Panzer Group in January 1942 and resumed the German-Italian operations against the British. One victory followed another until his troops reached El Alamein in Egypt in July 1942. At this point, the Germans and Italians were only approximately ten days away from Palestine.[595]

Palestine residents were apprehensive about the possibility of a German attack. The Jewish community actively supported the British war effort by serving in special units in the British army.[596] The Arab population admired General Rommel and hoped for an invasion to drive out the Jews. It is difficult to determine what the remaining Germans of Palestine thought about Rommel's advance. Their memoirs rarely mention their experiences in Palestine of the 1930s and 1940s, except for the fact that they were forced to leave the country which most of them called their homeland (*Heimat*).[597] In 1941–1942, the majority of the German population in Palestine were interned. Their radios had been confiscated by the British police in May 1940 after they had greeted the news of German war victories with great delight.[598] But this and similar measures did not result in total isolation. They were still in contact with their Arab workers, and free to read the local press. They were allowed to receive visitors in the presence of an officer or policeman,

---

595 See Klaus-Michael Mallmann and Martin Cüppers, *Halbmond und Hakenkreuz. Das Dritte Reich, die Araber und Palästina* (Darmstadt, 2006), 121–35, 182–90.

596 *Palestine Post*, 13 May 1941, 1; 14 May 1941, 3; 5 June 1941, 3.

597 Cf. Tempelgesellschaft Deutschland, ed., *Damals in Palästina – Templer erzählen vom Leben in ihren Gemeinden* (Stuttgart, 1990); Mallmann and Cüppers, *Halbmord und Hakenkreuz*, 157–58, 172–82.

598 Helmut Glenk, *From Desert Sands to Golden Oranges. The History of the German Settlement of Sarona in Palestine 1871–1947* (Victoria, 2005), 204–6, 214.

and could even leave the internment camp under certain circumstances. They certainly must have been aware of the sporadic German or Italian air raids on Haifa and Tel Aviv-Jaffa in the years 1940 to 1942.[599] There had even been alerts in the Jerusalem area. In September 1940, the German Jerusalemsverein journal, *Neueste Nachrichten aus dem Morgenlande*, published an article, "Der Krieg in Palästina," which spoke of the air raids on Haifa and gave a thorough account of the military situation and troop movements in North Africa of the British and the Italians (who were German allies).[600] The English-language daily *Palestine Post*, published several reports on the battles in North Africa in 1941 to 1942.[601] So, although the interned Germans must have know quite a lot about the war taking place only a few days distance from Palestine, it is not known if they were aware of the reasons for Jewish fears of German advances and the persecution which would likely follow any invasion of Palestine. In the memoirs and testimonies of Palestine-Germans, they assumed the reports of the destruction of European Jewry were merely the hostile propaganda of German enemies.[602]

The Jews of Palestine, by contrast, were acutely aware of the danger as the German army approached the country. They knew that even Jews outside of Europe were not safe, and it was no secret that Arab leaders, including the Mufti of Jerusalem, Haj Amin el-Husseini, were in touch with Nazi officials. Ruth Lapide remembered that she had heard about the Mufti's meeting with Hitler in Berlin and about Hitler's promise to deport thousands of Jews from Palestine to Auschwitz.[603] Reactions among the Jews were varied. Some thought of hiding in Christian monasteries; others purchased cyanide in order to be able to commit suicide in case of a German victory in Palestine. Sarah van Gelder (born 1907), a Dutch woman in Haifa, fled from Palestine to Indonesia with her three children; her husband wanted her to join her relatives there for safety, but they were all

---

599 *NNM* (Sept. 1940): 49; *Palestine Post*, 11 June 1941, 3 and 13 June 1941, 1; Mallmann and Cüppers *Halbmond und Hakenkreuz*, 174; Thomas Lackmann, "Hitlers Todesschwadron vor Palästina. Spektakulärer Fund deutscher Historiker: Wie die SS die Juden im Nahen Osten ermorden wollte," *Der Tagesspiegel*, 16 Apr. 2006.

600 *NNM* (Sept. 1940): 47–50.

601 *Palestine Post*, 1941–1942.

602 Naomi Ben Nathan, *Transport 222*, video documentary (Washington, D.C., USHMM, c. 1990); Brigitte Hoffmann, "Unsere Verantwortung in der Welt," *Der besondere Beitrag. Beilage der Warte des Tempels* (Stuttgart) 2 (1995): 7–14; Alfred Weller, "Gedanken über die Haltung der Tempelgesellschaft zum Nationalsozialismus," lecture, 1948, edited by Brigitte Hoffman, in *Der besondere Beitrag. Beilage der Warte des Tempels* (Stuttgart) 2 (1995): 3–7.

603 Lackmann, "Hitlers Todesschwadron."

interned by the Japanese.[604] The Yishuv (Jewish proto-government in Palestine) discussed options for its defense, intending to fight German occupying forces and evacuate Jews en masse. The Palmach, established in May–June 1941 by the Haganah (Jewish defense forces), with the assistance of the British, intensified its recruitment and training.[605] More than six hundred members were trained at Kibbutz Mishmar Haemek by the British Army. The British saw the Palmach as "the core of a guerilla army to fight the Germans should Rommel succeed in conquering Palestine."[606] The Haganah developed a plan to rescue as many civilian Jews as possible via Haifa and to resist the German forces and their collaborators in the north of the country as long as they could. In a German occupation, there would have been a desperate fight between the armed Jews and the Axis forces. It seems probably that it was only the ultimately successful British victory over the Afrika Korps saved the Jews of Palestine from total destruction.[607]

Thorough research on Arabic sources from the 1930s and 1940s has not been conducted, so it is uncertain how many Arabs living in Palestine admired Hitler and his antisemitic ideology. Did some sixty percent of the country's Arabs support the Nazis, or were there only a few Arab ideologues who admired Hitler, as Basheer M. Nafi claims?[608] However, one fact is very well documented: the connections of the Mufti of Jerusalem to the Nazi regime and his strong support for the Nazi goal of exterminating the Jews.

In March and April 1933, only a few weeks after Hitler's rise to power, Haj Amin el-Husseini (1895–1974) contacted German Consul Heinrich Wolff in Jerusalem. He spoke approvingly of the Nazis' anti-Jewish policy and demanded the termination of Jewish immigration to Palestine. In July 1937, he met with Consul Walter Doehle (who had succeeded Wolff), and proposed to dispatch an envoy to Germany to discuss German-Arab interests. The Mufti's demands were rejected, for Germany only gradually changed its political attitude towards the Arabs of the Middle East. In 1941, the Mufti helped to organize an Arab revolt against the

604 Heidemarie Wawrzyn, interview with Helen Benninga (cousin of Sarah van Gelder), Jerusalem, 13 Oct. 2007.

605 Haganah (lit., defense), the pre-State underground military organization that operated from 1920–1948. Although the British administration did not officially recognize the Haganah, British security forces cooperated with it during the Arab riots (1936–39) and World War II.

606 Benny Morris, *Righteous Victims. A History of the Zionist-Arab Conflict, 1881–2001* (New York, 2001), 174.

607 Mallmann and Cüppers, *Halbmond und Hakenkreuz*, 165–82; Tom Segev, *One Palestine Complete. Jews and Arabs under the British Mandate* (London, 2001), 452–53.

608 Basheer M. Nafi, "The Arabs and the Axis: 1933–1940," *Arab Studies Quarterly* 19, no. 2 (1997): 1–24, 2, 18; Segev, *One Palestine Complete*, 462–63.

British in Iraq. When it failed, he made his way to Berlin, where he remained until the end of World War II as the guest of Hitler. While there, he broadcast Nazi propaganda to the entire Middle East, and organized Muslims in Bosnia, Albania, and Kosovo for the German war effort and against the Jews. Germany and Italy delivered money and arms to support the Mufti and his followers in their efforts to stir up riots in the Middle East.[609] In 1941–42, the Mufti was in contact several times with Adolf Eichmann, who kept him informed on the mass murder of Jews in Europe. The Mufti promised his support for the "Final Solution" whenever he could.[610]

At a meeting with the Führer in Berlin at the end of November 1941,

> The Grand Mufti began by thanking the Führer for the great honor he had bestowed by receiving him. He wished to seize the opportunity to convey to the Führer of the Greater German Reich, admired by the entire Arab world, his thanks for the sympathy which he had always shown for the Arab and especially the Palestinian cause, and to which he had given clear expression in his public speeches. The Arab countries were firmly convinced that Germany would win the war and that the Arab cause would then prosper. The Arabs were Germany's natural friends because they had the same enemies as had Germany, namely the English, the Jews, and the Communists. They were therefore prepared to cooperate with Germany with all their hearts and stood ready to participate in the war, not only negatively by the commission of acts of sabotage and by the instigation of revolutions, but also positively by the formation of an Arab Legion. The Arabs could be more useful to Germany as allies than might be apparent at first glance, both for geographical reasons and because of the suffering inflicted upon them by the English and the Jews. Furthermore, they had close relations with all Moslem nations, of which they could make use in behalf of the common cause. The Arab Legion would be quite easy to raise. An appeal by the Mufti to the Arab countries and the prisoners of Arab, Algerian, Tunisian, and Moroccan nationality in Germany would produce a great number of volunteers eager to fight.[611]

The Führer rebuffed the Mufti's requests for a public declaration in support of the Arabs. But he promised him that

---

609 Schechtman, *The Mufti and the Führer*, 79, 82–84; cf. Mallmann and Cüppers, "'Beseitigung der jüdisch-nationalen Heimstätte in Palästina,'" 162; Mallmann and Cüppers, *Halbmond und Hakenkreuz*, 59–60, 108; Klaus Gensicke, *Der Mufti von Jerusalem, Amin el-Husseini, und die Nationalsozialisten* (Frankfurt a.M., 1988), 45–47; 50–53; 233–34; 236–37; Morris, *Righteous Victims*, 165–66.

610 Mallmann and Cüppers, "'Beseitigung der jüdisch-nationalen Heimstätte in Palästina,'" 167; Mallmann and Cüppers, *Halbmond und Hakenkreuz*, 152–54; Gensicke, *Der Mufti von Jerusalem*, 164–65, 288.

611 http://www.paulbogdanor.com/holocaust/mideast.pdf (Appendix 1: "Minutes of the meeting with Hitler and Husseini," 28 Nov. 1941, cited from *Documents on German Foreign Policy, 1918–1945*, Series D, Vol. 13: *The War Years. June 23, 1941 to December 11, 1941*, no. 515 (London, 1964).

> Germany stood for uncompromising war against the Jews. That naturally included active opposition to the Jewish national home in Palestine.... Germany would furnish positive and practical aid to the Arabs involved in the same struggle.... Germany's objective [is]...solely the destruction of the Jewish element residing in the Arab sphere under the protection of British power.[612]

Details of the meeting between Hitler and the Mufti point to the important role of the Mufti for the Nazis' further plans concerning the Middle East. The Grand Mufti was a strong guarantor of Arab collaboration with Germany, a hoped-for collaboration the SS sought for their future persecution of the Jews in Egypt and Palestine. According to numerous archival documents examined by Mallmann and Cüpper,[613] the Nazis planned to exterminate the Jewish population of Egypt and Palestine as soon as General Erwin Rommel and his Panzer Army Africa crossed the Nile.[614] Hitler believed the invasion of Eastern Europe and the Soviet Union in Operation Barbarossa on June 22, 1941, would be successfully completed by the autumn of that year. Following the expected defeat of the Soviet Union, the Nazis planned to destroy Great Britain's power by creating instability through local Arab riots and sabotage and by attacking the British in the Mediterranean region. In the case of a German victory, the Middle East would be easy prey. As early as June 11, 1941, the Armed Forces Operations Staff (Wehrmachtführungsstab) had published instruction no. 32, entitled "Preparation for the time after Barbarossa" containing technical and strategic details for an advance to the Near East, including Palestine.[615]

Encouraged by Rommel's victories in Libya in 1942, the Reichssicherheitshauptamt (Reich Central Security Office) decided in June of that year to assign an SS killing unit to Rommel's Panzer Army.[616] The new Einsatzkommando Egypt was to be led by Walther Rauff (1906–1984) who had been deeply involved in the mass murder in Eastern Europe. He had invented the gas vans to make the killing of thousands of Jews "easier" for the executioners.[617]

On July 20, 1942, Rauff flew to Tobruk in Libya to receive instructions from General Rommel. Rauff's unit was sent from Berlin to Athens on July 29, ordered to wait at Cape Sunion, Greece to be transferred to Africa.[618] The twenty-four mem-

612 Ibid.

613 Mallmann and Cüppers, *Halbmond und Hakenkreuz.*

614 From 22 Jan. 1942 the Panzer Group Africa was called Panzer Army Africa: Mallmann and Cüppers, *Halbmond und Hakenkreuz*, 121.

615 Ibid., 89–90; Segev, *One Palestine Complete*, 452–53.

616 Ibid., 137–38.

617 Ibid., 140–41.

618 Ibid., 138–39.

bers of the group probably expected to collaborate with the local Arab population once Egypt and Palestine were conquered, as had been frequently promised by the Mufti. The use of local collaborators had already worked well in Lithuania, Belarus, and other Eastern European regions in the campaign to murder Jews. There is no doubt that the Nazis would have used the same method to eliminate the Jews in Palestine.[619]

Rauff's Einsatzkommando expected to enter Egypt as soon as Rommel's Panzer Army crossed the Nile, but British and American troops confronted the German and Italian forces at El Alamein from the summer of 1942 to the spring 1943, forcing the Axis to withdraw to Tunisia. Rommel himself left North Africa in early March 1943, and on May 12, the Panzer Army Africa surrendered.[620] Rauff's death squad had already been ordered to leave Athens and return to Berlin months before, in September 1942.[621]

The German-Arab Operation Atlas in 1944

After the German defeat in North Africa, it became clear to the Allies and many Arab states that Germany would lose the war. Fanatic Nazis and the Mufti and his followers continued to maintain their belief in a German victory. They continued to fight and intensified their subversive activity in the Middle East. Several joint German-Arab parachute actions took place in 1943 and 1944 in order to smuggle weapons, as well as incite and recruit Arabs against Jews.[622] Three Germans who had left Palestine on the eve of World War II to enroll in the Wehrmacht participated in one of these actions.

After basic military training, many young Germans who had left Palestine in August 1939 became members of the Lehr-Regiment Brandenburg z.b.V. 800 (Brandenburg Training Regiment for Special Tasks) because they were familiar with the Arab language and culture.[623] The Brandenburg Commando Unit, a small but well-known formation, was the private army of the Abwehr military intelli-

619 Ibid., 145–47.

620 See ibid., 121–35, 182–90.

621 Ibid., 185–87. See Mallmann and Cüppers, "'Beseitigung der jüdisch-nationalen Heimstätte in Palästina,'" 168–69: At the end of 1942, the same unit, enlarged, was sent to Tunis to register the Jews of Tunisia for forced labor. In May 1943, the Einsatzkommando was transferred from Tunis to Naples. For more information see: *Rommels Schatz* and *Rommels Krieg*, documentaries, Zweites Deutsches Fernsehen, May 2007.

622 Mallmann and Cüppers *Halbmond und Hakenkreuz*, 239.

623 Ibid., 92.

gence service. Recruiting and training focused on language ability and cultural knowledge, to allow saboteurs to pose as enemy soldiers and civilians. The Brandenburgers' task was to conduct espionage, sabotage, and recruit collaborators in enemy land; former Palestine-Germans were assigned to the Middle East. Kurt Wieland, Friedrich Deininger, and Werner Frank were trained in Brandenburg in 1940 and took part in a parachute action in Palestine in 1944.[624]

Their small five-man commando was formed in Berlin in early 1944. Their mission, Operation Atlas, consisted of three Germans and two Arabs, led by Colonel Kurt Wieland, a Palestine-German from Sarona, born in 1917. Before leaving for Germany in 1939, he had been in 1938 the leader of the Hitler Youth in Palestine. Lieutenant Werner Frank was born in Haifa in 1917 and joined the HJ in Palestine in 1934. Master Sergeant Friedrich Deininger was also a Palestine-German. Abdul Latif was originally from Jerusalem and had worked for the Mufti in Berlin; and the fifth man was Hassan Salama.[625] The five were instructed by the Mufti himself, who was then based in Berlin and had sent the German authorities various suggestions on how to attack the Jews of Palestine, among other things, by dropping paratroopers in Palestine.[626] Operation Atlas intended to organize hostile activity through local Arabs, supplying them with cash and arms.

On October 6, taking off from Athens, the group parachuted into the area of Jericho. Unable to find their dropped cargo parachutes, they were unable to continue the operation. The parachutes were soon picked up by the British police, who then began to search for the suspected enemy paratroopers.[627] On October 11, 1944 the *Palestine Post* informed its readers that one or more paratroopers had been dropped over the Jordan Valley and the public was asked to report to the nearest police station any information leading to the apprehension of these men.[628] Shortly afterward, the paratroops were arrested and interrogated. Nikolai Schmidt, who led the Temple Society at that time, wrote in his article on "The End of the Temple Colonies" that an illegal alien, staying at Wilhelma and spying for the British, allegedly denounced a German paratroop.[629] The captives tried to deny that they were a commando unit, but their equipment (sub-machine guns, dynamite, a radio, a German-Arabic dictionary) left no room for doubt about the

624 Ibid., 239–40.
625 Ibid., 90–92, 239–40; BPRO, KV 2/400-402; BBC News, 5 July 2001, http://baltimore.indymedia.org/newswire/display/5200/index.php.
626 Segev, *One Palestine Complete*, 464.
627 Mallmann and Cüppers, *Halbmond und Hakenkreuz*, 239–40.
628 *Palestine Post*, 11 Oct. 1944, 3.
629 Nikolai Schmidt, report, p. 7, TGA, T-576b_1.

purpose of their operation.[630] Friedrich Deininger managed to flee. But he was captured in Egypt and held as a prisoner of war until his release in December 1946.[631]

While parts of the Arab population admired Hitler and hoped for a German invasion, many Palestinian Jews were aware of the advancing danger by the Nazi regime and its willing collaborators. They realized that even outside of Europe Jews were not safe, nor was the British Mandate of Palestine a safe haven for them either.

630 Mallmann and Cüppers, *Halbmond und Hakenkreuz*, 239–40.

631 Gertrud Wassermann-Deininger, *Wir haben hier keine bleibende Statt. Geschichte der Familie Deininger in Palästina 1868–1948* (self-published, n.p., 1982), 62.

13 Increasing Tensions and the Final Departure of Palestine-Germans in 1950

Until the beginning of the 1940s, the German internees felt quite secure in their restricted area. Guards at the internment camps provided a barrier against the outside unrest between Arabs, Jews, and the British. Several incidents occurred in 1943, however, that caused unease and anxiety among the Germans. Internees at Sarona had just left their morning roll call on June 16, 1943 when a bomb exploded in the assembly area, but no one was seriously injured or killed. In August 1943 additional bomb blasts occurred, one at the Sarona cemetery, and the other at the Sarona school building then occupied by British Police.[632] In October–November 1944, the British authorities transferred the Sarona internees to Wilhelma. Forty people were allowed to stay at Sarona in order to provide basic agricultural products to the British military; they remained there until August–September 1945.[633]

The war in Europe ended on May 8, 1945. As the full extent of the atrocities against the Jews in Europe became known, widespread hatred of Germans by the Jews in Palestine increased, and the interned Palestine-Germans remained in their guarded camps for their own safety in fear of potential Jewish attacks.

Thousands of European Jews found themselves in DP (displaced persons) camps after the war and had no place to go. The British refused to lift the ban on Jewish immigration to Palestine, and opposed a partition plan that would separate the region into a Jewish and an Arab state. In early October 1945, three Jewish underground organizations, Haganah, Etzel, and Lehi, made an operational pact and formed the Jewish Resistance Movement to carry out attacks against the British.[634] Their anti-British attacks intensified in 1946, peaking in July 1946 when members of the Etzel group bombed the British headquarters in the south wing of the King David Hotel in central Jerusalem. The Haganah condemned the attack

---

632 Helmut Glenk, *From Desert Sands to Golden Oranges. The History of the German Settlement of Sarona in Palestine 1871–1947* (Victoria, 2005), 215.

633 Ibid., 217–18; Paul Sauer, *Uns rief das Heilige Land. Die Tempelgesellschaft im Wandel der Zeit* (Stuttgart, 1985), 306.

634 Etzel (acronym, *Irgun Tzvai-Leumi*, national military organization) clandestine Jewish group operating during the British Mandate, 1931–1948. Lehi (acronym, *Lohamei Herut Israel* (fighters for the freedom of Israel), a self-proclaimed anti-British terrorist group, founded in 1940 by Avraham Stern; also known as the "Stern Gang."

and separated from the radical Etzel and Lehi groups, which continued their terrorist activities.[635]

Jewish militants also focused on the remaining Germans in Palestine, whom they perceived as Nazis they were no longer willing to tolerate. On March 22, 1946, Gotthilf Wagner, the last mayor of Sarona and secretary of the Templers, was assassinated by the Hebrew Resistance Movement. A 2007 Israeli television documentary noted that the decision for this act was probably taken by the Haganah.[636] "Wagner was killed in Tel Aviv" was the headline in Jewish newspapers. The *Palestine Post* reported on the liquidation of "the pro-war German *Bürgermeister* of the German village Sarona"[637]:

> Wagner was on his way from the internment camp Wilhelma to Sarona by car to pay Arab workers hired by the Templers. At about 9 o'clock in the morning, a car suddenly appeared on the road, blocked his way and forced Wagner's car to slow down. Two men ran over to the car and fired at him. Wagner died instantly from the bullet wounds in the head. With him in the car were his sister, Frida Wagner, Karl Steller, and a Jewish supernumerary policeman. These passengers remained unharmed.[638]

An eyewitness and participant in the assassination explained that the decision to liquidate Gotthilf Wagner was made under the assumption that Wagner and his firm had supported the Arabs during the 1936–1939 uprising. Furthermore, from the Jewish point of view Wagner was seen as an ardent Nazi and the leader of the Germans in Palestine, whom they learned had been named to be *Gauleiter* for the region had the Germans occupied Palestine. The assassination was intended to make it unmistakably clear that Palestine-Germans could no longer remain in the country. "They will not last here," was the headline in Jewish newspapers. According to the C.I.D., Wagner's murder took place in the context of land politics, for he had consistently instructed members of his settlement not to sell land to Jews.[639]

The Templers, however, considered Gotthilf Wagner an anti-Nazi and victim of Jewish terror. Richard Hornung, his nephew, described his uncle and his assassination as follows:

---

635 Tom Segev, *One Palestine Complete. Jews and Arabs under the British Mandate* (London, 2001), 475–76; Benny Morris, *Righteous Victims. A History of the Zionist-Arab Conflict, 1881–2001* (New York, 2001) 176–79.

636 Israel Television, Channel 1, *The True Story. The Templers — Secrets in Tel Aviv*, documentary, spring 2007.

637 *Palestine Post*, 24 Mar. 1946: 3.

638 Ibid.

639 Israel Television, Channel 1, *The True Story. The Templers — Secrets in Tel Aviv*, documentary, spring 2007.

The secretary of the Templers was Gotthilf Wagner, a man in his late forties, de facto the leader, very energetic, stubborn and unafraid of the "authorities," which were not that clearly defined, making negotiation particularly difficult. He was also one of the very few fluent English speakers of the group. In his view the Templers had earned the right to be guaranteed a future, preferably where they were, but if not, then somewhere else in the British Empire with just and fair compensation for real estate values of the possessions that would have to be relinquished. His negotiations involved discussions with the British, the Zionists, the Arabs – with all of whom he stuck to his guns, being convinced of the justification of the line he had adopted.

This was the time when he began to receive anonymous phone calls, messages to the effect that "We" will make certain that he would never see his grandchildren in Australia again. In 1941, large numbers of younger Templers and their wives and children had been shipped on the *Queen Elizabeth* to Australia, which brought about the tearing apart of many families.... The warning Gotthilf Wagner had received subsequently turned out to be a bomb explosion in the Sarona community hall, one of the Templer settlements near Tel Aviv, where he was presiding over the meeting of elders. A major mess with many dead bodies would have been the outcome had the meeting for that day not been postponed by 20 minutes or so, a mere non-routine coincidence. I never found out why the meeting had been postponed. Then, on the morning of 22 March 1946, Wagner drove with two others, one of them his sister Frida, from the inland settlement Wilhelma near Lydda, now Bene Atarot near Lod, to nearby Jaffa....

On this business trip unrest was all around: tensions, daily killings, mutual atrocities between Jews and Arabs and occasionally involving the British.... Gotthilf's wife, Lina, had pleaded with her husband not to go.... In his somewhat gruff manner, Wagner had brushed it all aside saying "Allah ma na" – God is with us – and although he wasn't a Muslim, many Templers were less reticent, less inhibited when using the Arab tongue in which some were as fluent as the native speakers. After he had driven off in the car, Frida observed two motorbike riders following the car at some distance. Close to the outskirts of Jaffa, in front of a cast iron bridge over the wadi (creek)..., a car across the whole road blocked their way. Two obviously seasoned killers jumped forward at the slowing car from behind a bush, each pumped a bullet into his head and disappeared on their motorbikes. The deed took less than a minute. Gotthilf was almost instantly dead, trying to frame a word resembling "Ende" – the end – and turning off the motor as an already automatic reflex action. Frida, in inexpressible panic, tried to mop up the blood pouring out of the fatal wounds.

By the afternoon of that day Wagner's body was returned to Wilhelma. The entire community, and later all Templers, were stunned, speechless, feeling that time had stood still, and wondering who and what would come next. They certainly felt that the end of their time in that area had come in one form or other. There was no one remotely capable of guiding them through that impossibly chaotic time on the same conviction that Wagner had done, of toughing it out with those in power....

I was a 13-year-old boy in the Templer community and I was Gotthilf's nephew and he was my mother's cousin.... My brother, Hans, and I both knew *Onkel* Gotthilf particularly well, were extremely fond and admiring of him, appreciated his generosity, his sense of humour

> and his general ability to have fun.... Gotthilf was a positive personality and a role model. Like me, many people puzzled over the need to kill this man. It had nothing to do with the strife in Europe. Wagner was a deeply convinced anti-Nazi.[640]

In fact, Gotthilf Wagner had been a member of the Nazi party in Palestine. His membership no. 7024779 is recorded at the Public Record Office in London and the United States Holocaust Memorial Museum in Washington, D.C. Why the Haganah killed him is still unclear. Was Wagner eliminated because Zionists wanted the land of Sarona, which Wagner had constantly refused to sell to them? This is unlikely, because the British authorities had already promulgated the Land Ordinance of 1943, which "enabled the Government to acquire land compulsorily for another party if deemed desirable.... From 1944 onwards, the British expropriated more and more land around Sarona in favour of the Tel Aviv City Council."[641] More likely is that Wagner's murder was intended to signal that there was no longer any place in Palestine for Germans. Further hostilities and attacks against them underline this assumption.

In November 1946, two young Germans, Mitscherlich (first name unknown) and Rolf Mueller, were shot on their way to Waldheim. Two others, Wilfried Schumacher and Ruppert (first name unknown), were beaten to death in Haifa. Two elderly Templer ladies were detained in Tel Aviv for several days before they could return to their homes.[642] Richard Otto Eppinger of the Temple Society reported shots fired from passing cars, and sporadic firing at buildings in Wilhelma which damaged windows and entrance doors. He also recalled a German widow who was assaulted and blindfolded by two Jewish boys.[643] At the end of November 1946, the British informed the Templers and leaders of the Lutheran Church of the Redeemer that it proposed the deportation of all remaining Germans. It took almost a year and a half before this was implemented. Reluctantly over time they had to accept the bitter reality that they would have to give up their settlements.[644]

In April 1948, the Haganah raided the three internment camps of Waldheim, Bethlehem in the Galilee, and Wilhelma. Gottfried and Anna Meyer, the Swiss

---

640 Richard Hornung, "Reminiscence from the Middle East," Adelaide, 21 Mar. 2002, *Adelaide Institute Newsletter*, no. 159 (May 2002). Although the Adelaide Institute in Australia is known for Holocaust denial, Richard Hornung's article was included here to illustrate his perception and memory of the 1940s in the Middle East.

641 Glenk, *From Desert Sands*, 228. For further details on the sale of Sarona, see ibid., 227–33.

642 Ibid., 222; Paul Sauer, *Uns rief das Heilige Land. Die Tempelgesellschaft im Wandel der Zeit* (Stuttgart, 1985), 308.

643 Richard Otto Eppinger, "Die Zypern-Gruppe. Tagebuch-Notizen vom Ende des Siedlungswerks der Templer in Palästina," in *Der besondere Beitrag. Beilage der Warte des Tempels* (Stuttgart) (Dec. 2005): 6; Glenk, *From Desert Sands*, 221; Sauer, *Uns rief das Heilige Land*, 308–9.

644 Glenk, *From Desert Sands*, 221–25; Sauer, *Uns rief das Heilige Land*, 311.

couple who were staying at Waldheim at the time, reported on the incident.[645] Richard Otto Eppinger, Hedwig Deininger, and Kurt Seidler of the Temple Society also recorded the events of 1947 and 1948[646]:

> The United Nations' decision on the partition plan was made on November 29th, 1947. The Arabs living in the British Mandate were not willing to accept the UN resolution. Violent clashes erupted as both Jews and Arabs engaged in sniping, raids, and bombings. Most of the Arab guards of the internment camps left their post and took their guns with them in order to join the fights. After the end of the war both Jews and Arabs claimed the German property and fought to gain control of it. The interment camps, where the Germans and other enemy aliens were still staying for their own protection, were at that time watched by only a few Arab and British guards, by approximately seven or eight armed men. This circumstance made it easy to attack them.
>
> On April 17, 1948, heavy machine gun fire woke the inhabitants of Waldheim. It was four o'clock in the morning. People hurried to get dressed, went back and forth in their houses from one window to the next to watch Jewish armed men enter the camp and search for armed Arabs. But no Arab was there. Jewish soldiers[647] pushed open the door to a house where a sick, bedridden woman lived. Her daughter was with her. One of the soldiers shot at her daughter but the shot missed her and hit the ceiling instead. The sick woman was allowed to remain inside the house. Her daughter was ordered to go into the courtyard. A few seconds later, soldiers ordered Gottfried and Anna Meyer to leave their house with raised hands. They had to wait in the courtyard while the Jewish militants were searching their house, barn, stable, and chicken coop for Arabs. But it was too early to find any suspects there, because Arab workers were not allowed to enter the camp before 4.30 AM. The soldiers pushed the Meyers from the courtyard into a garden. They confiscated the husband's money and the couple's Swiss passports. The couple was taken to a room where they met other people detained by the Jewish soldiers. No one was allowed to talk. More and more inhabitants were brought in. An armed soldier was posted outside the room with his machine gun aimed at the detainees inside. Three children and their aunt entered the room. Although it was prohibited from talking, the aunt informed those present that the parents of the three children, Karl and Regine Aimann, had been shot by Jewish soldiers in front of their nine-year-old daughter. Furthermore a sixty-five-year-old woman, Katharine (Katharina) Deininger, had been grazed by a bullet but survived.
>
> During the day the detainees received food several times. The children even got chocolate and biscuits. The Meyers' Swiss passports were returned. The sick and injured persons were transported to a hospital in Nazareth.
>
> In the evening, all members were taken to an empty barrack where they had to spend the night on the floor. The next morning, on April 18, a Jewish officer ordered the relatives of the

645 "Überfall in Waldheim von der Haganah am 17. April 1948," YVA P19/26.

646 Gertrud Wassermann-Deininger, "Wir haben hier keine bleibende Statt. Geschichte der Familie Deininger in Palästina, 1868–1948," memoir, 1982, 69–73.

647 The terms *soldier*, *officer*, and *commanding officer* are those used by the eyewitnesses.

dead couple to bury their dead. After the funeral, all detainees had to return to their houses to pack a few things for their final deportation from Palestine. While they were waiting at the gathering place for the transfer, their luggage was searched. Then the Jewish commanding officer held a speech on the "horror stories," as Kurt Seidler put it, how the Germans had persecuted and murdered the Jews of Europe. He accused the Germans present of being Nazis. Furthermore, he claimed that his men had found soap in the camp labeled with "produced out of Jew's fat" (*hergestellt aus Judenfett*). The officer pointed out that it would be easy to him and his men to kill everybody in the camp as the Germans did to the Jews. But he emphasized that he and his soldiers were more civilized and therefore they would let all Germans go. After the speech, six young German men were called to step out for a special examination. Jews with machine guns took them into a building nearby and searched them for tattooed SS marks. The six men returned unharmed. Meanwhile a car with six people from Bethlehem/Galilee arrived. They reported that about ninety internees of the Bethlehem camp had managed to flee from the Haganah, first to an Arab village and from there to Nazareth.

Later the day, British military and tanks arrived. The British transferred the inhabitants of Waldheim to a military camp near Acre. On April 19, the Germans of Bethlehem who had fled to Nazareth were also brought to Acre. Two days later on April 21, British military vehicles and tanks guided all of them to the port of Haifa where the *Empire Comfort* was already waiting. Already on board were their companions in distress from Wilhelma. A day before, the internees of the Wilhelma camp had been picked up in a convoy of eight buses and five trucks under the protection of three British tanks. Their journey had taken them via Lydda to Jaffa and then to Haifa. In the evening of April 21, the *Empire Comfort* left the port of Haifa with about 330 internees, mainly Germans. The ship was heading to Famagusta, Cyprus.[648] (End of the reports.)

As the *Palestine Post* reported:

The Haganah yesterday occupied the German village of Waldheim.... The action was taken when it was learned that Arab gangs were preparing to occupy the 9,000 dunams which have been under the direction of the Custodian of Enemy Property. The village was occupied by 75 enemy aliens who were under the guard of the British. None of the British was injured in the raid, but two of the Germans who joined the Arabs in resisting the occupation were killed. According to an official report, the attack was made by 50 Jews with one armoured car. The village...served as a base for Arab gangs during the 1936–39 riots. German settlers, who at that time numbered between 400 and 500, cooperated with the Arab gangs. The Jewish national institutions have been negotiating with the Palestine Government for the purchase of the property, according to the Haganah Radio. Recently the Government intimated that it was unable to conclude the negotiations, and with the impending evacuation of the British and Germans, still at Waldheim, Arab gangs planned to assume control.[649]

648 "Überfall in Waldheim von der Haganah am 17. April 1948," YVA P 19/26; Wassermann-Deininger, "Wir haben hier keine bleibende Statt," 68, 69–73; Eppinger, "Die Zypern-Gruppe," 7–10; Glenk, *From Desert Sands*, 225.
649 *Palestine Post*, 18 Apr. 1948, 1.

On April 22, 1948, the evacuated Germans arrived in Cyprus. Military buses brought them to the Golden Sands tent camp, located on the shore near Famagusta, only two miles from the camp where illegal Jewish immigrants to Palestine had been taken by the British. Six or seven internees, headed by Gottlob Loebert remained in Palestine to sell the Templers' stock and furniture, and see to the transport of the large luggage items of the deported internees. This group was ultimately taken to Cyprus as well. After seven to ten months of internment in Cyprus, the majority of them (Templers) were allowed to leave for Australia. Only a small number returned to Germany.[650]

Approximately fifty German settlers, mainly Templers and a few Sisters of the Kaiserswerth Order,[651] requested not to take part in the evacuation, and were allowed to go to Jerusalem, where they moved into their former homes in the German Colony or into the German Hospice, where the Sisters of St. Charles Borromeo, under Mother Superior Emiliana, looked after them.[652] Nikolai Schmidt, the head of the Templer community at that time, described the daily life of those days in Jerusalem:

> The remaining Germans tried to lead a regular life but the political and economic situation made it almost impossible. They missed their clean and cozy homes which had been plundered, vandalized and damaged while they were in the internment camps. The shortage of food and drinking water made life difficult. As the Refaim Valley and the German Hospice lay between the Jewish-Arab front lines, daily life was not only difficult but also dangerous. Gun fire, shots, and explosions were heard day and night. One attack followed the other. Sometimes bullets missed their original goal and hit the walls of the German Hospice. Many Arabs fled from the neighborhood after they had learned about massacres of Arab villagers conducted by Jewish forces. The horrible news from Deir Yassin particularly frightened them. The streets and shops in the German Colony were deserted. In the middle of May 1948 the British left the city and the country, and the establishment of the new State of Israel was declared. The buildings the British had occupied in the German Colony were immediately plundered by looters. As the rumbling of battle fire and explosions came closer to the Refaim Valley, the few Germans who were still living in their own home had to seek shelter at the already overcrowded German Hospice. Later on, thousands of poor Jewish families from the Old City and immigrants from Yemen, Morocco, the Balkans, etc. moved into the houses of the German Colony in Jerusalem. Once, the former owners of those houses, the Templers, tried to collect rent from them but they were refused.[653]

---

650 Glenk, *From Desert Sands*, 225. For more details on the internment in Cyprus see Eppinger, "Die Zypern-Gruppe," 5–31 (including photos).
651 One of them was Sister Theodore Barkhausen, the former head sister of the German Protestant guesthouse of the Auguste Victoria Foundation on the Mount of Olives in Jerusalem.
652 Nikolai Schmidt, report, TGA, T-576b_1.
653 Ibid., 13, 17.

A day before the Christian holiday of Pentecost in 1948, when fights erupted around the Zion Gate and the Refaim Valley, 250 Arabs found refuge with the Borromean Sisters. But several hours later, a Jewish military unit entered the hospice and arrested seventeen of them. Arab men over sixty were allowed to return to the guest rooms of the German Hospice. On June 3, 1948, nineteen padres fled from the Dormition Abbey, which was used by Haganah fighters, and took shelter at the already crowded German Hospice. On June 11, the first truce, elaborated and negotiated by neutral powers, came into effect. From July on, the economic situation in Jerusalem improved slightly, and from November on the shooting diminished.[654]

On November 14, 1948, the families of Hermann Imberger and Nikolai Schmidt were the first to receive the order to leave the country. It was explained to them that they had to leave the State of Israel because they had been members of the Nazi party. Further deportation orders followed. Nikolai Schmidt, who had entered the Nazi party in 1938, commented: "The reason that was given to us was the involvement in the Nazi party. We recognized that a protest against the deportation order was doomed to fail."[655] From December 1948 to autumn 1950, the remaining Germans left Israel for good. The majority of them joined their families and relatives in Australia. Only a few returned to Germany.[656] The departure of the Germans in 1950 brought the presence of the Nazis in the Holy Land to a definite end. A very few, who had Palestinian passports, were allowed to stay.[657]

654 Ibid., 16.

655 Ibid., 17.

656 Ibid., 1–18; Glenk, *From Desert Sands*, 221–25.

657 Brigitte Kneher, Temple Society, Germany to Heidemarie Wawrzyn, email, 22 Apr. 2008; Peter Lange, Temple Society Germany to Heidemarie Wawrzyn, email, 28 April 2008.

14 Was the NS Country Group Palestine Different?

A comparison of NS groups

The majority of NS groups abroad came into being before 1933 and witnessed a boost after Hitler's seizure of power, resulting in an increase of membership and activities.[658] All Nazi officials abroad concentrated their recruitment on German colonies and schools in the host countries. As Germans generally preferred to live in close-knit communities in which they preserved their German language and traditions, it was quite easy for Nazi officials to reach them and win them over to the idea of a racial community (Volksgemeinschaft). The NS country leaders abroad tried to create a miniature Third Reich by introducing NS units for juveniles, women, teachers, workers, and so on, and providing Nazi propaganda from Germany including films, brochures, and NS newsletters. Celebrations of national holidays generally attracted a huge number of German citizens abroad and ethnic Germans. Nazi party members were trained in regular meetings and special courses.

Almost every NS country group suffered internal conflicts and struggles for power and leadership. NS officials aggressively tried to gain influence over the German embassies through measures like denunciation of and spying on their

658 The comparison is mainly based on the following archival sources and publications: correspondence, 1933, ISTA, 823/8-פ; correspondence, Mar. 1934, ISTA, 822/15-פ; *Vorschläge zur NS-Schulungsarbeit im Ausland* (Nov. 1936): 1–2; H. Blumhagen *Südwestafrika einst und jetzt* (Berlin, 1934) (South West Africa); Victor Farias, *Die Nazis in Chile* (Vienna, 2002) (Chile); Barbara Geldermann, "Jewish Refugees Should Be Welcomed and Assisted Here!" Shanghai: Exile and Return," *Yearbook of the Leo Baeck Institute* 19 (1999): 227–43 (Shanghai); Warren Grover, *Nazis in Newark* (2003) (United States); Albrecht Hagemann, *Südafrika und das "Dritte Reich." Rassenpolitische Affinität und machtpolitische Rivalität* (Frankfurt a.M., 1989) (South Africa); Stefan Heym, *Nazis in U.S.A. An Exposé of Hitler's Aims and Agents in the U.S.A.* (New York, 1938) (United States); Frank D. McCann, "Vargas and the Destruction of the Brazilian Integralista and Nazi Parties," *The Americas* 26, no. 1 (July 1969): 15–34 (Brazil); McKale 1977a (Far East); Donald M. McKale, *The Swastika outside Germany* (Kent State, 1977); Jürgen Müller, *Nationalsozialismus in Lateinamerika: Auslandsorganisation der NSDAP in Argentinien, Brasilien, Chile und Mexiko, 1931–1945* (Stuttgart, 1997) (Latin America); John Perkins, "The Swastika Down Under: Nazi Activities in Australia, 1933–1939," *Journal of Contemporary History* 26, no. 1 (1991): 111–29 (Australia); H. Schmidt, "The Nazi Party in Palestine and the Levant 1932–9," *International Affairs* 28, no. 4 (1952): 460–69 (Palestine, Levant); Simone Schwarz, *Chile im Schatten faschistischer Bewegungen. Der Einfluß europäischer und chilenischer Strömungen in den 30er und 70er Jahren* (Frankfurt a.M., 1997) (Chile).

own diplomats, consuls, and consulate staff. To a greater or lesser extent, they conducted subversion by infiltrating local fascist groups, penetrating the host government, army, and economy; and distributing anti-democratic propaganda. They promoted racism and antisemitism by spreading antisemitic pamphlets, petitioning, bans on Jewish immigration, and urging company owners to dismiss Jewish employees.

At the beginning, almost every NS branch abroad faced opposition from ethnic German immigrants (Volksdeutsche) who had been living in their settlements since the 19th century. This opposition was mainly directed at the Nazi's demand for dominance and control over the established German colonies and institutions, rather than at National Socialism itself or Hitler's dictatorship. In general, Germans living abroad sympathized with Hitler and his new German policy, as they hoped for an improvement in Germany's reputation abroad.

The establishment of Nazi groups outside Europe was generally not welcomed, except by some nationalist individuals and groups. For example, support and great admiration for Hitler and his regime were recorded among the Arab populations in the Middle East and the Afrikaners in South Africa.[659] In general, it can be noted, the more aggressively the Third Reich's foreign policy developed, the more foreign governments were suspicious of Nazi activities among their German immigrants. Nazi branches abroad faced various restrictions or outright bans; some Nazi officials were even imprisoned or expelled. A few NS country groups dissolved themselves, while others were dismantled only after Germany's defeat.

Differences and common ground

At first glance, the NS country group in Palestine displays many similarities to other NS branches abroad. First, NS activities were developed in Palestine before 1933, with an increase in its activities and membership after Hitler's accession to power. As with other country groups, the efficiency of the local groups mainly depended on the National Socialist engagement and leadership skills of its head. When the Templer Cornelius Schwarz replaced Landesvertrauensmann Karl Ruff in 1935, the organization greatly strengthened its political dominance and control under his strict and ambitious leadership.

Landesgruppe Palestine mirrored the Nazi party with its local groups, organizations, and affiliated associations in Germany. With its regular party meetings and training courses, its leagues for women and teachers, as well as its Hitler

---

659 For more details on South Africa see Hagemann, *Südafrika und das "Dritte Reich"* (esp. 350–51).

Youth program and Winter Relief collections, it was indeed a miniature Third Reich. All Nazi groups in Palestine were established within the German colonies, where national holidays and sporting events were celebrated, accompanied by marches with the swastika flag, Nazi songs, and *Sieg Heil!* acclamations. Like party members in Germany and other branches abroad, the majority of the party members were middle class males who disliked the democratic system of the Weimar Republic and longed for a strong, renewed Germany with a powerful leader.

NS officials abroad, including those in Palestine, encountered some opposition at the beginning of their activity. A few Templers, ministers, and businessmen expressed concern that National Socialist activities would adversely effect their businesses and religious activities. Such objections decreased after 1935 when Cornelius Schwarz was appointed NS Landeskreisleiter (regional leader) and Walter Doehle became the consul general.

In all countries, NS officials abroad saw German schools as the preferred target for influencing youth. In the late 1930s, they planned to merge the German Protestant School and the Lyceum Tempelstift (the secondary school of the Temple Society) in Jerusalem. Lutheran Church of the Redeemer Provost Ernst Rhein and a few ministers tried to stop this project, but to no avail.[660]

In certain aspects, the Nazi party in Palestine differed from other NS country groups. Archival documents and newsletters presented in this study display fewer internal conflicts and leadership power struggles, except in the period of 1934–1935 when Cornelius Schwarz fervently sought to head the party and replaced Landesvertrauensmann Karl Ruff. When Consul General Heinrich Wolff was dismissed from his position in 1935 because his wife was a Jewish convert to Christianity, he was succeeded by Walter Doehle.[661] Under the new consul general, excellent cooperation began between local Nazi party representatives and the German consulate in Palestine. Compared to the rivalries between NS officials and German embassies in other country groups, the situation in Palestine was quite extraordinary.[662]

660 Ralf Balke, *Hakenkreuz im Heiligen Land. Die NSDAP-Landesgruppe Palästina* (Erfurt, 2001), 88–89; Roland Löffler, "Die Gemeinden des Jerusalemsvereins in Palästina im Kontext des kirchlichen und politischen Zeitgeschehens in der Mandatszeit," in *Seht, wir gehen hinauf nach Jerusalem. Festschrift zum 150jährigen Jubiläum von Talitha Kumi und des Jerusalemsvereins,* edited by Almut Nothnagle, Hans-Jürgen Abromeit, and Frank Foerster (Leipzig, 2000), 185–212, 208; idem, *Protestanten in Palästina* (Stuttgart, 2008), 167–91.

661 Eckart Conze, Norbert Frei, Peter Hayes, and Moshe Zimmermann, *Das Amt und die Vergangenheit: Deutsche Diplomaten im Dritten Reich und in der Bundesrepublik* (Munich, 2010), 107–8.

662 Balke, *Hakenkreuz im Heiligen Land*, 183. The NSDAP in Australia had developed similarly good cooperation between the party and the consulate. See previous chapter.

Although only 2,000 to 2,500 German nationals lived in the British Mandate of Palestine, almost nineteen percent of of them joined the Nazi party, whereas on average, barely five percent of all German citizens abroad belonged to the NSDAP.[663]

Compared to other German communities abroad, the Palestine-Germans were very homogeneous. The number of Volksdeutsche to be "won back" to the racial community, was very small.[664] Most Germans residing in the British Mandate of Palestine were German citizens, the majority of whom belonged to the Temple Society and the German-speaking Protestant churches. Many were active Christians who attended Sunday services and conducted welfare and missionary work. The Schneller family, the Templers, the Deaconesses of Kaiserswerth, and others had chosen the region and their work for religious reasons. The older generation of the Templers had come to Palestine to fulfill a very ambitious goal – to establish God's Kingdom in the Holy Land. They generally had good relations with each other and socialized regularly. Christian faith and German culture (language, traditions, and values) formed their common bond. Their ties to Germany were strong, although many of them had been living in Palestine since the second half of the 19th century, yet they felt very German, perhaps even too German. Being a German was a holy commitment to them, as Alfred Weller expressed it in 1948.[665] Families sent their children to Germany for their education or training programs. Studies on NS groups worldwide show that Christian churches and religious movements abroad usually did not play such an important role in establishing Nazi branches, as it did in Palestine.

While the Auslands-Organisation often sent NS officials abroad to establish, organize, or reorganize local NS groups, all the Nazi leaders in Palestine came from the Temple Society, except for Kurt Hegele and Eugen Faber.[666] These leaders were well known and respected among most Germans. A series of political "successes" in German foreign policy in 1938 had motivated the senior members of the Temple Society especially to enter the Nazi party. Opposition against young, ambitious Nazi officials, who had just arrived in the country and wanted to take

---

663 Donald M. McKale, *The Swastika Outside Germany* (Kent State, 1977), 120.

664 According to information from the archive of the Temple Society in Germany, only three or four younger women and a few senior Templers held Palestinian passports. One Templer woman had gained British citizenship as a result of her marriage. Brigitte Kneher, Temple Society Germany to Heidemarie Wawrzyn, email, 22 Apr. 2008; Peter Lange, Temple Society Germany to Heidemarie Wawrzyn, email, 28 Apr. 2008.

665 Alfred Weller, "Gedanken über die Haltung der Tempelgesellschaft zum Nationalsozialismus," lecture, 1948, edited by Brigitte Hoffnung in *Der besondere Beitrag. Beilage der Warte des Tempels* 2 (Stuttgart, 1995), 3–7.

666 Balke, *Hakenkreuz im Heiligen Land*, 79.

over German institutions and colonies, did not erupt, as had happened in Brazil, Chile, and other NS country groups. Furthermore, the entire German youth of Palestine was already organized in religious youth programs sponsored by the Temple Society and the Lutheran Church of the Redeemer. With the organizational infrastructure already in place and given the Hitler Jugend's strong attraction for juveniles, the program was easily and successfully established so that by 1937 almost every German boy and girl in Palestine belonged to the movement.

The German settlers' daily life depended on their Jewish customers, Arab workers, and the goodwill of the British. In the late 1930s, the Germans were caught between the Jews accusing them of training and arming Arab rebels, while the British suspected them of smuggling weapons into the country. At the same time, Arab rebels pressured them to provide financial and military support by attacking and blackmailing them. Such a difficult and even life-threatening situation was not faced by any other NS country group.

Studies on NS country groups reveal that subversion and antisemitic acts were carried out by German Nazis abroad, but those in Palestine were the only community abroad surrounded by a steadily increasing Jewish population that planned to establish a Jewish state. National Socialism targeted Jews as the most dangerous threat to the German people, the "Aryan race," and led Germans to believe that their superior race was entitled to rule other nations. It would not be surprising to find that some Nazis in Palestine would commit anti-Jewish acts. Nazi propaganda was spread by German missionaries, Christian welfare workers, and the DNB directed by Franz Reichert. Documents from archives in London and Jerusalem prove that arms were smuggled or attempts were made to send them from Germany. Hence, it can be concluded that a number of Nazis in Palestine tried to bring about National Socialism not only by establishing a strong racial community but also by supporting the Arab cause.

Conclusion

Hitler's Community in Palestine

In 1932, a handful of Nazi sympathizers and loyal German patriots gathered around Karl Ruff, an architect who had been born in Haifa in 1904. In the 1920s, Ruff had spent several years in Germany for his studies. On his return to Haifa, he became politically engaged, promoting National Socialism among his fellow Germans and applying for membership in the NSDAP in Germany. Encouraged by the Auslands-Abteilung, he and his Nazi friends began to spread NS propaganda and established Nazi groups in Palestine. Cornelius Schwarz, a fellow member of the Temple Society, replaced Ruff as leader in 1935. Under Schwarz's firm and determined leadership, the Nazi organization in Palestine flourished, extending its political influence and gaining control over the German colonies. Furthermore, the excellent cooperation between Schwarz and Consul General Doehle (who replaced Heinrich Wolff in 1935) helped strengthen the hegemony of the local NSDAP. On the occasion of Hitler's birthday in 1937, the NS organization in Palestine received the rank of a Landesgruppe with Cornelius Schwarz as NS country leader. Within a few years, between 1932 and 1939, a miniature Third Reich was established with local NS groups and support points in Haifa, Jaffa, Sarona, Jerusalem, Wilhelma, Waldheim, and Bethlehem in the Galilee. Hitler Youth, work groups for women, and associations for teachers, workers, employees, and others had also been founded.

Almost every fifth Palestine-German was a member of the Nazi party. Between 1932 and 1939, more than four hundred adults joined the NSDAP, representing almost 19% of all Germans in Palestine. This figure includes the Parteianwärter who had applied for party membership and were awaiting their membership books. More than three hundred Germans of all ages participated either in the Hitler Youth program or in various NS groups without being party members. In summary, almost every third German in Palestine took part in some program of the local NSDAP.

Although the majority of the local NSDAP was recruited from the Temple Society, it should be pointed out that some Protestants (including Kirchlers) and a few Catholics joined the NSDAP, participated in the NS groups or attended celebrations of the National Socialist holidays, such as Hitler's birthday and the anniversary of Hitler's seizure of power. Nazi party members and NS participants were 75% Templer, approximately 22% Protestant, and less than 1% Catholic. Letters of both party members and non-party members overwhelmingly display the Germans' great loyalty to the fatherland, their pride in the new, strong Reich and a positive attitude towards Hitler, often expressed as admiration, love, or loyalty.

Even those who disagreed with the establishment of the NSDAP in Palestine saw Hitler as "sent from God." Privately and inwardly, they felt themselves to be a part of Hitler's new community. They were Hitler's small community abroad, which consisted of NS party members, participants, sympathizers, and collaborators. "All of us are Hitler," wrote Schwarz to his son Erwin in early 1932.[667] Palestine-Germans followed political events in Germany with great interest, full of love for the new Reich, and a new national spirit could be sensed among them. Their devotion to the fatherland and sense of solidarity with the entire German people was seen in celebrations of the new National Socialist holidays, collections for the Winter Relief Organization, and sticking together as an ethnic community. They gathered to listen to the broadcast speeches of Hitler, Goebbels, and other Nazi politicians, and as Schwarz described it: "It was like a [Christian worship] service. The women's eyes were filled with tears and mine too."[668]

As personal and official letters prove, the majority of Palestine-Germans proudly and honestly welcomed the establishment of the NS government in Germany, as did even those who deliberately decided not to join the NSDAP. They had in common their admiration for the Führer, German pride, and a great longing for a strong, renewed German Reich. Their Christian religion and cultural background was another strong bond between them. Their Christianity, with its anti-Jewish and chauvinist ideas, made them receptive to Hitler's ideology long before his seizure of power.[669] Palestine-Germans agreed with the National Socialist motto "*Gemeinnutz kommt vor Eigennutz*" (Public interest goes before self-interest).[670] Those in the Temple Society were especially familiar with it, since it had always been the maxim of their organization. *Die Warte des Tempels* published articles equating the Third Reich with God's Kingdom, which they believed they were implementing by practicing charity, communal life, and mutual support. Nazi propaganda proclaimed the same virtues.[671]

Criticism of the totalitarian and racist Nazi regime was rare. There was some limited opposition at the introduction of a local Nazi party in Palestine and its increasing activities. This was never based on human rights, anti-racism, or pro-Jewish attitudes, but rather had to do with financial, religious, or personal concerns.

---

667 Cornelius Schwarz to Erwin Schwarz, 8 Feb. 1932, ISTA 821/3- פ.

668 C. Schwarz, Jaffa to Erwin Schwarz, Cairo, 5 Mar. 1933: "Es war ein Gottesdienst. Den Frauen hier und auch mir wurden die Augen nass," ISTA 821/3- פ.

669 See Heidemarie Wawrzyn, *Ham and Eggs in Palestine. The Auguste Victoria Foundation 1898–1939* (Marburg, 2005), 60–64.

670 See, for example, *Die Warte des Tempels* (Stuttgart), 31 May 1933, 73.

671 Brigitte Hoffmann: "Unsere Verantwortung in der Welt," *Der besondere Beitrag. Beilage der Warte des Tempels* (Stuttgart) 2 (1995): 7–14.

A few members of the Protestant churches and Temple Society opposed the German Faith Movement,[672] whose intention was to abolish the Old Testament and "liberate" the Christian religion from its Jewish roots.[673] They also protested the Hitler Youth organization's plan to keep the youth from attending church on important Christian holidays. A few members of the Lutheran Church of the Redeemer in Jerusalem tried to stop the installation of the Deutsche Schule with its National Socialist curriculum. Despite these disagreements, they did not want their protest to be taken as a negative reaction to the new German NS state.[674]

Older Templers generally hesitated to join the party because they feared that the local NS branch activities would split their community. Furthermore, they were concerned that the introduction of Nazi songs, uniforms, and swastika flags would endanger their situation in Palestine and increase conflicts with the British Mandatory government and the Yishuv. They therefore tried to dampen the pro-National Socialist enthusiasm and antisemitism of their young members. Germans in Palestine, especially the Templers, feared their property would be expropriated and they would be deported if they publicly showed their pride in and loyalty to the new German Reich. If they had had the choice, many would have preferred the strengthening of Deutschtum through the establishment of groups for ethnic Germans rather than erecting an organizational network of the NSDAP in Palestine.[675]

German businessmen protested a few anti-Jewish and pro-Nazi activities, such as the hoisting of the new German flag in Palestine in March 1933, and the anti-Jewish boycott in Germany the following month. They feared such acts could ruin their businesses and damage good relations with their Jewish customers. Particularly in the 1930s, when thousands of Jews immigrated to Palestine, German business was booming. The Bank of the Temple Society earned huge profits as a result of Jewish immigration and increased economic development in Palestine.[676] German shops and firms also benefitted from the huge influx of new immigrants. Cornelius Schwarz wrote to his son in Egypt in 1933 full of excitement that steamers were bringing hundreds of Jews from Germany. At that time, he still

672 The German Faith Movement was founded in 1933 by Jakob W. Hauer (1881–1962), with the goal of introducing a new form of "German" Christianity in order to provide the Third Reich with a new religious basis. See Shaul Baumann, *Die Deutsche Glaubensbewegung und ihr Gründer Jakob Wilhelm Hauer (1881–1962).* (Marburg, 2005).

673 Balke, *Hakenkreuz im Heiligen Land*, 84-85.

674 Letter 6 June 1934, *Jerusalemsverein*, B 536; annual reports, 1933, 1935, 1936–1937, Oertzen: Haifa-Waldheim, *Jerusalemsverein*, B 557.

675 *Jerusalemsverein*, B 557, additional report, Oertzen, Haifa-Waldheim 1934; Nikolai Schmidt, June 1934, ISTA, 3174/27-פ.

676 *Die Warte des Tempels*, 15 Apr. 1935, 50–51; 30 June 1935, 93–94; 31 Aug. 1935, 125; Paul Sauer, *Uns rief das Heilige Land. Die Tempelgesellschaft imWandel der Zeit* (Stuttgart, 1985). 260–61.

looked forward to the continuing arrival of Jews because it was good for German business.[677] He described his official behavior to Jews as intentionally and consciously friendly and polite, in order not to cause suspicion or conflict.[678] Other German businessmen also treated their Jewish customers in an extremely friendly and careful manner because they did not want to lose their clients.[679] They concealed their Hitler-friendly, pro-Nazi attitude in order not to aggravate their life in the "*Judenland*."[680]

German Protestant ministers in Jerusalem, Jaffa, Haifa, and Waldheim had other reasons for not joining the NSDAP. Provost Ernst Rhein (Jerusalem, 1930–1938) welcomed the new Nazi era. In 1933, he seriously considered joining the Nazi party in Jerusalem in order to publicly express his support for the German NS state. In the end, he chose not to do so, explaining that in the difficult political situation in Palestine, he could probably serve the NS state better and more efficiently as an official non-Nazi by voluntarily serving Hitler and his state without any alleged pressure from the party.[681] Furthermore, as with some of his colleagues, he was convinced that a minister should not be officially involved in political activity. Nevertheless, their strong Nazi sympathies were evident in their letters and annual reports.

The fact that the Palestine-Germans lived with Arabs and Jews shaped their antisemitism, and led them to focus on different issues than the majority in Germany, perceiving Jews not only as representatives of materialism and capitalism, but also as the enemies of the Arabs in Palestine. While anti-Judaism used "the Jew" as a negative background to make Christianity look superior, and NS antisemitism labeled Jews as a "degenerate race" and a danger to the "pure" German race, Palestine-Germans mainly pictured Jews and Arabs as hostile opponents.[682] The polarization of "the bad, materialistic Jew" and "the poor Arab victim" had already begun during World War I.[683] With the growing number of Jewish immigrants, Germans in Palestine generally contrasted the immigrant Jews negatively with the Arabs in Palestine. Jews were perceived as enemies of the Arabs, intrud-

---

677 Cornelius Schwarz, Jaffa to Erwin Schwarz, Cairo, 12 and 26 Feb. 1933, ISTA 821/2-פ.

678 C. Schwarz, Jaffa to Erwin Schwarz, Cairo, 22 Mar. 1933, ISTA 821/2-פ.

679 C. Schwarz, Jaffa to Erwin Schwarz, Cairo, 22 Mar. 1933, 8 Feb. 1932, and 11 Mar. 1932, ISTA 821/2- פ.

680 Nikolai Schmidt, June 1934, ISTA 3174/27-פ.

681 Ernst Rhein, Annual Report, October 1932–December 1933, EZA 56/188.

682 Cf. Robert S. Wistrich, *Antisemitism in the New Europe* (Oxford, 1994), 5; idem, *Antisemitism. The Longest Hatred* (London, 1992), Introduction; Heidemarie Wawrzyn, *Vaterland statt Menschenrecht. Formen der Judenfeindschaft in den Frauenbewegungen des Deutschen Kaiserreiches* (Marburg, 1999), 43–44.

683 Heidemarie Wawrzyn, *Ham and Eggs in Palestine. The Auguste Victoria Foundation 1898–1939* (Marburg, 2005), 54–58.

ers who changed the country profoundly by bringing Western civilization to the region, and destroying Arab culture. They were seen as part of "World Jewry," Zionists plotting with wealthy Americans and British. Young immigrant Jews were perceived as immoral communists or atheists, and occasionally were said to be a danger to German youth. Palestine-Germans intentionally spoke of their positive relations with the Arab population, even when Arab rebels attacked them or pressured them to take sides on their behalf. Germans, mainly Protestants, claimed that the Jews purchased all Arab lands, and dominated the local market so that many Arab families were reduced to poverty. Only a few Germans spoke positively about the improvements (infrastructure, transportation, libraries, a university, and other improvements) brought to the country by the Jews. The Germans' anti-Jewish and pro-Arab attitude is clearly evident in the articles, newsletters, and correspondence. Their officially declared neutrality was only lip-service.

The uneasy situation of the German minority, living in a crisis-riddled region, led them to oppose those decisions of the Third Reich which they thought would trouble and endanger their life in Palestine. While the NS policy of the 1930s was aimed at a *judenfreies* Germany by means of Jewish emigration, Palestine-Germans asked the German government to ban Jewish immigration to Palestine. They did not favor the idea of a Jewish state, fearing that German existence in the region would end as soon as a Jewish state was established.[684] Representatives of the Reich and the NSDAP in Palestine generally opposed the German-Zionist transfer agreement because it would inevitably lead to the establishment of a Jewish state. The Haavara agreement provided the Yishuv with finances, German products, and hundreds of craftsmen and intellectuals – actually with everything needed to build up a state. In 1937, Consul General Walter Doehle explained to the Foreign Office in Berlin that a Jewish state would fight the German settlers economically and politically. Germans would be forced to give up their colonies and return to Germany. Doehle believed that an Arab state, not a Jewish state, would enable Palestine's populations to live peacefully together.[685] When the British discussed the plan of dividing Palestine in 1937–1938, a delegation of German settlers, nominated by the representatives of the Reich and the NSDAP in Palestine, officially explained that they wanted to remain under British rule. It was unthinkable to them to live under Jewish rule.[686]

684 Letter, D. von Oertzen, 27 Oct. 1937, *Jerusalemsverein*, B 536; annual report, D. von Oertzen, Haifa and Waldheim, 1933, B557; letter, Christian Berg, Haifa, mid-May 1937, B 557.
685 Consul general to the Foreign Office, Berlin, 22 mar. 1937, YVA, R 3/27.
686 Correspondence, German consulates, 1937–1938, YVA, R 3/27; Balke, *Hakenkreuz im Heiligen Land. Die NSDAP-Landesgruppe Palästina* (Erfurt, 2001),132–34; Paul Sauer, *Uns rief das Heilige Land. Die Tempelgesellschaft im Wandel der Zeit* (Stuttgart, 1985), 266–67.

The attitude of Palestine-Germans towards National Socialism and antisemitism was very similar to that found in Germany. The historian Shulamit Volkov describes the mentality of Germans during the Weimar Republic and after as radically opposing modernity, and longing for a world that had long ago disappeared. Opposing democracy and liberalism, they emphasized the ethnic community and supported imperial and colonial efforts.[687] Germans in Palestine shared these attitudes, and lived in close-knit units in a German idyll separated from the surrounding Arab and Jewish environments. They did not like the idea of living in a democratic state with several political parties, but favored having a strong nation with one leader. Palestine-Germans felt superior to Arabs and Jews and were generally proud of not having intermarried with them. A great number of them attended National Socialist lectures on racial studies (*Rassenkunde*); and German mothers with many children were, as far as we know, willing to accept the Mother Cross given to honor them as carriers of the "Aryan" race.[688] Party members and NS participants occasionally expressed the importance of keeping the German "race" pure. *Die Warte des Tempels* kept its readers informed about the NS idea of racial purity, and agreed that:

> The base of National Socialism is faith, its action is love. National Socialism is...brotherly love. But the brother is not the '*Hottentot*' and the '*Zulukaffer,*' the brother is the ethnic comrade of our flesh and blood, because this is God's will and law.[689]

Like their contemporaries in Germany, they were proud of the strong and expanding Germany and therefore probably willing to follow Hitler wherever he might lead them. They accepted antisemitism; for the sake of Germany's increased strength, they bought into the whole package. It is therefore not surprising that antisemitism was hardly an issue among the Germans in Palestine. The antisemitic policy of the Third Reich was never discussed in detail except for a few articles published in the Templers' journal in 1932 and 1933.[690] No words or criticism were written to distance themselves from the Nazis. The *Kristallnacht* pogrom of 1938 was not

---

687 Shulamit Volkov, *Antisemitismus als kultureller Code*, 2nd ed. (Munich, 2000), 20.

688 List, 6 Mar. 1939, ISTA, 823/2-פ. We do not know if the proposed awards were actually given out.

689 *Die Warte des Tempels* (Stuttgart), 15 Nov. 1935, 161. "Das Wesen des Nationalsozialismus ist Glaube, seine Tat ist Liebe. So ist der Nationalsozialismus ... die Liebe zum Nächsten. Dieser Nächste aber ... ist für uns nicht der Hottentote oder Zulukaffer, sondern uns ist der Nächste der Volksgenosse aus unserem Fleisch und Blut, weil er nach Gottes Willen und Gesetz uns zunächst gesetzt worden ist."

690 *Die Warte des Tempels*, 2 Feb. 1932; 15 Mar. 1932; 15 June 1932; 15 Apr. 1933; 15 May 1933.

mentioned at all.[691] International news about discrimination and persecution of Jews was ignored or set aside as lies and hostile propaganda.[692] They behaved this way despite the fact that they were witnesses to the mass immigration of Jews from Germany, one of the direct consequences of National Socialist policy.

Many Germans complained about the immigration, but it seems that almost no one thought or talked about what made Jews flee to Palestine. When hundreds of denaturalizations for German-Jewish immigrants had to be conducted at the German consulate in Jerusalem, the consul general usually confirmed the procedure of denaturalization by noting: "There are no objections to the denaturalization." No doubts, no questions, no requests were apparently expressed regarding the central role of antisemitism in Nazi Germany and its cruel impact on Jews.[693] During the war when about four hundred Germans were exchanged for Jews from Germany and Eastern Europe, they hardly "wasted" a single thought or word about their exchange partners. On the contrary, they saw themselves as victims because they had to leave their chosen homeland (*Wahlheimat*). The same reaction occurred when more than six hundred, mainly Templers, were deported to Australia. In *Damals in Palästina*, a few memoirists wrote about the deportation to Australia but none saw it as a consequence of their involvement in the local NSDAP. Instead they showed complete incomprehension and dismay toward the decision of the British Mandatory government.[694] Yet, having arrived in the Australian internment camp, they soon established a strongly-organized party network in the German compound. Until the end of the war, they were torn between their hope for the end of the war and loyalty to the Third Reich. Following the announcement of Hitler's death in May 1945, they gathered for a funeral service inside the internment camp led by Hermann Schneller, former director of the Syrian Orphanage in Jerusalem. A few days later, ordered to turn in flags and symbols of the Third Reich, the German Nazis held a ceremony at which they burned these artifacts, as the youth performed songs praising German courage, loyalty, and faith.[695]

---

691 Brigitte Hoffmann, "Unsere Verantwortung in der Welt," in *Der bedondere Beitrag. Beilage der Warte des Tempels* (Stuttgart) 2 (1995): 7–14.

692 Tempelgesellschaft Deutschland, ed., *Damals in Palästina—Templer erzählen vom Leben in ihren Gemeinden* (Stuttgart, 1990), 389; Gertrud Wassermann-Deininger, *Wir haben hier keine bleibende Statt. Geschichte der Familie Deininger in Palästina 1868–1948* (self-published, n.p., 1982), 61.

693 Correspondence, German consulate in Jerusalem, ISTA, 1036/4-פ; Balke, *Hakenkreuz im Heiligen Land*, 107.

694 Tempelgesellschaft Deutschland (ed.), *Damals in Palästina*.

695 Thomas Greif, "Interniert am Ende der Welt," http://www.sonntagsblatt-bayern.de/archiv01/17/ woche2.htm; Sauer, *Uns rief das Heilige Land*, 290–91.

Historians depict the reaction of Germans to the racial legislation and anti-Jewish measures as generally passive and indifferent.[696] The majority in Germany tolerated discrimination against Jews. Apathy, widespread indifference, and depersonalization of the increasingly invisible Jews were the common response to the propaganda of anti-Jewish hatred, whereas in Palestine, Jews were neither depersonalized nor invisible. They were a part of the Germans' daily life, encountered as customers, business partners, physicians, competitors, and so on. Nevertheless, the Germans in Palestine excelled at ignoring the Nazi regime's persecution of its Jewish population. With the beginning of World War II, the German residents of Palestine had to face arrest, internment, expropriation, and deportation. Like most Germans in Germany who felt they suffered greatly during the war, the members of Hitler's small community in Palestine considered themselves victims, unfairly treated and falsely accused of supporting the Arab revolt. In their articles, memoirs, and testimonies, they displayed a shocking lack of sensibility and responsibility for having welcomed the totalitarian, racist Nazi regime and having participated in the organizations and celebrations of the NSDAP in Palestine.

696 Marion Kaplan, "Jewish Daily Life in Wartime Germany," in *Probing the Depths of German Antisemitism. German Society and the Persecution of the Jews, 1933–1941*, edited by David Bankier (New York, 2000), 410–11; Richard Breitman, "American Diplomatic Records Regarding German Public Opinion during the Nazi Regime," in ibid., 508; Leni Yahil, "The Double Consciousness of the Nazi Mind and Practice," in ibid., 47; Markus Fugmann, *Moderner Antisemitismus* (Frankfurt a.M., 1998), 65; cf. Otto Kulka and Aron Rodrigue, "The German Population and the Jews in the Third Reich. Recent Publications and Trends in Research on German Society and the Jewish Question," *Yad Vashem Studies* (Jerusalem) 16 (1984): 421–36, 420, 429.

Appendix I

Leaflet for German Travelers to Palestine[697]

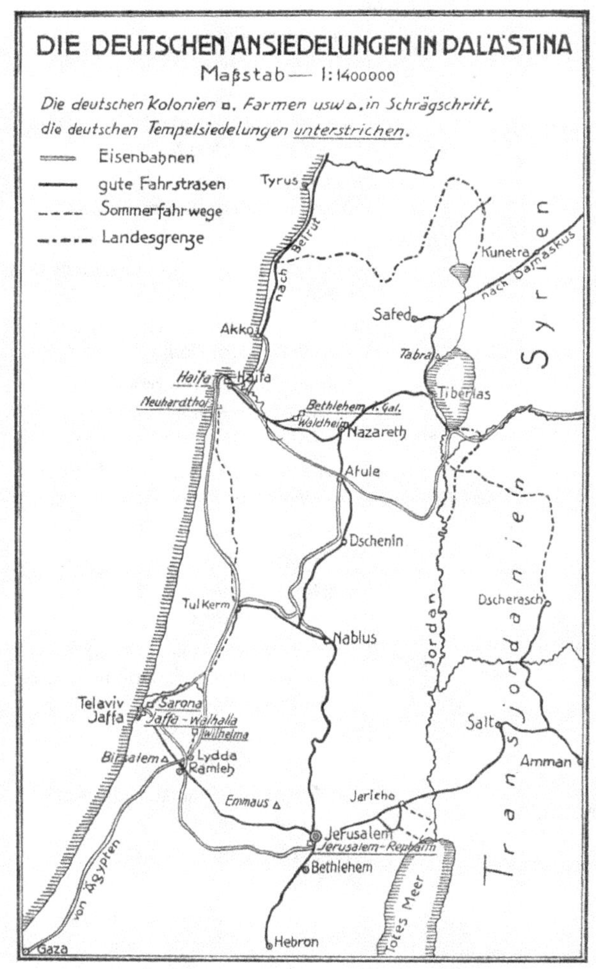

LEIPZIGER MESSE
Zweimal jährlich
Anfang März Ende August
Auskünfte erteilen das Leipziger Messamt, Leipzig und die Ehrenamtlichen Vertreter in den einzelnen Ländern.
In Palästina Bankdirector C. Hoffmann, Jaffa P. O. B. 24.

Buchdruckerei des Syrischen Waisenhauses, Jerusalem.

697 Archives of the Temple Society, Germany, date of document, late 1920s.

The Swabian colonies of the Temple Society in Palestine:

1. Haifa Colony:
Founded: 1869.
Inhabitants: more than 500 Germans, two thirds of them are Templers.
Information: Ph. Wurst, Mayor.

2. Bethlehem Colony in the Galilee:
Founded: 1906.
Inhabitants: 100.
Information: C. Kuhnle, Mayor.

3. Nazareth and Tiberias:
Inhabitants: some families.

4. Neuhardthof Farm:
Inhabitants: 3 families.
Administrated by Haifa Colony.

5. Jaffa Colony:
Founded: 1869.
Inhabitants: 225 (including the branch in Walhalla).
Information: G. Wagner sen., *Gemeindevorsteher*

6. Sarona Colony:
Founded: 1871.
Inhabitants: 225.
Information: R. Lippmann, Mayor.

7. Wilhelma Colony:
Founded: 1902.
Inhabitants: 200.
Information: A. Frank, Mayor.

8. Rephaim Colony, Jerusalem:
Founded: 1873.
Inhabitants: 160.
Information: C. Rohrer, President of the Temple Society, and N. Schmidt; Mayor.

Institutes of German Protestant churches and German Catholic orders:

Haifa:
Guest house and hospital of the Borromean Sisters, guest house of *Karmelmission.*

Waldheim:
Agricultural colony with 70 Protestants.

Nazareth:
Farm and branch of the Syrian Orphanage, Jerusalem.

Tabgha, Lake Kinnereth:
Guest house of the Catholic *Verein vom Heiligen Lande* (Pater Täpper).

Jaffa:
Protestant church, Minister Pätzold.

Birsalem, near Ramleh:
Farm, branch and school of agriculture of the Syrian Orphanage in Jerusalem.

Emmaus, West of Jerusalem:
Guest house of the Catholic *Verein vom Heiligen Lande* (Pater Müller).

Bethlehem, near Jerusalem:
Protestant church, Minister Jentzsch.

Jerusalem:
Syrian Orphanage, workshops, home for the blind, director: Minister Schneller.

Dormition Monastery: German Benedictine Abbey, Mt. of Zion.

Lutheran Church of the Redeemer: church, guest house, school, Provost Hertzberg (Muristan, Old City).

Auguste Victoria Foundation, Mt. of Olives, temporarily not in use.

Lepra Asylum *Jesus-Hilfe* near Temple Colony Rephaim.

Guest house of the Order of St. John, warden: Lorenz.

Monastery (*Mutterhaus*), girls' school and guest house of the Borromean Sisters, Emek Rephaim.

Girls' school of the Catholic *Verein vom Heiligen Lande.*

Görres Institute: Catholic Institute of Archaeology.

German Protestant Institute of Archaeology.

St. Paulus Hospice: currently used by the British Mandate government.

German Hospital: run by the Deaconesses (Sisters) of *Kaiserswerth* (Germany)

Talitah Kumi: Girls' school with the Deaconesses (Sisters) of *Kaiserswerth* in charge.

Source: Archives of the Temple Society, Germany; date of document, late 1920s.

Official Guidelines for Nazi Party Members Abroad

1. Observe the laws of the country whose guest you are.
2. Leave the politics of the country where you reside to its inhabitants. You are not concerned with the internal politics of a foreign country. Take no part in them, even in conversation.
3. Acknowledge yourself as a party member at all times and in all places.
4. Always speak and act in such a way that you bring honor to the National Socialist movement and thereby to the new Germany. Be upright, honorable, fearless and loyal.
5. Recognize every German abroad as your compatriot, a man of your blood and your kind. Extend your hand to him regardless of his position. We are all 'creators' of our people.
6. Help your German compatriots gladly and voluntarily when they are innocently in difficulty.
7. Do not be merely a member but also a fighter on the front line. Inform yourself thoroughly of the methods, content and aims of our movement.
8. Work and fight day after day for the entry of every honorable German into our movement. Convince him of the superiority and justness of our movement, of the necessity of our victory in order that Germany may live on! Fight with spiritual weapons!
9. Read our Party publication, our pamphlets and books.
10. Associate yourself with party members in your place of residence. If a local or city group exists there, be a disciplined and active worker. Not only should you not support dissension but you should also make every effort to settle disputes which arise.

Source: *Almanach der Nationalsozialistischen Revolution*, Berlin 1934: "The Foreign Organization of the NSDAP" by Ernst Wilhelm Bohle (page 90).

Appendix II

Table of Names and Data of Those who Joined the Nazi Groups in Palestine

The following list contains the names and data of those who joined the groups and subgroups of the Nazi party in Palestine. The table includes not only Nazi party members, but also membership applicants, members of the Hitler Youth, and fellows of NS associations for teachers, women, laborers, employed people, and so on.

The data were drawn from archives as the United States Holocaust Memorial Museum (Washington, D.C.), the Schumacher Institute (Haifa), the Yad Vashem Archives (Jerusalem), the Israel State Archives (Jerusalem), and the archives of the Temple Society in Germany. Further details were found in the journals *Evangelisches Gemeindeblatt* and *Die Warte des Tempels*, as well as in the publications by Ralf Balke and Paul Sauer.

The list does not claim to be complete.

Appendix IIa: List of names of Germans who joined the NS groups in Palestine

Membership no.	Name	Gender	Date of entry NSDAP or NS group	Age of entry, approx.	Year of birth	Place of birth	Address
	Aberle, Erhard	m	Spring 1934				Jerusalem
	Aberle, Ernst	m		12	1923		Jaffa-Sarona or Jerusalem
	Aberle, Gerd	m		13	1922		Jaffa or Jerusalem
	Aberle, Hanna	f		14-18			Haifa
	Aberle, Julius	m					Jaffa-Sarona
3722459	Aberle, Kurt	m	May 1,1936	24	1912	Jerusalem	Sarona, German Colony
	Aberle, Paul	m		18	1916		Jaffa
879371	Aberle, Walter	m	Jan. 1, 1932	27	1905	Jerusalem	Haifa, German Colony
	Albrecht, Walter	m		10-14			Bethlehem
	Albrecht, Wilhelm	m					
	Alle, Erika	f		14-18			Jaffa-Sarona
3551627	Allner, Friedrich	m		38	1901	Bitterfeld, Germany	Haifa
2275440	Appinger, Friedrich	m					Haifa, 1938: Stuttgart, Germany
3401707	Arndt, Erika Sophie	f	Feb. 1, 1934	25	1909	Jaffa	Jerusalem, German Colony
3401704	Arndt, Nikolai	m	Feb. 1, 1934	38	1896	Hulshof, S. Russia	Jerusalem, German Col.
	Asenstorfer, Charlotte	f		15	1920		Jaffa-Sarona
	Asenstorfer, Waltraud	f		14-18	1916		Jaffa
6990852	Bacher, Helmut	m	Oct. 1, 1938	29	1909	Jerusalem	Sarona
	Baldenhofer, Anneliese	f		20	1915		Jaffa-Sarona
3445374	Baldenhofer, Cecilie	f	Apr. 1, 1934	26	1908	Sarona	Sarona/Jaffa
1751803	Baldenhofer, Erhard	m	July 1, 1933	27	1906	Jaffa	Sarona/Jaffa
3402149	Baldenhofer, Friedrich	m	Feb. 1, 1934	46	1888	Sarona	Sarona/Jaffa Kellerstr.
	Baldenhofer, Hans Karl	m		12	1923		Jaffa-Sarona
	Bauer, Georg	m		14-18			Haifa
3475046	Bauer, Hans	m	March 1, 1936	22	1914	Haifa	Haifa, German Colony
	Bauer, Meta	f					Haifa
	Baumert, Emma	f		13	1922		Jaffa-Sarona
	Baumert, Ernst	m					Jerusalem

Occupation	NS post and/or membership	Source
	Party member, applied in 1933.	ISTA, 822/15-פ; YVA, R 3/25.
	JV, HJ	ISTA, 822/3-פ; ISTA, 1879/1-פ.
	JV, HJ	ISTA, 822/6-פ; ISTA, 822/3-פ; ISTA, 1879/1-פ.
	BDM	ISTA, 1879/1-פ.
	DAF *Sozialwalter* (officer for social affairs)	ISTA, 823/4-פ.
Merchant	Party member, DAF	USHMM, membership records; ISTA, 823/4-פ.
	Party member	ISTA, 822/3-פ; ISTA, 822/6-פ.
Engineer	Party member	USHMM, membership records, ISTA, 3162/31-פ; ISTA, 821/1-פ.
	JV	ISTA, 1879/1-פ.
	DAF	ISTA, 821/11-פ.
	BDM	ISTA, 822/3-פ.
	Party member	ISTA, 821/9-פ.
	Party member	YVA, R3/18.
None	Party member, applied in 1933.	USHMM, Membership records; ISTA, 822/15-פ; YVA, R 3/25.
Merchant	Party member, applied in 1933.	USHMM, membership records; ISTA, 822/15-פ; YVA, R 3/25.
	BDM	ISTA, 822/3-פ.
	BDM	ISTA, 822/6-פ.
Assembler	Party member	USHMM, membership records.
	BDM	ISTA, 822/3-פ; ISTA, 822/6-פ.
None	Party member	USHMM, membership records; ISTA, 833/15-פ.
Engineer	Party member	USHMM, membership records; ISTA, 822/15-פ.
Bank official	Party member	USHMM, membership records; ISTA, 822/15-פ.
	JV, HJ	ISTA, 822/3-פ; ISTA, 822/6-פ.
	HJ	ISTA, 1879/1-פ.
Bank official (Temple Bank)	Party member, DAF	ISTA, 821/11-פ.
	Party member, WHW	ISTA, 821/9-פ.
	BDM	ISTA, 822/3-פ; ISTA, 822/6-פ.
Chancellor, German consulate	Party member	ISTA, 3162/11-פ.

Membership no.	Name	Gender	Date of entry NSDAP or NS group	Age of entry, approx.	Year of birth	Place of birth	Address
	Baumert, Hermann	m	Spring 1934	14-18			Jerusalem
3402147	Baumert, Wilhelm	m	Feb. 1, 1934	42	1892	Jaffa	1. Jaffa, Walhalla, 2. Sarona
	Baumkamp, Hulda née Bulach	f	Spring 1934	10-18			Jaffa
	Baumkamp, Volker	m		10-18			
	Beck, Alfred	m		14-18			Haifa
6990854	Beck, Christian	m	Oct. 1, 1938	56	1882	Haifa	Haifa, German Colony
3726017	Beck, Christian Walter	m			1911	Haifa	Haifa, German Colony
	Beck, Else	f		14-17	1919		Haifa
3402150	Beck, Gottlob	m	Feb. 1, 1934	34	1900	Jaffa	Sarona
3402131	Beck, Hans	m	Feb. 1, 1934	25	1909	Haifa	Jaffa, German Colony
	Beck, Heinz	m		10-14			Bethlehem
6990857	Beck, Konrad	m	Oct. 1, 1938	31	1907	Haifa	Haifa, German Colony
6990858	Beck, Lotte	f	Oct. 1, 1938	28	1910	Stuttgart	Haifa, German Colony
3401844	Beck, Ludwig	m	Feb. 1, 1934	45	1889	Jaffa	Jaffa
	Beck, Martha	f		10-14			Haifa
3726015	Beck, Oskar	m	July 01, 1936	34	1902	Haifa	Haifa, German Colony
3726016	Beck, Paul	m	July 01, 1936	47	1889	Haifa	Haifa, German Colony
3709983	Beck, Rosa	f	May 01, 1936	53	1883	Murrhardt	Haifa, German Colony
	Beck, Tine	f		14-18			Bethlehem
6990856	Beck, Urban	m	Oct. 1, 1938	31	1907	Haifa	Sarona, Jägerstr.
3726017	Beck, Walter	m	July 1, 1936	25	1911	Haifa	Haifa, German Colony
370219	Behrens, Georg	m					Jaffa-Sarona, 1937: Baghdad
	Beilharz, Erich	m		14-18			Jerusalem
	Beilharz, Gerhard	m		10-14			Wilhelma
	Beilharz, Gertrud	f		10-14			Wilhelma
	Beilharz, Gustav						Haifa
3455025	Beilharz, Heinrich	m	June 1, 1934	28	1906	Haifa	Haifa, German Colony
	Beilharz, Herbert	m		10-14			Haifa
	Beilharz, Hulda	f					Haifa
3709973	Beilharz, Imanuel	m	May 1, 1936		1914	Haifa	Haifa, German Colony
	Beilharz, Irene	f		10-14			Haifa

Occupation	NS post and/or membership	Source
	HJ	ISTA, 822/15-פ.
Commercial official	Party member, applied in 1933, *Gebietswalter* of DAF, Jaffa	USHMM, membership records; ISTA, 822/15-פ; ISTA, 821/11-פ; ISTA, 823/4-פ; YVA, R 3/25.
	Party member, applied in 1933.	ISTA, 822/15-פ; YVA, R 3/25; EvGB, Aug. 1931.
	JV or HJ	YVA, R 3/25; EvGB, Aug. 1931.
	HJ	ISTA, 1879/1-פ.
Cabinetmaker	Party member	USHMM, membership records.
Merchant	Party member	USHMM, membership records.
	BDM	ISTA, 1879/1-פ.
Merchant	Party member, DAF *Zellenwalter* in Sarona.	USHMM, membership records; ISTA, 822/15-פ.
Machinist	Party member, applied in 1933; DAF *Betriebswalter*	USHMM, membership records; YVA, R 3/25; ISTA, 822/15-פ; ISTA, 823/6-פ.
	JV	ISTA, 1879/1-פ.
Merchant	Party member, DAF	USHMM, membership records; ISTA, 823/6-פ.
Housewife	Party member, AGdFA	USHMM, membership records; *Die Warte des Tempels*, May 31, 1938: 76.
Mechanic	Party member	USHMM, membership records.
	JM	ISTA, 1879/1-פ.
Merchant	Party member, DAF leader in Haifa	USHMM, membership records.
Cabinetmaker	Party member	USHMM, membership records; YVA, R3/18.
Housewife	Party member	USHMM, membership records.
	BDM	ISTA, 1879/1-פ.
Technician	Party member	USHMM, membership records.
Merchant	Party member, HJ sports leader	USHMM, membership records; ISTA, 821/9-פ; YVA, R 3/18; R 3/25.
	Party member	YVA, R 3/25.
	HJ	ISTA, 1879/1-פ.
	JV	ISTA, 1879/1-פ
	JM	ISTA, 1879/1-פ.
	DAF *Betriebszellenwalter*	ISTA, 823/6-פ.
Mechanic	Party member	USHMM, membership records; ISTA, 821/9-פ.
	JV	ISTA, 1879/1-פ.
	Party member, collected money for WHW, DAF	ISTA, 821/9-פ; ISTA, 823/6-פ.
Merchant	Party member	USHMM, membership records.
	JM	ISTA, 1879/1-פ.

Membership no.	Name	Gender	Date of entry NSDAP or NS group	Age of entry, approx.	Year of birth	Place of birth	Address
	Beilharz, Käthe	f		31	1907		Haifa
3526110	Beilharz, Konrad	m	Dec. 1, 1935	29	1906	Haifa	Haifa, German Colony
	Beilharz, Oskar	m		14-18			Haifa
	Beilharz, Rudi	m		10-14			Haifa
	Beilharz, Waldemar	m		14-18			Haifa
	Beilharz, Willi (Willy)	m		14-18			Jerusalem
3455039	Bender, Wilhelm	m	June 1, 1934	31	1903	Hoffenheim	Bethlehem-Waldheim, 1936: Germany
3401927	Bez, Irma Johanna	f	Spring 1934, active since 1933.				Haifa; 1938: Germany.
	Bez, Karl	m	July 1, 1932	28		Haifa	Haifa, 1937: Germany.
3401928	Bez, Maria Werra	f	Spring 1934, active since 1933.				Haifa, 1938: Germany.
3726043	Bienzle, Helmut	m	July 1, 1936	27	1909	Jerusalem	Jerusalem, German Colony
	Bisse	m					
3455034	Blaich, Albert	m	June 1, 1934	32	1902	Haifa	Haifa, German Colony
	Blaich, Hedwig	f		10-14			Waldheim
	Blaich, Ilse	f		10-18			Jaffa-Sarona
	Bracher, Otto	m	Joined OG Haifa from Dec. 1936 on.	29	1907		Haifa, 1938: Germany
6990861	Breisch, Gerhard	m	Oct. 1, 1938	24	1914	Jaffa	Haifa, German Colony
3401688	Brons, Hans	m	Feb. 1, 1934	28	1906	Wuppertal-Elberfeld	Jerusalem, Syrian Orphanage
3455021	Bubeck, Ernst Karl	m	June 1, 1934	31	1903	Haifa	Haifa, Allenby
3401708	Buchhalter, Hildegard	f	Feb. 1, 1934	24	1910	Jerusalem	Jerusalem, German Colony
	Buchhalter, Ida	f		30	1907	Tantah	Jaffa
1751392	Buchhalter, Ludwig	m	July 1, 1933	23	1910	Alexandria, Egypt	Jerusalem, German Colony
	Bühler, Hildegard	f		14-18			Haifa
3402136	Bulach, Anna	f	Feb. 1, 1934	57	1877	Haifa	Jaffa-Sarona
	Bulach, Anne	f					Wilhelma
6990862	Bulach, Erich	m	Oct. 1, 1938	30	1908	Jaffa	Haifa, German Colony

Occupation	NS post and/or membership	Source
Kindergarten teacher	Party applicant (1937-38), NSLB	ISTA, 821/9-פ; YVA, R3/18.
Construction contractor	Party member	ISTA, 821/9-פ; USHMM, membership records.
	HJ	ISTA, 1879/1-פ,.
	JV	ISTA, 1879/1-פ.
	HJ	ISTA, 1879/1-פ.
	HJ	ISTA, 1879/1-פ,
Teacher (1932-1936)	Party member, NSLB	ISTA, 822/15-פ; EvGB, Dec. 1934.
	Party member	ISTA, 822/15-פ.
Mechanic	Party applicant, *Pressewart*	ISTA, 822/15-פ; USHMM, membership records.
	Party member	ISTA, 822/15-פ.
Engineer	Party member, DAF	ISTA, 821/11-פ; USHMM, membership records.
	Party member	YVA, R 3/10.
Saddle maker	Party member	USHMM, membership records.
	JM	ISTA, 1879/1-פ.
	JM or BDM	YVA, R 3/25.
Worked in a bakery.	Party applicant	ISTA, 821/9-פ.
Teacher	Party member, NSLB member, HJ official	ISTA, 821/9-פ; USHMM, membership records.
Bookkeeper	Party member, applied in 1933.	ISTA, 822/15-פ; USHMM, membership records; YVA, R 3/25.
Electro engineer	Party member	ISTA, 821/9-פ; USHMM, membership records.
Housewife	Party member	USHMM, membership records.
	DAF	ISTA, 821/11-פ.
Teacher	Party member, OGL Jerusalem, NSLB member	ISTA, 822/15-פ; ISTA, 821/9-פ; ISTA, 823/8-פ; USHMM, membership records.
	BDM	ISTA, 1879/1-פ.
Housewife	Party member, applied 1933.	ISTA, 822/15-פ; USHMM, membership records; YVA, R 3/25.
Farmer, Orange planter	AGdFA	ISTA, 823/2-פ.
Pharmacist	Party member	USHMM, membership records.

Membership no.	Name	Gender	Date of entry NSDAP or NS group	Age of entry, approx.	Year of birth	Place of birth	Address
1587502	Bulach, Frieder (Friedrich)	m	May 1, 1933	19	1914	Jaffa	Jaffa
3726018	Bulach, Luise	f	July 1, 1936	30	1906	Jaffa	Haifa, German Colony
	Damek, Elfriede	f					Jaffa-Sarona, 1937: Germany
	Daxer, Kurt	m					Jerusalem
	Decker, Fritz	m		14-18			Jerusalem
	Decker, Gerda	f		10-14			Wilhelma
	Decker, Helene	f		14-18			Wilhelma
	Decker, Irma	f		10-14			Wilhelma
2756233	Decker, Jakob	m	Oct. 1, 1934	37	1897	Welikolu-jascheskye	Wilhelma near Jaffa
	Decker, Johanna	f					Wilhelma
3726032	Decker, Peter	m	July 1, 1936	41	1895	Wohldemfürst (Russia)	Wilhelma
	Deininger, Friedrich Wilhelm	m	Applied for membership in 1936.				Bethlehem-Waldheim
	Deininger, Gertrud(e)	f		10-13	1923		Waldheim
	Deininger, Otto	m		18	1918		Haifa
	Dietrich, Lina	f		35	1904	Althangstett	Wilhelma, spring 1939: Germany
4009185	Doehle, E(r)na	f	Feb. 1, 1937	24	1913	Rotterdam	Jerusalem, German consulate
	Doehle, Elisabeth	f					Jerusalem
3398410	Doehle, Walter	m		51	1884		Jerusalem
	Doh, Anneliese	f		10-14			Haifa
	Doh, Elfriede	f		14-18			Haifa
	Doh, Gerhard	m		14-18			Haifa
	Doh, Hermann	m	Feb. 1, 1934	25	1909	Alexandria, Egypt	Sarona
	Doh, Luise	f		14-18			Jerusalem
	Doh, Theodor	m		10-14			Jerusalem
3726019	Doh, Walter	m	July 1, 1936	22	1914	Alexandria, Egypt	Haifa, German Colony
	Doh, Willy (Wilhelm)	m	Feb. 1, 1934	23	1911	Alexandria, Egypt	Jerusalem, German Colony
1587582	Doster, Alfred	m	May 1, 1933	27	1906	Jaffa	Jaffa
6990864	Doster, Hermann	m	Oct. 1, 1938	29	1909	Jaffa	Jaffa
	Dreher, Ella	f		14-18			Wilhelma
	Dreher, Gerhard	m					
6990865	Dreher, Hanna	f	Oct. 1, 1938	62	1876	Stuttgart	Wilhelma

Occupation	NS post and/or membership	Source
Commercial official	Party member, *Landesjugendführer*	ISTA, 822/15-פ; USHMM, membership records.
(Kindergarten) teacher	Party member, BDM leader, NSLB	ISTA, 821/9-פ; USHMM, membership records; YVA, R 3/1.
	Party member	YVA, R 37/25.
Vicar	Party member, NSV (1935), WHW (1936).	ISTA, 821/5-פ; YVA, R 3/25.
	HJ	ISTA, 1879/1-פ.
	JM	ISTA, 1879/1-פ.
	BDM	ISTA, 1879/1-פ.
	JM	ISTA, 1879/1-פ.
Chauffeur	Party member, *Standortführer*	USHMM, membership records; YVA, R 3/1.
	AGdFA	ISTA, 823/2-פ.
Farmer	Party member, DAF	ISTA, 823/4-פ; USHMM, membership records.
	Party applicant	ISTA, 821/7-פ.
	JM	ISTA, 1879/1-פ; PA AA, R 41529.
	HJ, DAF	ISTA, 1879/1-פ.
	AGdFA	ISTA, 823,/2-פ.
Graduate political economist	Party applicant	YVA, R3/25
	Party member	YVA, R3/25.
Consul General	Party member	YVA, R 3/25; BArch, PK/Q106, pic. no. 686.
	JM	ISTA,1879/1-פ.
	BDM	ISTA, 1879/1-פ.
	HJ	ISTA, 1879/1-פ.
Electro engine fitter	Party member, DAF	ISTA, 822/15-פ; USHMM, membership records.
	BDM	ISTA, 1879/1-פ.
	DJ	ISTA, 1879/1-פ.
Merchant	Party member	USHMM, membership records.
Innkeeper	Party member, applied in 1933; *Propandawart* (1934), KdF officer (1937), DAF	ISTA, 821/5-פ, ; USHMM, membership records; YVA, R 3/25.
Cabinetmaker	Party member, DAF	ISTA, 822/15-פ; ISTA, 823/4-פ; USHMM, membership records.
Cabinetmaker	Party member	USHMM, membership records.
	BDM	ISTA, 1879/1-פ.
	DAF	YVA, R3/25.
Housewife	Party member, AGdFA	ISTA, 823,/2-פ; USHMM, membership records.

Membership no.	Name	Gender	Date of entry NSDAP or NS group	Age of entry, approx.	Year of birth	Place of birth	Address
	Dreher, Heinz	m		18	1916		Jaffa
	Dreher, Jakob	m		14-18			Wilhelma
	Dreher, Lotte	f		14-18			Wilhelma
2755377	Dreher, Ludwig	m	Oct. 1, 1934				Wilhelma
3726033	Dreher, Luise	f	June 1, 1936	35	1901	Jaffa	Wilhelma
	Drescher, Werner						Sarona
3709984	Duerr, Emil	m	May 1, 1936	22	1914	Pforzheim	Haifa, 1937: Jerusalem
	Dukkek, Helene	f		10-14			Jerusalem
6990866	Dukkek, Jacob	m	Oct. 1,1 938	54	1885	Oberholzheim	Nazareth
	Dukkek, Ruth	f		10-14			Jerusalem
3401693	Dyck, Abraham	m	Feb. 1, 1934	31	1903	Jerusalem	Jerusalem, German Colony
2556600	Ebe, Max	m		28	1911		Jerusalem, 1938: Frankfurt a. M.
	Eckert	m					Jerusalem
	Edelmaier, Anna	f		14-18			Wilhelma
3402158	Edelmaier, Hugo	m	Feb. 1, 1934	24	1910	Wilhelma	Sarona
3455033	Ehmann, Georg	m	June 2, 1934	45	1889	Haifa	Haifa, German Colony
	Ehmann, Grete	f		14-18			Haifa or Jerusalem?
	Ehmann, Hertha	f		14-18			Bethlehem-Waldheim
	Ehmann, Hugo	m					Jaffa-Sarona
	Ehmann, Karl	m		10-14			Jerusalem
	Ehmann, Karl W.	m	Spring 1934	35	1899	Möhringen/ Stuttgart	Jaffa-Sarona
	Ehnis, Eleonore	f		10-18			Jaffa-Sarona
	Ehnis, Kurt	m		14	1921		Jaffa-Sarona or Jerusalem
1587707	Eppinger, Arnolf	m	Spring 1934				Jaffa
3726044	Eppinger, Bruno	m	July 1, 1936	30	1906	Jerusalem	Jerusalem, German Colony
	Eppinger, Helga	f		10-14			Jerusalem
	Eppinger, Linda	f		14-18			Jaffa-Sarona
	Eppinger, Martha	f	Spring 1934				Jerusalem
	Eppinger, Richard	m				Jaffa	Wilhelma
7024777	Eppinger, Sieglinde	f	Mar. 1, 1939	23	1916	Jaffa	Sarona
	Eppinger, Theodor	m	Spring 1934	14-18			Jerusalem
	Eppinger, Wilhelm	m					Jerusalem
1549757	Faber, Eugen	m	Spring 1934	37	1897	Jerusalem	Jaffa

Occupation	NS post and/or membership	Source
	HJ	ISTA, 822/15-פ.
	HJ	ISTA, 1879/1-פ.
	BDM	ISTA, 1879/1-פ.
Farmer	Party member	USHMM, membership records.
Assistant teacher	Party member, NSLB member, JM leader	ISTA, 821/9-פ; USHMM, membership records; YVA, R 3/1.
	DAF-*Betriebszellenwalter*	ISTA, 823/6-פ.
Butcher	Party member, DAF	ISTA, 821/11-פ; USHMM, membership records.
	JM	ISTA, 1879/1-פ.
Manager	Party member	USHMM, membership records.
	JM	ISTA, 1879/1-פ.
Bank official	Party member, applied in 1933; DAF-leader in Jerusalem	ISTA, 822/15-פ; YVA, R 3/25; USHMM, membership records.
	Party member	YVA, R 3/22.
Vice Consul	Party member	YVA, R 3/25.
	BDM	ISTA, 1879/1-פ.
Mechanic	Party member, applied in 1933.	ISTA, 822/15-פ; USHMM, membership records; YVA, R 3/25.
Building contractor	Party member	ISTA, 822/15-פ; USHMM, membership records.
	BDM	ISTA, 1879/1-פ.
	BDM	ISTA, 821/7-פ
Teacher, headmaster	Party member; 1937-39: SD informant in Cairo	Balke 2001: 49; Sauer 1985: 235.
	DJ	ISTA, 1879/1-פ.
Teacher	Party member, vice-leader of Sarona (Dec. 1934)	ISTA, 821/8-פ; ISTA, 823/8-פ; ISTA, 822/15-פ.
	JM or BDM	YVA, R 3/25.
	JV, HJ	ISTA, 822/6-פ; ISTA, 1879/1-פ.
	Party member, applied in 1933; WHW 1936.	ISTA, 822/15-פ; YVA, R 3/25, R 3/20.
Construction engineer	Party member	USHMM, membership records.
	JM	ISTA, 1879/1-פ.
	BDM	ISTA, 822/3-פ.
	Party member, applied in 1933.	ISTA, 822/15-פ; YVA, R 3/25.
	DAF, *Betriebszellenwalter* in Wilhelma.	ISTA, 821/13-פ.
Piano teacher	Party member	USHMM, membership records.
	HJ	ISTA, 822/15-פ.
Teacher	NSLB (March 1, 1938)	ISTA, 821/9-פ.
	Party member, applied in 1933, HJ leader	ISTA, 822/15-פ; YVA, R 3/25; Sauer 1985: 247.

Member-ship no.	Name	Gen-der	Date of entry NSDAP or NS group	Age of entry, approx.	Year of birth	Place of birth	Address
3401719	Faig, Arnold	m	Feb. 1, 1934	19	1915		Jerusalem
	Faig, Elisabeth	f	Feb. 1, 1934				Jerusalem
3.4E+07	Faig, Eugen	m	Feb. 1, 1934	29	1905	Jerusalem	Jerusalem
3401720	Faig, Hans	m	Feb. 1, 1934	19	1915	Jerusalem	Jerusalem
	Faig, Johanna	f		14-18			Jerusalem
3402143	Faig, Johannes	m					1. Jerusalem, 2. Sarona
	Faig, Lore	f					Jerusalem
2755361	Faig, Maria	f					Jerusalem
3401718	Faig, Paul	m	Feb. 1, 1934	20	1914	Jerusalem	Jerusalem
3402143	Faig, Theodor Johannes	m	Feb. 1, 1934	31	1903	Jerusalem	Sarona
7025322	Fast, Hanna	f	Apr. 1, 1939	49	1890	Tempelhof (Russia)	Jerusalem
	Fast, Lilli	f		14-18			Jerusalem
	Fast, Waldemar	m	Spring 1934	23	1911		Jerusalem
1587402	Fechner, Grete	f	Spring 1934				Jaffa
	Feubel, Friedrich	m					Jerusalem, German Colony
2755361	Feubel, Maria	f	Oct. 1, 1934	21	1913	Jerusalem	Stuttgart (last address)
3709985	Fitterling, Carl	m	May 1,1 936	25	1911	Ulm a. D.	Haifa
	Frank, Albrecht	m		18	1916		Jaffa
	Frank, Edwin	m					
	Frank, Elisabeth	f		14-18	1923		Jaffa
	Frank, Erika	f		14-18			Wilhelma
	Frank, Gottlob	m					Jerusalem
7025386	Frank, Gudrun	f	Apr. 1, 1939	24	1915	Nazareth	Haifa, Jaffa, Bethlehem?
7332429	Frank, Hans	m	Dec. 1, 1939	24	1915	Wilhelma	Wilhelma
	Frank, Helga	f		10-14			Jerusalem
	Frank, Hildegard née Kaulfuss	f					Jerusalem
	Frank, Hulda	f		28	1911		Haifa

Occupation	NS post and/or membership	Source
Assistant teacher or mechanic	Party member, applied in 1933.	ISTA, 821/9-פ; USHMM, membership records; YVA, R 3/25.
	Party member, applied in 1933.	ISTA, 822/15-פ.
Pastry cook	Party member, applied in 1933.	ISTA, 822/15-פ; USHMM, membership records; YVA, R 3/25.
Commercial clerk	Party member, applied in 1933.	ISTA, 822/15-פ; membership record, USHMM; YVA, R 3/25.
	BDM	ISTA, 1879/1-פ.
	Party member, DAF	ISTA, 821/11-פ; ISTA, 823/4-פ.
Owner of a hairdressing salon	Party member	ISTA, 821/11-פ.
	Party member	YVA, R 3/25.
Clerk	Party member, applied in 1933; DAF	ISTA, 822/15-פ; USHMM, membership records; YVA, R 3/25.
Engineer	Party member, applied in 1933; DAF	ISTA, 822/15-פ; USHMM, membership records; YVA, R 3/25.
Housewife	Party member	USHMM, membership records.
	BDM	ISTA, 1879/1-פ.
	Party member	ISTA, 822/15-פ; Mallmann/Cüppers 2006: 98.
	Party member, applied in 1933; *Landesjugendführerin*	ISTA, 822/15-פ, 1934; YVA, R 3/25.
Tailor	DAF	ISTA, 821/11-פ.
Housewife	Party member	USHMM, membership records.
Merchant	Party member	USHMM, membership records.
	Party member (1934); HJ	ISTA, 822/6-פ.
	SA	ISTA, 822/15-פ; ISTA, 823/8-פ.
	BDM	ISTA, 822/6-פ.
	BDM	ISTA, 1879/1-פ.
2nd secretary, German consulate, from 4/1936 on: *Oberinspektor*.	Party member	ISTA, 3162/10-פ.
Kindergarten teacher	Party member, NSLB	USHMM, membership records.
Farmer	Party member	USHMM, membership records.
	JM	ISTA, 1879/1-פ.
	Party member, applied in 1933.	ISTA, 3162/10-פ; ISTA, 822/15-פ; YVA, R 3/25.
	Party member, collected money for WHW	ISTA, 821/9-פ.

Member-ship no.	Name	Gen-der	Date of entry NSDAP or NS group	Age of entry, approx.	Year of birth	Place of birth	Address
	Frank, Isolde	f		10-14			Haifa
6990869	Frank, Kurt	m	Oct. 1, 1938	29	1909	Jaffa	Jaffa
	Frank, Manfred	m		10-14			Wilhelma
	Frank, Mausi	f		10-14			Jaffa-Sarona
3455018	Frank, Max	m	June 1, 1934	37	1897	Jaffa	Sarona-Jaffa
	Frank, Olga	f					Sarona
3402132	Frank, Otto	m	Feb. 1, 1934	20	1914	Wilhelma	Jaffa
6990870	Frank, Roland	m	Oct. 1, 1938	33	1905	Jaffa	Jaffa
	Frank, Werner	m	Spring 1934	17	1917	Haifa	Jerusalem
	Franz, Edith	f					
	Fritz, Adolf	m					Haifa
	Froehlich, Ernst	m					
6990872	Gassmann, Friedrich	m	Oct. 1, 1938	44	1894	Beyreuth/Syria	Haifa
	Gassmann, Rudi	m		14-18			Bethlehem/Galilee
	Gassmann, Rudolf	m	June 1,1932	32	1900	Beyreuth/ Syria	Bethlehem/Galilee
	Gassmann, Sunhild	f		10-14			Haifa
	Gassmann, Sylvia	f		39	1899		Haifa
	Gassmann, Wilhelm	m		50	1888		Haifa
1751034	Glenk, Ewald	m	July 1, 1933	24	1909	Sarona	Sarona
	Glunkler, Grete	f		14-18			Jerusalem
	Glunkler, Hans	m		10-14			Jerusalem
	Gmelin, Eberhard	m	Spring 1934				Jerusalem
	Gmelin, Elli (Elly)	f	Spring 1934				Jerusalem
	Gollmer, Ilse	f		10-18			Jaffa-Sarona
	Gollmer, Rudolf	m	Spring 1934				Sarona
6990876	Graze, Edmund	m	Oct. 1, 1938	31	1907	Sarona	Sarona
2755261	Groendahl, Anita	f	Oct. 1, 1934	31	1903	Vienna	Jerusalem, Old City, Muristan Hospice
1751833	Groetzinger (Groezinger), Willy	m	July 1, 1933 or Spring 1934	27	1907		Sarona
3445367	Groll, Wilhelm	m	April 1, 1934	31	1903	Sarona	Sarona
	Guenthner, Doris	f		17	1918		Haifa, (1934/35: Jaffa-Sarona)
	Guenthner, Dorothea	f		14-18			Jaffa-Sarona
	Haar, Gisela	f		10-14			Haifa
3709971	Haar, Herbert Willi	m	May 1, 1936	24	1912	Haifa	Haifa, German Colony

Occupation	NS post and/or membership	Source
	JM	ISTA, 1879/1-פ.
Bank official	Party member	USHMM, membership records.
	JV	ISTA, 1879/1-פ.
	JM	ISTA, 822/3-פ.
Bank official	Party member	USHMM, membership records.
Teacher	Party member, NSLB	ISTA, 821/9-פ; YVA, R3/18.
Store clerk	Party member, applied in 1933.	ISTA, 822/15-פ; USHMM, membership records; YVA, R 3/25.
Manager	Party member	USHMM, membership records.
	HJ	ISTA, 822/15-פ; ISTA, 3162/10-פ; Mallmann/Cüppers 2006b: 240.
Kindergarten teacher	NSLB	ISTA, 821/9-פ.
Teacher a. D. (retired)	NSLB	ISTA, 821/9-פ.
	DAF	ISTA, 821/11-פ.
Hotel expert	Party member	USHMM, membership records.
	HJ	ISTA, 1879/1-פ.
Farmer	Party member, DAF, HJ leader in Bethlehem	ISTA, 822/15-פ; ISTA 821/7-פ; USHMM, membership records.
	JM	ISTA, 1879/1-פ.
	Party applicant (1936-1938)	YVA, R3/18.
	Party applicant (1936-38)	YVA, R3/18.
Bank official	Party member	ISTA, 822/15-פ; USHMM, membership records.
	BDM	ISTA, 1879/1-פ.
	DJ	ISTA, 1879/1-פ.
Physician	Party member, applied in 1933; vice-OGL Jerusalem 1935, DAF	YVA, R 3/25; ISTA, 821/5-פ; ISTA,821/11-פ; ISTA, 822/15-פ.
	Party member, applied in 1933.	ISTA, 822/15-פ; YVA, R 3/25.
	JM or BDM	YVA, R 3/25.
	Party member, applied in 1933.	ISTA, 822/15-פ; YVA, R 3/25.
Electro technician	Party member	USHMM, membership records.
Pastor's assistant	Party member; resigned in 1936.	USHMM, membership records.
Butcher	Party member	ISTA, 822/15-פ; USHMM, membership records.
Farmer	Party member	ISTA, 822/15-פ; USHMM, membership records.
	BDM, DAF	ISTA, 822/6-פ.
	BDM	ISTA, 1879/1-פ.
	JM	ISTA, 1879/1-פ.
Cabinetmaker	Party member	USHMM, membership records.

Membership no.	Name	Gender	Date of entry NSDAP or NS group	Age of entry, approx.	Year of birth	Place of birth	Address
3230061	Haar, Hermann	m	May 1, 1933	21	1913	Haifa	Haifa, German Colony
	Haar, Irene	f					Haifa
	Haar, Kurt Christian	m		28	1911		Haifa
	Haar, Leni	f		14-18			Haifa
	Haar, Ruth	f		10-14			Haifa
3445366	Haering, Erwin	m	April 1, 1934	26	1908	Sarona	Sarona
3445370	Haering, Rosa	f	April 1, 1934	30	1904	Sarona	Sarona, German Colony
	Hahn, Erich	m		10-18			Sarona
1587433	Hahn, Hugo	m	May 1, 1933 or Spring 1934	28	1906	Jaffa	Jaffa
	Hahn, Ida	f	Spring 1934				Jaffa
	Hahn, Magda	f		14-18			Wilhelma
3726034	Hahn, Oskar	m	July 1, 1936	26	1910	Wilhelma	Wilhelma
3455409	Hahn, Paula	f					Sarona
	Hahn, Siegfried	m		10	1924/ 1925		Jaffa-Sarona
	Haigis, Matthias	m					Palestine, 1936: Germany
	Hanssmann, Fritz	m					Jerusalem
	Hardegg, Maria	f		67/68	1871	Jaffa	*Ortsgruppe* Wilhelma?
	Hase, Walter	m		14-18			Wilhelma
	Hasenpflug, Elsa	f		10-12	1923		Jaffa-Sarona
	Hasenpflug, Heiner	m		14	1921		Jaffa-Sarona
	Hasenpflug, Heinrich	m	Spring 1934				Sarona
	Hasenpflug, Rosemarie	f		10-18			Jaffa-Sarona
	Hasenpflug, Siegfried	m		10-18			Sarona
	Haussmann, Friedrich (Fritz)	m					Jerusalem, June 1937: Cyprus
2342539	Hegele, Kurt Dr.	m	May 1, 1933	23	1910	Feuerbach/ Wttbg.	Jerusalem, German Colony
	Heinrici, Johannes	m		14-18			Haifa
	Heinrici, Johannes	m	Spring 1934				Haifa
	Hennig, Elfriede	f		17	1919	Leipzig	Jaffa-Sarona (1935+1939), Haifa
	Hennig, Erna	f		14-18			Jaffa-Sarona
	Hennig, Gisela	f		10-18			Jaffa-Sarona
	Herrmann, Bruno	m		10-14			Bethlehem
	Herrmann, Cornelia	f					Haifa
	Herrmann, Emma	f		14-18			Bethlehem

Occupation	NS post and/or membership	Source
Construction technician	Party member	USHMM, membership records.
	Party member, collected money for WHW	ISTA, 821/9-פ.
	Party applicant (1936-38)	YVA, R3/18.
	BDM	ISTA, 1879/1-פ.
	JM	ISTA, 1879/1-פ.
Farmer	Party member	ISTA, 822/15-פ; USHMM, membership records.
Housewife	Party member	USHMM, membership records.
	JV or HJ	YVA, R3/25.
Master borer	Party member	ISTA, 822/15-פ; USHMM, membership records; YVA, R 3/25.
	Party member, applied in 1933.	ISTA, 822/15-פ; YVA, R 3/25.
	BDM	ISTA, 1879/1-פ.
Farmer	Party member	USHMM, membership records.
Teacher	Party member, NSLB member, 1935: BDM, 1937/38: leading position.	ISTA, 821/9-פ; YVA, R 3/1.
	JV	ISTA, 822/6-פ.
	Party member, *Filmwart, Funkwart* (1935)	ISTA, 821/5-פ; YVA, R 3 /20.
	Party member or applicant	YVA, R3/25.
	AGdFA	ISTA, 823/2-פ.
	HJ	ISTA, 1879/1-פ.
	JM	ISTA, 8232/3-פ; PA AA, R 41529.
	JV, HJ	ISTA, 1879/1-פ; ISTA, 822/6-פ.
	Party member	ISTA, 822/15-פ.
	JM or BDM	YVA, R 3/25.
	JV or HJ	YVA, R 3/25,.
	Party member, DAF	YVA, R 3/25.
Teacher, Dr. of Philosophy	Party member, NSLB officer, *Schulungswart*	USHMM, membership record.
	HJ	ISTA, 1879/1-פ.
Missionary	Party member	ISTA, 822/15-פ.
	BDM, DAF, joined the German Labor Service for Women in 1937.	ISTA, 822/6-פ; YVA, R3/18.
	BDM	ISTA, 822/3-פ.
	JM or BDM	YVA, R 3/25.
	JV	ISTA, 1879/1-פ.
	Party applicant (1937-38)	YVA, R3/18.
	BDM	ISTA, 1879/1-פ.

Membership no.	Name	Gender	Date of entry NSDAP or NS group	Age of entry, approx.	Year of birth	Place of birth	Address
3280666	Herrmann, Erich	m	July 1, 1933	23	1910	Bethlehem near Haifa	Jerusalem, German Colony
	Herrmann, Ewald	m		10-14			Bethlehem
	Herrmann, Frieder	m		14-18			Bethlehem
	Herrmann, Gerhard	m		14-18			Bethlehem
	Herrmann, Gertrud	f		14-18			Bethlehem
3709982	Herrmann, Heinrich Gotthilf	m	May 1, 1936	33	1903	Haifa	Haifa, German Colony
	Herrmann, Johannes	m	Applied for a membership book, 1938				Haifa
3455037	Herrmann, Karl (Carl)	m	June 1, 1934	25	1909	Haifa	Haifa or Bethlehem
	Herrmann, Kurt	m		14-18			Jerusalem
	Herrmann, Manfred	m		10-14			Bethlehem
	Herrmann, Max Walter	m		25	1912	Erdmannshain	Jerusalem
	Herrmann, Ruth	f		14-18			Bethlehem
3445385	Herrmann, Theodor	m	April 1, 1934	21	1913	Haifa	Bethlehem near Haifa
7025324	Herrmann, Walter	m	April 1, 1939	29	1910	Haifa	Haifa, 1938: Germany
6990880	Herrmann, Wilhelm	m	Oct. 1, 1938	41	1897	Haifa	Bethlehem
	Heselschwerdt, Nelli	f		10-14			Jerusalem
	Heselschwerdt, Philipp	m	July 12, 1933 or Spring 1934				Haifa
	Heselschwerdt, Theodora	f		21	1917	Nazareth	Haifa
	Hess, Gertrud	f		14-18			Jerusalem
3401705	Hess, Marie-Luise	f	Spring 1934				Jerusalem, 1937: Germany
	Hiendlmayer (Hientlmayer), Charlotte	f					Sarona
6990882	Hiendlmayer, Thietmar Kunz	m	Oct. 1, 1938	32	1906	Stuttgart	Sarona near Jaffa, German Colony
3710250	Hoefer, Friedrich	m	May 1, 1936	78	1858	Wolfsölden	Wilhelma near Jaffa
2756219	Hoefer, Gottlob	m	Oct. 1, 1934	64	1870	Wolfsölden	Wilhelma near Jaffa
	Hoefer, Johannes	m		14-18			Wilhelma
3401698	Hoefer, Luise	f	Spring 1934	25	1909	Wilhelma	Jerusalem, Wilhelma, 1938: Haifa
3726035	Hoefer, Wilhelm	m	June 1, 1936	32	1904	Sarona	Wilhelma near Jaffa
2756170	Hoenig, Alfred	m	Oct. 1, 1934	35	1899	Stuttgart	Wilhelma, German Colony

Occupation	NS post and/or membership	Source
Teacher	Party member, NSLB member, engaged in establishing the OG Jerusalem.	ISTA, 821/5-פ; YVA, R 3/25; USHMM, membership records; EvGB, May 1934.
	JV	ISTA, 1879/1-פ.
	JV, HJ	ISTA, 1879/1-פ.
	HJ	ISTA, 1879/1-פ.
	BDM	ISTA, 1879/1-פ.
Mechanic	Party member	USHMM, membership records.
	Party member	ISTA, 821/9-פ.
Farmer	Party member	ISTA, 822/15-פ; USHMM, membership records.
	HJ	ISTA, 1879/1-פ.
	JV	ISTA, 1879/1-פ.
Hairdresser at Lore Faig's shop.	DAF	ISTA, 821/11-פ.
	BDM	ISTA, 1879/1-פ.
Farmer	Party member	ISTA, 822/15-פ; USHMM, membership records.
Mechanic	Party member, DAF	ISTA, 821/9-פ; USHMM, membership records.
Farmer	Party member	USHMM, membership records.
	JM	ISTA, 1879/1-פ.
	Party member	ISTA, 822/15-פ.
	BDM	ISTA, 821/9-פ.
	BDM	ISTA, 1879/1-פ; EvGB, Mar. 1932.
	Party member, applied in 1933.	YVA, R 3/25; EvGB, Mar. 1932; ISTA, 822/15-פ.
	AGdFA	ISTA 823/2-פ.
Merchant	Party member	USHMM, membership records.
Farmer	Party member	USHMM, membership records.
Planter	Party member	USHMM, membership records
	HJ	ISTA, 1879/1-פ.
	Party member, applied in 1933	ISTA, 822/15-פ; YVA, R 3/25, R3/18.
Farmer	Party member	USHMM, membership records
Teacher	Party member, NSLB, DAF-*Zellenwalter*.	ISTA, 821/9-פ.

Member-ship no.	Name	Gen-der	Date of entry NSDAP or NS group	Age of entry, approx.	Year of birth	Place of birth	Address
	Hoenig, Berta	f					Wilhelma?
	Hoenig, Erika	f		10-14			Wilhelma
	Hoenig, Mrs.	f					
111695	Hoersch, Hermann	m	May 1, 1933 or Spring 1934	31	1903	Oberemsingen	Haifa, Deutsches Sportheim
	Hoever, Hans	m					Nazareth (OG Haifa), 1936: Germany
	Hofer, Fritz						Jaffa
	Hofer, Rudolf	m		15	1920		Jaffa-Sarona or Jerusalem?
	Hoffmann, Beate	f		21	1914	Jerusalem	Jaffa-Sarona
	Hoffmann, Charlotte	f		14	1921		Jaffa-Sarona
	Hoffmann, Hugo	m		10-18	1927	Jaffa	
7258296	Hoffmann, Ida	f	Oct. 1, 1939	49	1890	Termsalem	Jaffa, Walhalla
	Hoffmann, Klaus	m		10-18			Jaffa-Sarona
	Hoffmann, Luise	f					Sarona
3722463	Hoffmann, Martha	f	May 1, 1936	25	1911	Tripolis, Syria	Sarona, German Colony
	Hoffmann, Oskar	m		13	1922		Jaffa-Sarona
3445375	Hoffmann, Richard Otto Dr.	m	April 1, 1934	26	1908	Jerusalem	Sarona
3445377	Hoffmann, Theodor	m	April 1, 1934	25	1909	Jerusalem	Sarona
1636167	Hoffmann, Theodor Samuel	m	June 1, 1933	40	1893	Jerusalem	Jaffa-Sarona
3445376	Hoffmann, Walter	m	April 1, 1934	39	1895	Jerusalem	Jerusalem
	Horn, Walter	m					Sarona
3726036	Hornung, Anna	f	July 1, 1936	30	1906	Wilhelma	Wilhelma
3726037	Hornung, Friedrich	m	July 1, 1936	35	1901	Sarona	Wilhelma
	Hornung, Helene (or Helena)	f					Wilhelma?
	Imberger, Alma	f		14-18			Wilhelma
3477505	Imberger, Edith Babette	f	March 1, 1936	30	1906	Jerusalem	Jerusalem, German Colony
3401701	Imberger, Erich	m	Feb. 1, 1934	21	1913	Jerusalem	Jerusalem, German Colony
6990884	Imberger, Fritz	m	Oct. 1, 1938	25	1913	Jerusalem	Jerusalem, German Colony
	Imberger, Gertrud	f	Spring 1934				Jerusalem
	Imberger, Heinrich	m	Spring 1934				Sarona
3474884	Imberger, Hermann Karl	m	March 1, 1936	52	1884	Jerusalem	Jerusalem, German Colony
	Imberger, Manfred	m	Spring 1934	14-18			Jerusalem

Occupation	NS post and/or membership	Source
	AGdFA	ISTA, 823,/2-פ.
	JM	ISTA, 1879/1-פ.
	AGdFA	ISTA, 823/2-פ.
Master cooper	Party member	USHMM, membership records.
	Party member, DAF	ISTA, 821/11-פ.
	Party member, DAF	ISTA 821/13-פ.
	HJ	ISTA, 1879/1-פ.
Kindergarten teacher	BDM	ISTA, 822/3-פ.
	JM, BDM	ISTA, 1879/1-פ; ISTA, 822/6-פ.
	JV or HJ	YVA, R 3/25; *Rundbrief d. Familiengemeinschaft GPH*, 43, June 2002.
Housewife	Party member	USHMM, membership records.
	JV or HJ	YVA, R 3/20.
	AGdFA	ISTA 823/2-פ.
Official clerk	Party member	USHMM, membership records.
	JV, HJ	ISTA, 1879/1-פ; ISTA, 822/6-פ.
Doctor of law	Party member, DAF-*Rechtswalter*	ISTA, 822/15-פ; USHMM, membership records.
Bank official	Party member	USHMM, membership records.
Merchant	Party member; OGL in Sarona-Jaffa, DAF treasurer; vice-*Landeskreisleiter (1935ff)*	ISTA, 821/7-פ; ISTA 821/9-פ, ISTA 823/4-פ, ISTA 822/15-פ.
Director	Party member, WHW	ISTA, 822/15-פ; USHMM, membership records.
Teacher	Party applicant, NSLB, DAF *Bücherwart*	ISTA, 821/9-פ.
Nursery school teacher	Party member, BDM leader	USHMM, membership records; YVA, R 3/1.
Farmer	Party member	USHMM, membership records.
Teacher (?)	AGdFA	ISTA, 823/2-פ.
	BDM	ISTA, 1879/1-פ.
Housewife	Party member	USHMM, membership records.
Bank official	Party member, applied in 1933.	ISTA, 822/15-פ; USHMM, membership records; YVA, R 3/25, R 3/22.
none	Party member, DAF-treasurer	USHMM, membership records; ISTA, 823/6-פ.
	Party member, applied in 1933.	ISTA, 822/15-פ; YVA, R 3/25.
	Party member	ISTA, 822/15-פ.
Architect	Party member, DAF	USHMM, membership records.
	HJ	ISTA, 822/15-פ.

Membership no.	Name	Gender	Date of entry NSDAP or NS group	Age of entry, approx.	Year of birth	Place of birth	Address
	Imberger, Otto	m	Spring 1934				Jerusalem
3726038	Imberger, Richard	m	July 1, 1936	21	1915	Wilhelma	Wilhelma
7024778	Imberger, Rudolf	m	March 1, 1939	33	1906	Mannheim	Jaffa, German Colony
3402134	Imberger, Wilfried	m	Feb. 1, 1934	26	1908	Jerusalem	Sarona
	Jaeger, Emma	f					
2754599	Jentzsch, Gerhard	m					Jerusalem
	Jentzsch, Kaethe	f	Spring 1934				Jerusalem
	Jentzsch, Ute	f		10-14			Jerusalem
	Jentzsch, Werner	m		10-14			Jerusalem
	Jung, Hulda	f					Haifa
	Kahlow, Erika	f		14-18			Jaffa-Sarona
6990886	Kaltenbach, Adolf	m	Oct. 1, 1938	27	1911	Haifa	Haifa, German Colony
3455023	Kaltenbach, Christian	m	June 1,1934	59	1875	Haifa	Haifa, German Colony
3455022	Kaltenbach, Ernst Gottlieb	m	June 1, 1934	25	1909	Haifa	Haifa, German Colony
	Kaltenbach, Fritz	m		10-14			Haifa
	Kaltenbach, Gretel	f		10-14			Haifa
6990887	Kaltenbach, Imanuel	m	Oct. 1, 1938	46	1892	Haifa	Haifa, German Colony
6??0888	Kaltenbach, Magdalene	f	Oct. 1, 1938	38	1900	Haifa	Haifa, German Colony
	Kastorff, Hans	m		39	1899		Port-Said, 1938: Haifa
	Katz, Fritz	m		10-14			Wilhelma
6990889	Katz, Meta	f	Oct. 1, 1938	24	1914	Haifa	Haifa, German Colony
	Katz, Werner	m		14-18			Waldheim
3901189	Kaufmann, Arthur	m	Mar. 16, 1937	26	1911	Kornwestheim	Haifa, German Colony
	Kaufmann, Hans	m					Jerusalem
3401687	Kaulfuss, (Egon) Reinhold	m	Feb. 1, 1934	46	1888	Wermsdorf	Jerusalem, German Colony
	Kaulfuss, Edith née Lange	f	Spring 1934				Jerusalem
	Kaulfuss, Emilie Bertha	f					Jerusalem
	Kaulfuss, Feriha	f		14-18			Jerusalem
	Kaulfuss, Inge	f		10-14			Jerusalem
6990891	Keller, Albert Philipp	m	Oct. 1, 1938	46	1892	Haifa	Haifa, German Colony

Occupation	NS post and/or membership	Source
	Party member, applied in 1933.	ISTA, 822/15-פ; YVA, R 3/25.
Farmer	Party member	USHMM, membership records.
Engineer	Party member	USHMM, membership records.
Merchant	Party member, DAF-*Pressewalter*	ISTA, 822/15-פ; USHMM, membership records; YVA, R 3/25.
	DAF	ISTA, 821/11-פ.
Minister	Party member, NSLB member	ISTA, 821/9-פ; Loeffler 2000: 207.
	Party member, applied in 1933.	ISTA, 822/15-פ; YVA, R 3/25.
	JM	ISTA, 1879/1-פ.
	DJ	ISTA, 1879/1-פ.
	Party member, collected money for WHW	ISTA, 821/9-פ; cf. EvGB, Aug. 1932.
	BDM	ISTA, 822/3-פ.
Machine engineer	Party member	USHMM, membership records.
Master workman	Party member	USHMM, membership records.
Machine engineer	Party member, DAF, *Filmstellenleiter*	USHMM, membership records; YVA, R 3/20.
	JV	ISTA, 1879/1-פ.
	JM	ISTA, 1879/1-פ.
Technician	Party member	USHMM, membership records.
Housewife	Party member	USHMM, membership records.
	Party member	YVA, R3/18.
	JV	ISTA, 1879/1-פ.
none	Party member	ISTA, 821/9-פ; USHMM, membership records.
	HJ	ISTA, 1879/1-פ.
Cook	Party applicant, DAF	ISTA, 821/11-פ; USHMM, membership records.
Teacher, Studien-assessor	Party applicant, NSLB, DAF	ISTA, 821/9-פ.
Painter	Party member, applied in 1933; treasurer (Kassenwart) 1934	ISTA, 821/5-פ, 822/15-פ; YVA, R 3/25; USHMM, membership records.
	Party member, applied in 1933.	ISTA, 822/15-פ; YVA, R 3 /25.
	Party member	ISTA, 3162/10-פ.
	BDM	ISTA, 1879/1-פ.
	JM	ISTA, 1879/1-פ.
Merchant	Party member, DAF	USHMM, membership records.

Membership no.	Name	Gender	Date of entry NSDAP or NS group	Age of entry, approx.	Year of birth	Place of birth	Address
1369604	Keller, Herbert	m	Feb. 1, 1933	28	1905	Jerusalem	Haifa, German Colony
	Keller, Hermann	m					Jerusalem, Dormition Abbey
	Kirchner, Hans (-Juergen)	m		14-18			Jerusalem
1751590	Kirchner, Hans E.	m	July 1, 1933	27	1906	Jerusalem	Jerusalem, German Colony
3401717	Kirchner, Mathilde Sophie	f	Spring 1934				Jerusalem or Haifa, 1938: Tübingen, Germany
3401930	Kirchner, Oskar	m	Feb. 1, 1934	24	1910	Tersalem	Haifa, German Colony
	Kirchner, Rolf	m					Haifa
3709976	Kirchner, Rudolf Ernst	m	May 1, 1936	31	1905	Jerusalem	Haifa, German Colony
	Kirchner, Ruth	f		14-18			Jerusalem
2643112	Klause, Helmut	m					Jaffa-Sarona
2756134	Klink, Friedrich	m	Oct. 1, 1934	73	1861	Wilhelma	Wilhelma
2756169	Klink, Hans	m	Oct. 1, 1934	38	1896	Jaffa	Wilhelma
3803836	Klink, Siegfried Dr.	m	June 15, 1936	31	1905	Haifa	Haifa, German Colony
	Klink, Theodor	m		10-14			Wilhelma
	Klisch, Helene	f					Jerusalem
1636182	Knoll, Erich	m	June 1, 1933				Sarona, 1938: Germany
2755531	Knoll, Erna	f	Oct. 1, 1934	28	1906	Sarona	Jerusalem, German Colony
	Knoll, Helene	f		21	1914		Jaffa-Sarona
3402153	Knoll, Karl Friedrich	m	Feb. 1, 1934	58	1876	Sarona	Sarona or Stuttgart
3445371	Knoll, Lydia née Sawatzky	f	April 1, 1934	52	1882	Wohldemfürst/Russ.	Sarona or Stuttgart
1636169	Knoll, Oswald	m	June 1, 1933				Sarona
	Knoll, Rosa	f	Spring 1934				Sarona
2612910	Koch, Eugen Dr.	m		41	1895	Waiblingen	Sarona
	Koch, Gertrud	f	1932				Jaffa

Occupation	NS post and/or membership	Source
Mechanic	Party member, NSKK, DAF	ISTA, 822/15-פ; ISTA, 823/8-פ; USHMM, membership records.
Temp. head of Dormition Abbey	Party member, SD	*The Jerusalem Post*, Oct. 9, 1998.
	HJ	ISTA, 1879/1-פ.
Bank official	Party member, HJ leader	ISTA, 821/5-פ; USHMM, membership records.
	Party member, applied in 1933.	ISTA, 822/15-פ; YVA, R3/18; YVA, R 3/25.
Merchant	Party member, port service (*Hafendienst*)	ISTA, 822/15-פ; USHMM, membership records; YVA, R 3/1.
	DAF-*Betriebszellenwalter*	ISTA-823/6-פ.
Merchant	Party member, appointed *Landesfilmwart*	ISTA, 821/9-פ; USHMM, membership records.
	BDM	ISTA, 1879/1-פ.
	Party member	YVA, R 3/25.
none	Party member	USHMM, membership records.
Farmer	Party member	USHMM, membership records.
Teacher	Party applicant (1936-38), NSLB, DAF	ISTA, 821/9-פ; USHMM, membership records.
	JV	ISTA, 1879/1-פ.
Dentist's assistant (Dr. Burhan Abdulhadie, Mamillah Rd.)	DAF	ISTA, 821/11-פ.
	Party member, DAF	ISTA, 822/15-פ; ISTA, 823/4-פ.
Teacher	Party member	ISTA, 821/5-פ; USHMM, membership records.
	BDM	ISTA, 822/6-פ.
Bank official	Party member	ISTA, 822/15-פ; USHMM, membership records.
Housewife	Party member	ISTA, 822/15-פ; USHMM, membership records.
	Party member	ISTA, 822/15-פ.
	Party member	ISTA, 822/15-פ.
Teacher at the Temple Soc. in Sarona-Jaffa from Oct. 1934.	Party member, NSLB officer, *Pressestellenleiter in 1936.*	ISTA, 821/9-פ; YVA, R 3/20.
Manager of the Ottoman Bank	Party member; DAF-*Kassenwalter*; she left the party, no money to pay the membership.	ISTA, 821/1-פ.

Membership no.	Name	Gender	Date of entry NSDAP or NS group	Age of entry, approx.	Year of birth	Place of birth	Address
	Koenig, Karl	m	Spring 1934	25	1909		Jerusalem, Sarona-Jaffa, 1937: Haifa
3402151	Koeper, Werner	m	Feb. 1, 1934	27	1907	Leipzig	Sarona
	Kolb, Horst	m	1932	11	1924		Jaffa-Sarona
2755822	Kopp, Karl	m	Oct. 1, 1934	51	1883	Althengstett	Wilhelma
858379	Kotzenberg, Karl	m	Dec. 1, 1931	21	1910	Schloss Naumburg	Jerusalem
3726021	Krafft, August	m	July 1, 1936	32	1904	Haifa	Haifa, German Colony
6990894	Krafft, Edith Irmgard	f	Oct. 1, 1938	23	1915	Haifa	Haifa, German Colony
	Krafft, Ewald	m	Spring 1934				Jerusalem
3726022	Krafft, Georg	m	July 1, 1936	55	1881	Haifa	Haifa, German Colony
	Krafft, Hildegard	f		29	1909		Haifa
3726023	Krafft, Philipp	m	July 1, 1936	62	1874	Haifa	Haifa, German Colony
3401252	Krautmacher, Alfred	m		28	1909	Elberfeld	Sarona
	Krockenberger, Frieder	m		14-18			Jerusalem
	Krockenberger, Irene	f		14-18			Bethlehem
	Krockenberger, Karl	m	Applied for membership in 1936.				Bethlehem-Waldheim
	Krockenberger, Oskar	m		10-14			Bethlehem
6990898	Kruegler, Anna	f	Oct. 1, 1938	34	1904	Haifa	Haifa, German Colony
3455026	Kruegler, Anna	f	June 1, 1934	28	1906	Jaffa	Haifa or Esslingen
3401926	Kruegler, Christian	m	Feb. 1, 1934	34	1900	Haifa	Haifa, German Colony
6990896	Kruegler, Dorothea Luise	f	Oct. 1, 1938	36	1902	Haifa	Haifa, German Colony
6990899	Kruegler, Else	f	Oct. 1, 1938	29	1909	Haifa	Haifa, German Colony
6990900	Kruegler, Friedrich	m	Oct. 1, 1938	39	1899	Haifa	Haifa, German Colony
3709972	Kruegler, Maria	f	May 1, 1936	30	1906	Haifa	Haifa, German Colony
6990897	Kruegler, Otto Alexander	m	Oct. 1, 1938	31	1907	Haifa	Haifa, German Colony
	Kuebler, Anni	f		10-18			Jaffa-Sarona
	Kuebler, Egon	m		10-18			Sarona

Occupation	NS post and/or membership	Source
	Party member	ISTA, 822/15-פ; YVA, R3/18.
Printing-shop owner	Party member	ISTA, 822/15-פ; USHMM, membership records:
	JV, HJ	ISTA, 822/6-פ.
Smith	Party member, *Kassenstellenleiter*	USHMM, membership records; YVA, R 3/1.
Student	Party member	USHMM, membership records.
Technician	Party member, *Filmwart*	ISTA, 821/9-פ; USHMM, membership records; YVA, R 3/1.
None	Party member	USHMM, membership records.
	Party member, applied in 1933.	ISTA, 822/15-פ; YVA, R 3/25; EvGB, Jan. 1931.
Innkeeper	Party member	ISTA, 821/9-פ; USHMM, membership records.
	Party applicant (1936-1938)	YVA, R3/18.
Merchant	Party member	ISTA, 821/9-פ; USHMM, membership records.
	Party member, DAF-*Betriebswalter*	YVA, R 3/1.
	HJ	ISTA, 1879/1-פ.
	BDM	ISTA, 1879/1-פ.
	Party applicant	ISTA, 821/7-פ.
	JV	ISTA, 1879/1-פ.
Bank official	Party member	USHMM, membership records.
none	Party member	USHMM, membership records.
Teacher	Party member, NSLB officer, DAF	ISTA, 821/9-פ; USHMM, membership records.
none	Party member	USHMM, membership records.
none	Party member, collected money for WHW	USHMM, membership records:
Merchant	Party member	USHMM, membership records.
none	Party member	USHMM, membership records.
Watchmaker	Party member, DAF	ISTA, 821/9-פ; ISTA, 823/6-פ; USHMM, membership records.
	JM or BDM	YVA, R 3/25.
	JV or HJ	YVA, R 3/25.

Member-ship no.	Name	Gen-der	Date of entry NSDAP or NS group	Age of entry, approx.	Year of birth	Place of birth	Address
3402145	Kuebler, Fritz	m	Feb. 1, 1934	46	1888	Sarona	Sarona
	Kuebler, Gerda	f		14	1921		Jaffa-Sarona
3497559	Kuebler, Hedwig	f	Nov.1, 1935	41	1894	Stuttgart	Jaffa, Hotel Jerusalem, German Colony
	Kuebler, Heinz	m		10-18			Jaffa-Sarona
	Kuebler, Herbert	m		10-14			Jaffa-Sarona
6990892	Kuebler, Hermann	m	Oct. 1, 1938	33	1905	Sarona	Sarona, Heinrichstr.
	Kuebler, Hilde	f		10-14			Jaffa-Sarona
3455014	Kuebler, Rudolf	m	June 1, 1934	22	1912	Sarona	Sarona
	Kuebler, Theodor	m		14-18			Haifa-Waldheim
1636193	Kuebler, Walter	m	June 1, 1933				Sarona
	Kuhnle, Eberhard	m					Jerusalem
	Kuhnle, Ella	f		14-18			Haifa
	Kuhnle, Else	f		14-18			Bethlehem
3455027	Kuhnle, Hans	m					Sarona-Jaffa, 1936: Haifa
	Kuhnle, Hermann Wilhelm	m	Spring 1934				Haifa
	Kuhnle, Hilda	f		14-18			Bethlehem
3455029	Kuhnle, Hugo Helmut	m					Haifa, 1936-1937: German army.
	Kuhnle, Rudolf	m		10-14			Haifa
	Kuhnle, Werner	m		14-18			Bethlehem
6990903	Kuhnle, Wilhelm	m	Oct. 1, 1938	50	1888	Haifa	Bethlehem
2755992	Kunert, Robert	m		37	1901		Jerusalem, Syrian Orphanage, 1938: Böblingen
3402156	Laemmle, Otto	m	Feb. 1, 1934	23	1911	Sarona	Sarona
6990904	Lange, Gerhard	m	Oct. 1, 1938	37	1901	Haifa	Jerusalem, German Colony
2739381	Lange, Grete	f	Oct. 1, 1934	25	1909	Jaffa	Jaffa, German Colony
3445381	Lange, Hanna	f	April 1, 1934	39	1895	Jaffa	Bethlehem Port Haifa
	Lange, Hans	m					Sarona
3401932	Lange, Kurt	m	Feb. 1, 1934	34	1900	Haifa	Approx. 1938: Bethlehem-Waldheim, 1934: Haifa.
	Lange, Nikolaus Gerhardt	m					1. Jerusalem, 2. Jaffa

Occupation	NS post and/or membership	Source
Farmer	Party member, applied in 1933.	ISTA, 822/15-פ; USHMM, membership records; YVA, R 3/25.
	JM, BDM	ISTA, 822/6-פ.
Cook	Party member	USHMM, membership records.
	JV or HJ	YVA, R 3/25.
	JV	ISTA, 822/3-פ.
Engineer	Party member, DAF-*Pressewalter*	USHMM, membership records.
	JM	ISTA, 822/3-פ.
Cooper	Party member	USHMM, membership records.
	HJ	ISTA, 1879/1-פ.
	Party member	ISTA, 822/15-פ.
Teacher	Party applicant, NSLB	ISTA, 821/9-פ.
	BDM	ISTA, 1879/1-פ.
	BDM	ISTA, 1879/1-פ.
	Party member	YVA, R3/18.
	Party member	ISTA, 822/15-פ.
	BDM	ISTA, 1879/1-פ.
	Party member	YVA, R3/18.
	JV	ISTA, 1879/1-פ.
	HJ	ISTA, 1879/1-פ.
Farmer	Party member	USHMM, membership records.
	Party member	YVA, R 3/22.
Farmer	Party member	ISTA, 822/15-פ; USHMM, membership records.
Mechanic	Party member	USHMM, membership records.
Housewife	Party member	USHMM, membership records.
none	Party member	ISTA, 822/15-פ; USHMM, membership records.
	DAF-*Berufswalter*	ISTA, 823/6-פ.
Teacher	Party member, Vice- *Ortsgruppen-leiter* Beth.-Waldheim, NSLB, DAF, temp. leader of HJ	ISTA, 3160/18-פ, ISTA, 822/15-פ; USHMM, membership records; YVA, R3/25.
	Party applicant	YVA, R 3/25.

Member-ship no.	Name	Gen-der	Date of entry NSDAP or NS group	Age of entry, approx.	Year of birth	Place of birth	Address
3726024	Lange, Oskar	m	Dec. 5, 1934	23	1911	Haifa	Haifa, German Colony; 1935: Stuttgart?
	Lauer, Emil	m		22	1914		Haifa until Jan. 1939, later: near Graz
3280667	Lauer, Hermann Christian	m	July 1, 1933	27	1906	Trieste	Haifa, German Colony
6990855	Lendholt, Erika	f	Oct. 1, 1938	23	1915	Haifa	Haifa, German Colony
3474756	Lendholt, Eugen	m	March 1, 1936	25	1911	Jerusalem	Haifa, German Colony
	Liebmann, Herbert	m	Spring 1934				Jerusalem
3402146	Lippmann, Friedrich Wilhelm	m	Feb. 1, 1934	34	1900	Sarona	Sarona
3445373	Lippmann, Mathilde	f	April 1, 1934	30	1904	Jaffa	Sarona
	Loebert, Helga	f		10-14			Wilhelma
	Loebert, Olga	f		10-14			Wilhelma
	Loebert, Otto	m		10-14			Wilhelma
	Loebert, Werner	m		10-14			Wilhelma
	Lorch, Fritz	m	Spring 1934				Jaffa
	Lorch, Karl	m	1934		1880	Jaffa	Palestine, Sept. 1934: Germany
7024775	Lorenz, Agnes	f	March 1, 1939	22	1917	Petershagen	Jaffa-Sarona
	Lorenz, Alfred	m		12	1923		Jaffa-Sarona
	Lorenz, Anni	f		18	1917		Jaffa-Sarona
	Lorenz, Friedrich	m	Spring 1934				Jerusalem
	Lorenz, Kurt	m		10-18			Jaffa-Sarona
	Lorenz, Richard	m		14-18	1920		Jaffa
7332431	Lorenz, Rudolf	m	Dec. 1, 1939	37	1902	Jerusalem	Jaffa, German Colony
3709986	Lutz, Berta	f					Haifa, 1938: Stuttgart, Germany
	Lutz, Carmen	f		10-14			Haifa
	Lutz, Marianne	f		10-14			Jerusalem
3455028	Lutz, Otto	m	June 1, 1934	53	1881	Heilbronn	Haifa, German Colony
	Lutz, Wilhelm	m	Spring 1934				Jerusalem, 1937: Germany
	Lutz, Wolfgang	m		10-14			Haifa
6990908	Maier, Erich	m	Oct. 1, 1938	36	1902	Berlin	Jerusalem
3445389	Maier, Karl	m	Spring 1934				Jerusalem, 1937: Enzweihingen

Occupation	NS post and/or membership	Source
Machinist	Party applicant	USHMM, membership records.
	Party member	ISTA, 821/9-פ; ISTA, 821/7-פ.
Merchant	Party member, DAF, NSV, WHW	USHMM, membership records; YVA, R 3/1.
Housewife	Party member	USHMM, membership records.
Technician	Party member	USHMM, membership records.
Teacher	Party member, applied in 1933.	ISTA, 822/15-פ; ISTA, 821/9-פ.
Farmer	Party member, applied in 1933	ISTA, 822/15-פ; USHMM, membership records; YVA, R 3/25.
none	Party member	ISTA, 822/15-פ; USHMM, membership records.
	JM	ISTA, 1879/1-פ.
	JM	ISTA, 1879/1-פ.
	JV	ISTA, 1879/1-פ.
	JV	ISTA, 1879/1-פ.
	Party member, applied in 1933.	ISTA, 822/15-פ; YVA, R 3/25.
Dentist	Party member, SA	Schumacher Institute, P-LK-01.
none	Party member	USHMM, membership records.
	JV, HJ	ISTA, 822/6-פ.
	BDM	ISTA, 822/6-פ.
Employee, Syrian Orphanage	Party member	ISTA, 822/15-פ.
	JV or HJ	YVA, R 3/25.
	JV, HJ	ISTA, 822/3-פ, ISTA, 822/6-פ.
Employee	Party member, DAF-KdF officer	ISTA, 823/4-פ; ISTA, 823/4-פ; USHMM, membership records.
	Party member	YVA, R3/18; EvGB, Jan. 1931.
	JM	ISTA, 1879/1-פ; EvGB Jan. 1931.
	BDM	ISTA, 1879/1-פ; EvGB Jan. 1931.
Architect	Party member, Committee of Veterans, *Schriftstellenleiter*	USHMM, membership records.
Employee, Syrian Orphanage	Party member, applied in 1933; DAF	ISTA, 822/15-פ; YVA, R 3/25; EvGB, Jan.1931.
	JV	ISTA, 1879/1-פ; EvGB, Jan.1931.
Auditor	Party member	USHMM, membership records.
	Party member	ISTA, 822/15-פ; YVA, R 3/25.

Membership no.	Name	Gender	Date of entry NSDAP or NS group	Age of entry, approx.	Year of birth	Place of birth	Address
	Maier, Maria	f		10-18			Jaffa-Sarona
	Maier, Ursula	f		10-14			Jerusalem
	Melchers, Wilhelm	m					Haifa
3429815	Memmi, Eugen	m	May 1, 1933	31	1902	Heilbronn	Sarona
3224145	Merz, Erwin	m					Jerusalem, *Propstei*
	Messerle, Christian	m	Spring 1934				Jerusalem
	Messerle, Grete (Gretel)	f		17	1917		Jaffa-Sarona
	Messerle, Hilde	f		18	1918		Jaffa-Sarona
7024776	Messerle, Margarete	f	Mar. 1, 1939	22	1917	Jaffa	Jaffa, Tel Aviv St.
3497623	Messerle, Marta Friederike	f	Nov. 1, 1935	25	1910	Jerusalem	Jaffa, German Colony
	Messerle, Martha	f		14-18			Jaffa-Sarona
7024773	Messerle, Paul	m	Mar. 1, 1939	23	1916	Jaffa	Jaffa, Tel Aviv St.
	Michel, Erwin	m					Jerusalem
	Minzenmay, Erich	m		10-14			Haifa
6990909	Minzenmay, Herta	f	Oct. 1, 1938	26	1912	Haifa	Haifa, German Colony
	Minzenmay, Kurt	m		10-14			Jerusalem
	Minzenmay, Werner	m		10-14			Haifa
3709981	Minzenmay, Wilhelm Fr.	m	May 1, 1936	46	1890	Haifa	Haifa, German Colony
3455036	Moessner, Karl	m	June 1, 1934	27	1907	Erdmanns-hausen	Haifa
6990911	Müller, Christian	m	Oct. 1, 1938	66	1872	Heidelberg	Haifa, German Colony
	Nachbauer, Xaver	m					Haifa, German Colony; from 1937 unknown.
	Neun, Eugen	m	Spring 1934				Sarona
	Noth, Christian	m		39	1898	Nehren-Tübingen	Jerusalem
6990912	Noz, Elfriede	f	Oct. 1, 1938	23	1915	Sarona	Sarona, Christophstr.
	Noz, Emma	f		10-18			Jaffa-Sarona
6990913	Orth, Friedrich	m	Oct. 1, 1938	42	1896	Sarona	Sarona, German Colony
	Orth, Hetty	f		10-18			Jaffa-Sarona
	Orth, Manfred	m		10-18			Jaffa-Sarona
	Orth, Reinhold	m		10-18			Jaffa-Sarona
	Pfaender, Albert	m					Haifa
	Pfaender, Erich	m		10-14			Haifa
	Pfaender, Erwin	m		10-14			Haifa

Occupation	NS post and/or membership	Source
	JM or BDM	YVA, R 3/25,.
	JM	ISTA, 1879/1-פ.
Consul in Haifa	Party member	ISTA, 821/9-פ.
Teacher	Party member	USHMM, membership records.
Teacher	Party member, NSLB member	ISTA, 821/9-פ.
	Party member, applied in 1933.	ISTA, 822/15-פ; YVA, R 3/25.
	BDM	ISTA, 822/6-פ.
	BDM	ISTA, 1879/1-פ; ISTA, 822/6-פ.
none	Party member	USHMM, membership records.
Official clerk	Party member	USHMM, membership records.
	BDM	ISTA, 822/3-פ.
Butcher	Party member, HJ	USHMM, membership records.
Employed at the office of the Syrian Orphanage	DAF	ISTA, 821/11-פ.
	JV	ISTA, 1879/1-פ.
none	Party member	USHMM, membership records.
	DJ	ISTA, 1879/1-פ.
	JV	ISTA, 1879/1-פ.
Watchmaker	Party member	USHMM, membership records.
Butcher	Party member	USHMM, membership records.
Engineer	Party member	USHMM, membership records.
	Party applicant or party member, DAF	ISTA, 821/11-פ; YVA, R/18.
Teacher	Party member	ISTA, 822/15-פ; Sauer 1985: 235.
	Party member, DAF	ISTA, 821/11-פ.
Maid	Party member	USHMM, membership records.
	JM or BDM	YVA, R 3/25.
Apiarist	Party member	USHMM, membership records.
	JM or BDM	YVA, R 3/25.
	JV or HJ	YVA, R 3/25.
	JV or HJ	YVA, R 3/25.
	Party member, DAF	YVA, R3/25.
	JV	ISTA, 1879/1-פ.
	JV	ISTA, 1879/1-פ.

Membership no.	Name	Gender	Date of entry NSDAP or NS group	Age of entry, approx.	Year of birth	Place of birth	Address
	Pfaender, Ilse	f		10-14			Haifa
	Pfaender, Margarete	f		10-14			Haifa
3709984	Pfaender, Paul Gustav	m	May 1, 1936	51	1885	Haifa	Haifa, German Colony
3455020	Pfeiffer, Elisabeth	f	approx. 1936				1. Haifa, 2. Germany in 1939
	Pfeiffer, Elly	f		14-18			Haifa
3726025	Pfeiffer, Ida	f		24	1913	Alexandria, Egypt	Haifa (until March 1939), later: Germany (marriage)
3709975	Pfeiffer, Ludwig	m	May 1, 1936	57	1879	Alexandria, Egypt	Haifa, German Colony
7025325	Plzak, Franz	m	Apr. 1, 1939	47	1892	Neu-Bistriz-Neuhaus	Haifa, German Colony
	Pommerenke, Charlotte	f					Jerusalem, German Colony, Pension Lenholt
	Reichardt, Uli	m		14-18			Jaffa-Sarona
	Reichert, Elfriede	f		14-18			Wilhelma
	Reichert, Franz Dr.						
3402138	Reichert, Gottlob	m	Feb. 1, 1934	23	1911	Wilhelma	Sarona, German Colony
3726039	Reichert, Gustav Friedrich	m	July 1,1936	28	1908	Wilhelma	Wilhelma
	Reichert, Helga	f		10-14			Jerusalem
	Reichert, Willi	m		14-18			Wilhelma
	Reimann, Kurt	m	Spring 1934				Jerusalem
	Reinhard(t), Ulrich	m		14	1921		Jaffa
	Reinhardt, Helmuth	m		10-18			Jaffa-Sarona
	Reinhardt, Klaus	m		10-18			
	Rhein, Hans Werner	m		14-18			Jerusalem
	Richter, Erika	f		14-18			Wilhelma
2756111	Richter, Hans	m	Oct. 1, 1934	52	1882	Willingshausen	Wilhelma
	Richter, Karl	m		10-14			Wilhelma
	Richter, Meta	f		14-18			Wilhelma
	Richter, Theo	m		14-18			Wilhelma
3726040	Richter, Theodor	m	July 1, 1936	23	1913	Jerusalem	Wilhelma
	Richter, Willi	m		10-14			Wilhelma
	Ringelmann	m					Jerusalem
	Rippert, H.	m					Acre

Occupation	NS post and/or membership	Source
	JM	ISTA, 1879/1-פ.
	JM	ISTA, 1879/1-פ.
Merchant	Party member	USHMM, membership records.
	Party member	ISTA, 821/9-פ.
	BDM; JM. leader	ISTA, 1879/1-פ; YVA, R 3/1.
Teacher	Party member, NSLB member, BDM leader in Bethlehem/Galilee.	YVA, R 3/1.
Piano tuner	Party member	ISTA, 821/9-פ; USHMM, membership records.
Master workman	Party member	USHMM, membership records:
	DAF	ISTA, 821/11-פ.
	HJ	ISTA, 1879/1-פ.
	BDM	ISTA, 1879/1-פ.
	Head of the DNB in Palestine, SD	BPRO, FO 371/23237+23238+23222; Balke 2001: 113-15.
Machinist	Party member, applied in 1933.	ISTA, 822/15-פ; USHMM, membership records; YVA, R 3/25.
Farmer	Party member	USHMM, membership records.
	JM	ISTA, 1879/1-פ.
	HJ	ISTA, 1879/1-פ.
	Party member	ISTA, 822/15-פ.
	JV, HJ	ISTA, 822/3-פ; ISTA, 822/6-פ.
	JV or HJ	YVA, R 3/25.
	JV or HJ	YVA, R 3/25.
	HJ	ISTA, 1879/1-פ.
	BDM	ISTA, 1879/1-פ.
Farmer	Party member, DAF	ISTA, 1879/1-פ; USHMM, membership records.
	JV	ISTA, 1879/1-פ.
	BDM	ISTA, 1879/1-פ.
	HJ	ISTA, 1879/1-פ.
Farmer	Party member	USHMM, membership records.
	JV	ISTA, 1879/1-פ.
Vice consul	Party member	YVA, R 3/25, R 3/20.
Missions-baumeister (missionary constructor)	Party member	Jerusalemsverein, B 536.

Membership no.	Name	Gender	Date of entry NSDAP or NS group	Age of entry, approx.	Year of birth	Place of birth	Address
3455038	Rippert, Jakob	m	June 1, 1934	35	1899	Querlack, Hess.	Acre, German Farm
	Roedenbeck						
6990914	Rohrer, Anna	f	Oct. 1, 1938	61	1877	Jerusalem	Jerusalem, German Colony
3401694	Rohrer, Herbert Dr.	m	Feb. 1, 1934	31	1903	Jerusalem	1. Jerusalem, German Colony, 2. Jaffa-Sarona.
1486054	Rohrer, Richard	m	Spring 1934				Jaffa
	Rohwer, Edelgard	f		10-18			Jaffa-Sarona
	Rossteuscher, Otto	m		10-14			Haifa
3726026	Rothenberger, Georg Friedrich	m	Nov. 29, 1934	33	1901	Hornberg	Haifa, German Colony
	Rubitschung, O. Dr.	m					Jaffa
	Rubitschung, Paul	m		10-18			Jaffa-Sarona
	Ruesen, Ruth	f					Jerusalem
	Ruff, Brunhilde	f		14-18			Bethlehem
	Ruff, Dieter	m		10-14			Haifa
	Ruff, Eva	f		10-14			Haifa
	Ruff, Gerhard	m		14-18	1918	Bethlehem/ Haifa	Haifa
3726027	Ruff, Gottlieb Samuel	m	July 1, 1936	46	1890	Haifa	Haifa, German Colony
879372	Ruff, Karl	m	Jan. 1, 1932	28	1904	Haifa	Haifa, German Colony
	Ruff, Paul	m		20	1919	Haifa	Haifa
3401931	Ruff, Ruth	f	Feb. 1, 1934	25	1909	Hochstetten	Haifa, German Colony
3726041	Sawatzky, Anne or Anna	f	July 1, 1936	45	1891	Willingshausen	Wilhelma
	Sawatzky, Beate	f					Wilhelma
	Sawatzky, Helene	f		14-18			Wilhelma
	Sawatzky, Karl	m		14-18			Wilhelma
	Sawatzky, Otto	m		14-18			Wilhelma
	Sawatzky, Wilhelm	m		10-14			Wilhelma
6990916	Schanz, Anna Maria	f	Oct. 1, 1938	38	1900	Jaffa	Waldheim, German Colony
3710253	Schanz, Magdalena Katharina	f	May 1, 1936	42	1894	Jaffa	Waldheim
6990917	Schanz, Maria	f	Oct. 1, 1938	33	1905	Jaffa	Waldheim, German Colony
3445384	Schanz, Peter	m	Apr. 1,1 934	27	1907	Jerusalem	Waldheim
	Schanz, Sophie	f			1861	Waldenbuch	Wilhelma
	Scharf, Georg	m	1933/34				Jerusalem

Occupation	NS post and/or membership	Source
Farmer, engineer	Party member	ISTA, 822/15-פ; USHMM, membership records.
	Party member	YVA, R3/25.
Widow	Party member	USHMM, membership records.
Teacher in Jerusalem, later in Sarona-Jaffa.	Party member, applied in 1933; Vice-OGL Jerusalem	ISTA, 822/15-פ; USHMM, membership records; YVA, R 3/25.
	Party member, applied in 1933, DAF	ISTA, 822/15-פ; YVA, R 3/25.
	JM or BDM	YVA, R 3/25; EvGB, Mar. 1932.
	JV	ISTA, 1879/1-פ.
Mechanist	Party applicant	USHMM, membership records.
	DAF, Committee of Veterans	ISTA, 823/3-פ; ISTA, 823/4-פ.
	JV or HJ	YVA, R 3/25.
	Party applicant	YVA, R 3/25.
	BDM	ISTA, 1879/1-פ.
	JV	ISTA, 1879/1-פ.
	JM	ISTA,1879/1-פ.
Carpenter (*Tischler*)	HJ	ISTA, 1879/1-פ; Schumacher Inst., P-RK 63 (Jan. 1, 1937).
Cabinetmaker	Party member, *Schulungswart*	ISTA, 821/9-פ; USHMM, membership records.
Architect	Party member, head of NS movement until 1935.	ISTA, 821/9-פ; USHMM, membership records.
	HJ; Feb.. 1939: RAD in Germany.	Schumacher Inst., P-RK-63.
Housewife	Party member	ISTA, 822/15-פ; USHMM, membership records.
Housewife	Party member, AGdFA	USHMM, membership records.
	AGdFA-youth group	ISTA, 823/2-פ.
	BDM	ISTA, 1879/1-פ.
	HJ	ISTA, 1879/1-פ.
	HJ, DAF	ISTA, 1879/1-פ.
	JV	ISTA, 1879/1-פ.
Nurse	Party member	USHMM, membership records.
none	Party member	USHMM, membership records.
none	Party member	USHMM, membership records.
Farmer	Party member	ISTA, 822/15-פ; USHMM, membership records.
	AGdFA	ISTA, 822/5-פ, membership card.
	Party member, applied in 1933, excluded in 1934.	ISTA, 822/15-פ; YVA, R 3/16, R 3/25.

Membership no.	Name	Gender	Date of entry NSDAP or NS group	Age of entry, approx.	Year of birth	Place of birth	Address
	Scheerer, Annemarie	f		22	1916		Haifa
	Scheerer, Eberhard	m		20	1919	Haifa	Haifa
	Scheerer, Elsa	f		10-14			Wilhelma
	Scheerer, Erna	f		10-14			Wilhelma
	Scheerer, Gertrud	f		10-14			Wilhelma
	Schirling, Andreas	m		39	1901	Marburg	1. Bir-Salem, 2. Haifa
	Schmelzle, Gerhard	m		17	1918		Jaffa-Sarona
	Schmelzle, Luise	f		10-14			Haifa
	Schmid, Walter (Werner?)	m					
6990921	Schmidt, Babette	f	Oct. 1, 1938	54	1884	Jerusalem	Jerusalem, German Colony
3401929	Schmidt, Baltram	m	Feb. 1, 1934	23	1911	Haifa	Haifa, German Colony
3709979	Schmidt, Edeline	f	May 1, 1936	51	1885	Orbeljanovka	Haifa, German Colony
	Schmidt, Erkentrud	f					Haifa
6990922	Schmidt, Ingri(e)d	f	Oct. 1, 1938	22	1916	Haifa	Haifa, German Colony
3709978	Schmidt, Johannes David	m	May 1, 1936	54	1882	Haifa	Haifa, German Colony
3401698	Schmidt, Luise	f	Feb. 1, 1934	25	1909	Wilhelma	Wilhelma
6990946	Schmidt, Nicolai (Nikolai)	m	Oct. 1, 1938	62	1876	Jerusalem	Jerusalem, German Colony
3401690	Schmidt, Nikolai	m	Feb. 1, 1934	36	1898	Olgino, Russia	Jerusalem, 1937: Jaffa
	Schmidt, Thusnelda	f		14-18			Haifa
	Schneider, Rudolf	m		28	1910		Haifa
6990944	Schneller, Agnes	f	Oct. 1, 1938	39	1899	Tübingen	Jerusalem, Syrian Orphanage
6990945	Schneller, Erika	f			1904		Jerusalem
3401713	Schneller, Ernst	m	Feb. 1, 1934	33	1901		Jerusalem
3401686	Schneller, Hermann	m	Feb. 1, 1934	41	1893	Jerusalem	Jerusalem, Syrian Orphanage
	Schneller, Ursula	f		10-14			Jerusalem
3401702	Schnerring, Carl Jr.	m	Feb. 1, 1934	20	1914	Haifa	Jerusalem, German Colony
	Schnerring, Karl	m	Feb. 1, 1934	54	1880	Jerusalem	Jerusalem
	Schnerring, Manfred	m		18	1916		Jaffa
2755843	Schoenecke, Johanna	f	Oct. 1, 1934	53	1881	Jerusalem	Jerusalem, Prophetenstr.

Occupation	NS post and/or membership	Source
	Party applicant (Parteinanwärterin) (1937-38)	YVA, R3/18.
	HJ; Feb.. 1939: RAD in Germany	ISTA, 821/9-פ.
	JM	ISTA, 1879/1-פ.
	JM	ISTA, 1879/1-פ.
	JM	ISTA, 1879/1-פ.
Mechanic	Party member, DAF	ISTA, 821/9-פ; ISTA, 823/4-פ.
	HJ, resigned Feb. 1935	ISTA, 822/3-פ; EvGB, Aug. 1932.
	JM	ISTA, 1879/1-פ; cf. EvGB, Aug. 1932.
	DAF-*Pressewalter*	ISTA, 821/11-פ.
Housewife	Party member	USHMM, membership records.
Merchant	Party member	ISTA, 822/15-פ; USHMM, membership records.
Housewife	Party member, AGdFA leader in Haifa	*Die Warte des Tempels*, May 31, 1938: 76; USHMM, membership records.
	Party member, WHW collector	ISTA, 821/9-פ.
none	Party member	USHMM, membership records.
Merchant	Party member	USHMM, membership records.
Housewife	Party member	USHMM, membership records.
Mayor	Party member	USHMM, membership records.
Merchant	Party member, applied in 1933.	ISTA, 822/15-פ; YVA, R 3/25; USHMM, membership records.
	BDM	ISTA, 1879/1-פ.
	Party applicant (1937-38), DAF-*Pressewart*	YVA, R3/18; ISTA, 823/6-פ.
Housewife	Party member	USHMM, membership records.
	Party applicant(1938)	YVA, R3/25, R 3/22; BArch, PK/Q106, pic. no.. 498-504.
Syrian Orphanage	Party member, applied in 1933; economic adviser (1935), DAF	ISTA, 821/5-פ; YVA, R 3/25; BArch, PK/Q106. pic. no.. 498-504.
Director of the Syrian. Orphanage	Party member, applied in 1933; *Presseleiter* 1935	ISTA, 821/5-פ; YVA, R 3/25; USHMM, membership records.
	JM	ISTA, 1879/1-פ.
Clerk	Party member	USHMM, membership records.
	Party member, DAF	ISTA, 822/15-פ; ISTA, 823/6-פ; YVA, R 3/25.
	HJ	ISTA, 822/15-פ; ISTA, 823/8-פ.
Teacher	Party member, NSLB	ISTA, 821/9-פ; USHMM, membership records.

Member-ship no.	Name	Gen-der	Date of entry NSDAP or NS group	Age of entry, approx.	Year of birth	Place of birth	Address
3250010	Schrade, Helmut	m	May 1, 1933	22	1911	Kirchheim	1. Jerusalem, 2. Haifa
	Schraitle, Herbert	m		14-18			Haifa
	Schreiber, Else	f					Jerusalem
	Schuetzinger, Doris	f		10-14			Jerusalem
3401697	Schultz, Egon	m	Feb. 1, 1934	27	1907		Jerusalem, Syrian Orphanage
6990924	Schumacher, Christof	m	Oct. 1, 1938	41	1897	Haifa	Haifa, German Colony
3445372	Schurr, Anne	f	Apr. 1, 1934	25	1909	Geislingen Stg.	Sarona
1587418	Schwarz, Cornelius	m	May 1, 1933	55	1878	Kornthal	Jaffa, German Colony
1587579	Schwarz, Gottfried	m	Spring 1934				Jaffa
1587359	Schwarz, Hanna (Nanna) Bertha	f	May 1, 1933	57	1876	Jaffa	Jaffa, Wahalla
3445368	Schwenker, Emil	m	Spring 1934				Sarona
3474877	Seebass, Ernst	m					Jerusalem
7025326	Seeger, Friedrich	m	Apr. 1, 1939	39	1900	Bösingen	Haifa
	Seering, Elsbeth	f					
	Sickinger, Paul	m		14	1921		Jaffa-Sarona
	Sickinger, Rolf	m		10-14			Waldheim
	Sickinger, Stephan	m		14-18			Haifa-Waldheim
3455412	Spohn (Sponn), Johannes	m	June 1, 1934	36	1898	Bir-Salem	Bir-Salem near Ramleh
	Staden, Irmgard von	f		14-18			Haifa
	Staib, Karl	m		14-18			Waldheim
1275871	Staib, Sam(uel)	m	Aug. 1, 1932	19	1913	Waldheim	Bethlehem-Waldheim, Haifa
	Stark, Gertrude (Gertraude)	f	Spring 1934				Haifa
	Steller, Bruno	m		14	1921		Jaffa-Sarona or Jerusalem
3455019	Steller, Edmund	m	June 1, 1934	25	1909	Sarona	Sarona
1730799	Steller, Erich	m	June 1, 1933	24	1909	Sarona	Sarona
3402159	Steller, Eugen	m	Feb. 1, 1934	30	1904	Sarona	Sarona
3497581	Steller, Friedrich (Fritz)	m			1908	Sarona	Wilhelma, later: Jerusalem
	Steller, Herbert	m		10-14			Wilhelma
3455016	Steller, Hugo	m	June 1, 1934	20	1914	Sarona	Sarona
4457262	Steller, Johannes	m	Oct. 1, 1937	43	1894	Sarona	Wilhelma

Occupation	NS post and/or membership	Source
Teacher	Party member, NSLB, active for HJ	ISTA, 821/9-פ; USHMM, membership records; YVA, R3/25.
	HJ	ISTA, 1879/1-פ; EvGB, Jan. 1930.
Worked at Hotel Darouti	DAF	ISTA, 821/11-פ.
	JM	ISTA, 1879/1-פ.
Master mechanic	Party member, applied in 1933; resigned 1936/37 because of "non-Aryan" spouse; DAF.	ISTA, 822/15-פ; YVA, R 3/25.
Bank official	Party member	USHMM, membership records.
Housekeeper	Party member	ISTA, 822/15-פ; USHMM, membership records.
Clerk	Party member, applied in 1933; head of the NS country group (1937)	ISTA, 822/15-פ; YVA, R 3/25; USHMM, membership records.
	Party member, applied in 1933.	ISTA, 822/15-פ; YVA, R 3/25.
Housewife	Party member	ISTA, 822/15-פ; USHMM, membership records.
	Party member	ISTA, 822/15-פ; YVA, R 3/25.
Teacher	Party member, NSLB, WHW	ISTA, 821/9-פ.
Cartwright	Party member; from 1937 to 1938: party applicant	ISTA, 821/9-פ; YVA, R3/18; USHMM, membership records.
	DAF	ISTA, 821/11-פ.
	JV, HJ	ISTA, 1879/1-פ; ISTA, 822/6-פ.
	DJ	ISTA, 1879/1-פ.
	HJ	ISTA, 822/9-פ; EvGB, June 1934.
Technician	Party member	USHMM, membership records; EvGB, Mar. 1932.
	BDM	ISTA, 1879/1-פ.
	HJ	ISTA, 1879/1-פ.
Student, teacher	Party member, NSLB, DAF-treasurer	ISTA, 821/9-פ.
	Party member	ISTA, 822/15-פ.
	JV, HJ	ISTA, 1879/1-פ; ISTA, 822/6-פ.
Farmer	Party member	USHMM, membership records.
Manager	Party member	ISTA, 822/15-פ; YVA, R 3/25; USHMM, membership records.
Merchant	Party member, applied in 1933.	ISTA, 822/15-פ; YVA, R 3/25; USHMM, membership records.
Architect	Party member	YVA, R 3/22; *Rundbrief d. Familiengemeinschaft GPH*, 41, June 2000.
	JV	ISTA, 1879/1-פ.
Farmer	Party member	USHMM, membership records.
Farmer	Party member	USHMM, membership records.

Member-ship no.	Name	Gen-der	Date of entry NSDAP or NS group	Age of entry, approx.	Year of birth	Place of birth	Address
	Steller, Kurt	m		11	1925	Wilhelma	Wilhelma
	Steller, Liselotte	f		10-18			Jaffa-Sarona
2754051	Stiefel, Gottfried	m	Oct. 1, 1934	33	1901	Erzingen	Jerusalem Syrian Orphanage
	Strasser, Udo	m		14-18			Jaffa-Sarona or Jerusalem?
3726028	Stre(c)ker, Daniel	m	July 1, 1936	45	1891	Jaffa	Haifa, German Colony
	Strecker, Helene	f		14	1921		Jaffa-Sarona
	Strecker, Horst	m		14-18			Haifa
	Strecker, Lieselotte	f		10-14			Haifa
	Streker, Helene	f		10-18			Jaffa-Sarona
3455413	Streker, Karl	m	June 1, 1934	46	1888	Jaffa	Jaffa, German Colony
	Streker, Maria	f		10-18			Jaffa-Sarona
3726029	Struve, Hulda	f	July 1, 1936	48	1888	Jerusalem	Haifa, German Colony
	Struve, Oskar	m		14-18			Haifa
3445387	Struve, Paul	m	Apr. 1, 1934	29	1905	Haifa	Haifa, German Colony
	Struve, Werner	m		14-18			Haifa
	Stuetz, Elfriede	f		10-14			Haifa
	Stuetz, Ilse	f		10-14			Haifa
3401933	Sus, Hermann	m	Feb. 1, 1934	21	1913	Waldheim	Waldheim near Haifa
	Sus, Georg	m		10-14			Haifa-Waldheim
	Sus, Guenther	m		10-14			Waldheim
3445383	Sus, Hans	m	Apr. 1, 1934	37	1897	Haifa	1938: Bethlehem-Waldheim, 1934: Haifa.
3710252	Sus, Olga Hedwig	f	May 1, 1936	34	1902	Jaffa	Waldheim
6990925	Tietz, Erna	f	Oct. 1, 1938	32	1906	Jaffa	Haifa
3445379	Tietz, Hermann	m	Apr. 1, 1934	45	1889	Jaffa	Haifa, German Colony
6990926	Tornau, Johannes (Harry) von	m	Oct. 1, 1938	28	1910	Muri	Jerusalem, Syrian Orphanage
	Tornau, Maria née Lösinger	f					Jerusalem
	Trefz, Amelie	f		10-14			Jaffa-Sarona
	Trefz, Anneluise	f					
	Trefz, Annemarie	f		10-14			Jaffa-Sarona
	Trefz, Elly	f		14-18	1916		Jaffa
	Trefz, Ida	f		22	1914		Jaffa-Sarona
	Trefz, Karl	m		18	1918		Jaffa

Occupation	NS post and/or membership	Source
	JV	ISTA, 1879/1-פ.
	JM or BDM	YVA, R 3/25.
Deacon	Party member	USHMM, membership records.
	JV, HJ	ISTA, 1879/1-פ.
Clerk	Party member	ISTA, 821/9-פ; USHMM, membership records.
	BDM	ISTA, 822/3-פ; ISTA, 822/6-פ
	HJ	ISTA, 1879/1-פ.
	JM	ISTA, 1879/1-פ.
	JM or BDM	YVA, R 3/25.
Cabinetmaker	Party member	USHMM, membership records.
	JM or BDM	YVA, R 3/25.
None	Party member	ISTA, 821/9-פ; USHMM, membership records:
	HJ	ISTA, 1879/1-פ.
Chemist	Party member, *Standortführer*	ISTA, 822/15-פ; YVA, R 3/1; USHMM, membership records.
	HJ	ISTA, 1879/1-פ.
	JM	ISTA, 1879/1-פ; EvGB, Nov. 1934.
	JM	ISTA, 1879/1-פ; EvGB, Nov. 1934.
Farmer	Party member, SA, HJ leader in Waldheim	ISTA, 822/15-פ; USHMM, membership records.
	JV	ISTA, 1879/1-פ; EvGB; June 1934.
	DJ	ISTA, 1879/1-פ.
Farmer	Party member, OGL, DAF	ISTA, 3160/18-פ; ISTA 821/11-פ; USHMM, membership records.
Housewife	Party member	USHMM, membership records.
Housewife	Party member	USHMM, membership records.
Merchant	Party member	ISTA, 822/15-פ; YVA, R 3/1; USHMM, membership records.
Secretary	Party member, DAF	USHMM, membership records.
	DAF	ISTA, 821/11-פ.
	JM	ISTA, 822/3-פ.
	Party member, treasurer of BDM, member of AGdFA	YVA, R 3/25.
	JM	ISTA, 822/3-פ.
	BDM	ISTA, 822/6-פ; EvGB, Jan.1931.
	BDM	ISTA, 1879/1-פ; ISTA, 822/6-פ; EvGB, Jan. 1931 and June 1934.
	HJ	ISTA, 1879/1-פ; ISTA, 822/6-פ; EvGB, June 1934.

Membership no.	Name	Gender	Date of entry NSDAP or NS group	Age of entry, approx.	Year of birth	Place of birth	Address
1587536	Trefz, Otto	m	Spring 1934				Jaffa
3402139	Uhlherr, Herbert	m	Feb. 1, 1934	28	1906	Jaffa	Jaffa
	Unger, Ernst	m		14-18			Waldheim
3455032	Unger, Fritz	m	June 1, 1934	24	1910	Haifa	Waldheim
	Unger, Gerhard	m		14-18			Waldheim
	Unger, Kurt	m		10-14			Waldheim
	Unger, Rudolf	m		14-18			Jerusalem
	Unger, Ruth	f		10-14			Haifa
	Unger, Walter	m		14-18			Haifa
	Venus, Bruno	m		10-18			Sarona, German Colony
2613290	Venus, Otto	m	Aug. 1, 1935	45	1890	Sarona	Sarona, German Colony
2755136	Voegelin, Walter	m					1. Jerusalem, 2. Haifa
	Vollhardt, Adam						
	Volk, Hans	m	Spring 1934				Jerusalem
2756174	Vollmer, Max	m	Oct. 1, 1934	37	1897	Ludwigsburg	Wilhelma
1587548	Wagner, Adolf jr.	m	May 1, 1933	19	1914	Jaffa	Jaffa
6990928	Wagner, Elsa	f	Oct. 1,1 938	44	1894	Jaffa	Jaffa
3722458	Wagner, Eugen	m	May 1, 1936	25	1911	Jaffa	Jaffa
	Wagner, Ewald	m		10-14			Bethlehem
7332430	Wagner, Frida	f	Dec. 1, 1939	48	1891	Jaffa	Jaffa
3445378	Wagner, Friedrich	m	Apr. 1,1 934	48	1886	Jerusalem	Haifa
6990929	Wagner, Georg	m	Oct. 1, 1938	45	1893	Jaffa	Jaffa
	Wagner, Gerhard	m		10-18			Jaffa-Sarona
7024779	Wagner, Gotthilf	m	Mar. 1, 1939	52	1887	Stuttgart	Jaffa, German Colony
	Wagner, Helene	f		10-14			Haifa
	Wagner, Helmut	m		14-18			Bethlehem
6990934	Wagner, Ilse	f	Oct. 1, 1938	28	1910	Nazareth	Haifa or Jerusalem
6990930	Wagner, Johanna	f	Oct. 1, 1938	50	1888	Haifa	Haifa, German Colony
	Wagner, Karl	m		10-14			Bethlehem
7024780	Wagner, Karoline	f	Mar. 1, 1939	60	1879	Cologne	Jaffa, German Colony
7332432	Wagner, Lieselotte	f	Dec. 1, 1939	21	1918	Bethlehem	Jaffa
	Wagner, Lore	f		10-14			Haifa
	Wagner, Margret	f		13	1922		Jaffa-Sarona
	Wagner, Theo(dor)	m		11	1924		Jaffa-Sarona
	Wagner, Ursula	f		10-14			Haifa

Occupation	NS post and/or membership	Source
	Party member, applied in 1933; JV leader	ISTA, 822/15-פ; YVA, R 3/25, R 3/10,
Assembler	Party member, applied in 1933; DAF	ISTA, 822/15-פ; ISTA, 823/4-פ; YVA, R 3/25; USHMM, membership records.
	HJ	ISTA, 1879/1-פ.
Farmer	Party member, DAF-leader in Bethlehem-Waldheim	USHMM, membership records.
	HJ	ISTA, 1879/1-פ.
	DJ	ISTA, 1879/1-פ.
	HJ	ISTA, 1879/1-פ.
	JM	ISTA, 1879/1-פ.
	HJ	ISTA, 1879/1-פ.
	JV or HJ	YVA, R 3/25.
Cabinetmaker	Party member	USHMM, membership records.
Employee at Syrian Orphanage	Party member	YVA, R 3/25.
	DNB, F. Reichert's assistant	BPRO, FO 371/23237+23238+23222; Balke 2001: 119.
	Party member	ISTA, 822/15-פ.
Merchant	Party member, DAF-treasurer	YVA, R 3/25; USHMM, membership records.
Founder	Party member	ISTA, 822/15-פ; YVA, R3/25; USHMM, membership records.
None	Party member	USHMM, membership records.
Orange planter	Party member	USHMM, membership records.
	JV	ISTA, 1879/1-פ.
Clerk	Party member	USHMM, membership records.
None	Party member, OGL Haifa	ISTA, 822/15-פ; USHMM, membership records.
Engineer	Party member	USHMM, membership records.
	JV or HJ	YVA, R 3/25.
Merchant	Party member	USHMM, membership records.
	JM	ISTA, 1879/1-פ.
	HJ	ISTA, 1879/1-פ.
Tailor	Party member	USHMM, membership records.
Housewife	Party member	USHMM, membership records.
	JV	ISTA, 1879/1-פ.
None	Party member	USHMM, membership records.
None	Party member, BDM	USHMM, membership records.
	JM	ISTA, 1879/1-פ.
	BDM	ISTA, 822/6-פ.
	JV, HJ	ISTA, 822/6-פ.
	JM	ISTA, 1879/1-פ.

Membership no.	Name	Gender	Date of entry NSDAP or NS group	Age of entry, approx.	Year of birth	Place of birth	Address
	Wagner, Wally	f		14-18			Haifa
3497457	Wagner, Walter	m	Nov. 1, 1935	25	1910	Haifa	Sarona
	Walla, Mrs.	f					
	Weber, Georg Heinrich	m	Spring 1934				Sarona
	Weber, Hermann	m		20	1919		Haifa
	Weber, Irmgard	f		14-18			Bethlehem
1484999	Weber, Waldemar	m	Apr. 11, 1933	21	1912	Bethlehem	Haifa, German Colony
	Weberruss, Agnes	f		14-18			Haifa
	Weberruss, Bernhard	m		14-18			Bethlehem
3726030	Weberruss, Bruno	m	Mar. 21, 1935	23	1912	Haifa	Haifa, German Colony
	Weberruss, Erika	f		14-18			Bethlehem
	Weberruss, Friede (Frieda)	f		14-18			Bethlehem
6990933	Weberruss, Friedrich W.	m	Oct. 1, 1933	46	1887	Haifa	Bethlehem
	Weberruss, Fritz	m		10-14			Bethlehem
	Weberruss, Gerda	f		14-18			Bethlehem
1636190	Weberruss, Herbert	m	June 2, 1933 or Spring 1934				Haifa 1933: Jaffa
	Weberruss, Hermann	m		14-18			Haifa or Jerusalem?
3709970	Weberruss, Jacob Adam	m	May 1, 1936	55	1881	Undingen	Haifa, German Colony
6990932	Weberruss, Katharina	f	Oct. 1, 1938	53	1885	Haifa	Haifa, German Colony
	Weberruss, Luise	f		10-14			Haifa
	Weberruss, Paul	m		14-18			Bethlehem
	Weberruss, Wilhelm	m	Applied for membership in 1936.				Bethlehem-Waldheim
	Weberruss, Willy	m		14-18			Bethlehem
6990935	Weiberle, Maria	f	Oct. 1, 1938	51	1887	Sarona	Wilhelma
	Weidemann, Gerhard	m					Jerusalem
3401714	Weigold, Hermann	m	Feb. 1, 1934	28	1906	Wilhelma	Jerusalem, German Colony
3445380	Weigold, Wilhelm Friedrich	m	Apr. 1, 1934	32	1902	Jaffa	Waldheim near Haifa
3402157	Weinmann, Georg Friedrich	m	Feb. 1, 1934	30	1904	Sarona	Sarona

Occupation	NS post and/or membership	Source
	BDM	ISTA, 1879/1-פ.
Clerk	Party member	USHMM, membership records.
	Party applicant	ISTA, 821/5-פ.
	Party member	ISTA, 822/15-פ.
	HJ; March 1939: RAD in Germany.	ISTA, 821/9-פ.
	BDM	ISTA, 1879/1-פ.
Mechanic	Party member	ISTA, 822/15-פ; USHMM, membership records.
	BDM	ISTA, 1879/1-פ.
	HJ	ISTA, 1879/1-פ.
Machinist	Party applicant, HJ leader in Haifa	ISTA, 822/9-פ; USHMM, membership records.
	BDM	ISTA, 1879/1-פ.
	BDM	ISTA, 1879/1-פ.
Farmer	Party member	USHMM, membership records.
	JV	ISTA, 1879/1-פ.
	BDM	ISTA, 1879/1-פ.
	Party member, DJ leader	ISTA, 822/15-פ; ISTA, 823/8-פ; ISTA, 823/8-פ; YVA, R 3/1.
	HJ	ISTA, 1879/1-פ.
Mechanic	Party member	USHMM, membership records.
None	Party member	USHMM, membership records.
	JM	ISTA, 1879/1-פ.
	HJ	ISTA, 1879/1-פ.
	Party applicant	ISTA, 821/7-פ.
	HJ	ISTA, 1879/1-פ.
Nurse	Party member	USHMM, membership records.
Teacher at the Syrian Orphanage	NSLB	ISTA, 821/9-פ.
	Party member, applied in 1933.	ISTA, 822/15-פ; YVA, R 3/25; USHMM, membership records.
Farmer	Party member	ISTA, 822/15-פ; USHMM, membership records.
Farmer	Party member, applied in 1933.	ISTA, 822/15-פ; YVA, R 3/25; USHMM, membership records; EvGB, Jan. 1933; EvGB, Jan. 1933.

Member-ship no.	Name	Gen-der	Date of entry NSDAP or NS group	Age of entry, approx.	Year of birth	Place of birth	Address
3445364	Weiss, Christian	m	Apr. 1, 1934	39	1895	Sarona	Sarona, Christophst. 554
771515	Weiss, Georg	m	Apr. 1, 1934	26	1908	Neustadt	Jerusalem, Prophet's St.; 1937: Nürnberg
	Weiss, Inge(borg)	f		14	1921		Sarona
3401716	Weiss, Irmgard	f	Feb. 1, 1934	25	1909	Jerusalem	Jerusalem, German Colony
6990936	Weiss, Johannes	m	Oct. 1, 1938	50	1888	Sarona	Sarona, German Colony
	Weller, Edgar	m		12	1922		Sarona
3709980	Weller, Erich	m	May, 1936	31	1905	Jaffa	Haifa, German Colony
	Weller, Hugo	m		10-18			Jaffa-Sarona
	Weller, Ingeborg (Inge)	f		10-18			Jaffa-Sarona
3402152	Weller, Karl	m	Feb. 1, 1934	24	1910	Sarona	Sarona
	Weller, Rolf	m		10-14			Jaffa-Sarona
	Weller, Ruth	f		10-14			Jaffa
2707311	Weller, Samuel	m	Oct. 1, 1934	39	1895	Sarona	Sarona
	Weller, Theo	m		14	1921		Jaffa-Sarona
3722460	Wennagel, Herbert Kurt	m	May 1, 1936	24	1912	Haifa	Jaffa-Sarona
7025328	Wennagel, Hugo	m	Apr. 1, 1939	32	1907	Jaffa	Sarona
2755564	Weno, Luzie	f	Oct. 1, 1934	31	1903	Lippine O/Schl.	Jerusalem
	Wenz, Eleonore	f					Jerusalem
2613022	Wied, Hermann	m	Aug. 1, 1935	27	1908	Wilhelma	Sarona
3445365	Wied, Karl	m	Apr. 1, 1934	24	1910	Wilhelma	Sarona, Christophstreet
3726042	Wied, Konrad	m	July 1, 1936	25	1911	Wilhelma	Wilhelma
	Wieland, Bruno	m	Spring 1934	24	1910		Jaffa
	Wieland, Eva	f		10-18			Jaffa-Sarona
	Wieland, Hans(-Joachim)	m		12	1922		Jaffa or Jerusalem
1751640	Wieland, Heinz	m	July 1, 1933	21	1912	Jerusalem	Jaffa
	Wieland, Hildegard	f					Jerusalem, 1938: Stuttgart
	Wieland, Kurt	m		18	1917	Illertissen	Jaffa
	Wieland, Marianne	f		10-14			Jerusalem
	Wieland, Paul	m		14-18	1919		Jaffa
6990939	Wieland, Rudolf	m	Oct. 1, 1938	56	1882	Jerusalem	Beisan
	Wieland, Theodor	m					Jaffa-Sarona

Occupation	NS post and/or membership	Source
Merchant	Party member	ISTA, 822/15-פ; USHMM, membership records.
City vicar, teacher	Party member	YVA, R 3/25; USHMM, membership records:
	JM, BDM	ISTA, 822/6-פ.
None	Party member, applied in 1933.	ISTA, 822/15-פ; YVA, R 3/25; USHMM, membership records.
Farmer	Party member, DAF-leader in Sarona	USHMM, membership records.
	HJ (Apr. 16, 1934)	ISTA, 822/6-פ.
Construction engineer	Party member	USHMM, membership records.
	JV or HJ	YVA, R 3/25.
	JM or BDM	YVA, R 3/25.
Planter	Party member	ISTA, 822/15-פ; USHMM, membership records.
	JV	ISTA, 822/3-פ.
	JM	ISTA, 822/3-פ.
Farmer	Party member	USHMM, membership records.
	JV, HJ	ISTA, 822/6-פ.
Bank official	Party member	YVA, R 3/25; USHMM, membership records.
Architect	Party member	USHMM, membership records.
Schmidt's Girls School (1932-1935), teacher	Party member, WHW collector	ISTA, 821/9-פ.
	Party applicant	YVA, R 3/25, R 3/22.
Cabinetmaker	Party member	USHMM, membership records.
Mechanic	Party member	ISTA, 822/15-פ; USHMM, membership records.
Farmer	Party member	USHMM, membership records.
	Party member, DAF	ISTA, 822/15-פ; YVA, R 3 /25; Sauer 1985: 270.
	JM or BDM	YVA, R 3/25.
	JV, HJ (Apr. 10, 1934)	ISTA, 822/3-פ.
Store clerk	Party member, DAF, Vice-leader of the national youth (*Landesjugend-führer*)	ISTA, 822/15-פ; YVA, R 3/25 and R 3/1; USHMM, membership records.
	Party applicant	YVA, R 3/22; EvGB, Mar. 1932.
	HJ; approx. 1936: DAF;1938: HJ leader	ISTA, 822/3-פ.
	JM	ISTA, 1879/1-פ; Ev.GB, Mar. 1932.
	JV, HJ	ISTA, 822/3-פ; ISTA 822/6.
Merchant	Party member	USHMM, membership records.
	Party member	YVA, R 3/25.

Membership no.	Name	Gender	Date of entry NSDAP or NS group	Age of entry, approx.	Year of birth	Place of birth	Address
2755622	Wilkens, Paul	m	Oct. 1, 1934	36	1898	Oldenburg	Jerusalem, Syrian Orphanage
	Wille, Friedrich	m					Jerusalem
	Woerner, Gustav	m	Spring 1934				Jerusalem
7025329	Woerz, Gottlieb	m	Apr. 1, 1939	36	1903	Haifa	Haifa, German Colony
	Wohlberts, Friedrich Wilh.	m					Jerusalem
789382	Wohlfarth, Maria	f	1932				Jerusalem
	Wolberts, Friedrich Wilh.	m					Jerusalem
	Wolff, Heinrich	m					Jerusalem
	Wollmer, Friedrich	m		14-18			Wilhelma
	Wollmer, Hedwig	f		10-14			Wilhelma
	Wollmer, Luise	f		10-14			Wilhelma
	Wollmer, Margot	f		10-14			Wilhelma
	Wollmer, Ruth	f		10-14			Wilhelma
	Wurst, Alfred	m		14-18			Haifa or Jerusalem?
	Wurst, Beate	f					Jaffa-Sarona
	Wurst, Eberhard	m		14-18	1920		Jaffa
3726031	Wurst, Emil	m	July 1, 1936	23	1913	Wolfsölden	Haifa, 1938: Germany
	Wurst, Gisela	f		14	1921		Sarona
3445369	Wurst, Heinrich	m	Apr. 1, 1934	21	1913	Jaffa	Sarona
6990943	Wurst, Philipp	m	Oct. 1, 1938	54	1882	Jerusalem	Jerusalem, German Colony
	Zimmermann, Eberhard	m					Jerusalem, 1937: Hamburg
	Zitzmann			35	1903	Steinbach	Jaffa
	Zo(e)llinger, Aline	f		14-18			Jaffa-Sarona
	Zuelow	m					Haifa

Occupation	NS post and/or membership	Source
Deacon	Party member	USHMM, membership records.
	Party applicant	YVA, R3/25, R 3/22.
	Party member, applied in 1933.	ISTA, 822/15-פ; YVA, R 3/25.
Mechanic	Party member	USHMM, membership records.
	Party applicant	YVA, R 3/25.
	Party member	ISTA, 821/1-פ; ISTA, 823/8-פ.
	Party member	YVA, R 3/25.
Consul General	Party applicant (*Parteianwärter*), autumn 1933	ISTA, 3162/19-פ; YVA, R 3/25.
	HJ	ISTA, 1879/1-פ.
	JM	ISTA, 1879/1-פ.
	JM	ISTA, 1879/1-פ.
	JM	ISTA, 1879/1-פ.
	JM	ISTA, 1879/1-פ.
	HJ	ISTA, 1879/1-פ.
Teacher	Party member, head of AGdFA in Palestine	Die Warte des Tempels, May 31, 1938: 76; ISTA 823/2-פ.
	JV, HJ	ISTA, 822/3-פ; ISTA 822/6-פ.
Butcher	Party member	USHMM, membership records.
	JM, BDM, DAF	ISTA, 822/6-פ.
Clerk	Party member	ISTA, 822/15-פ; YVA, R 3/1; USHMM, membership records.
Teacher, head of the Temple Society	Party member	USHMM, membership records.
	Party applicant, DAF	ISTA, 821/11-פ; YVA, R 3/25.
	Party member = *Saisonmitglied* (a seasonal member), DAF	ISTA, 821/1-פ; ISTA, 823/4-פ.
	JM, BDM	YVA, R 3/25.
	Party member	ISTA, 821/9-פ.

Appendix IIb: List of names of Palestine-born Germans who joined Nazi branches abroad

Membership no.	Name	Date of entry	Y. of birth	Place of birth
7025176	Asenstorfer, Anton	Apr. 1, 1939	1913	Jerusalem
3751916	Bäuerle, August	Oct. 1, 1936	1885	Jerusalem
3766083	Bäuerle, Christian	Dec. 1, 1936	1881	Jaffa
2707796	Bäuerle, Hans	Oct. 1, 1934	1882	Jerusalem
1484819	Bäuerle, Hugo	Apr. 1, 1933	1893	Jerusalem
3936249	Bäuerle, Otto	June 1,1 937	1915	Wilhelma
2636965	Bäuerle, Wilhelm Gottlob	Oct. 1, 1935	1879	Jaffa
3604555	Egger, Robert	Mar. 1, 1935	1910	Jaffa
5988930	Faber, Herbert	Oct. 1, 1937	1904	Jaffa
2872490	Hoffmann, Christoph	Oct. 1, 1934	1896	Jerusalem
3281229	Kaiser, Adalbert	July 01, 1933	1905	Jerusalem
3445068	Kappus, Samuel	Apr. 1, 1934	1890	Jaffa
2755035	Liebmann, Margarethe	Oct. 1, 1934	1902	Jerusalem
3500174	Mohr, Dr. Ernst Günther	Nov. 1, 1935	1904	Waldheim
3400241	Neef, Walter Ernst	Mar. 1, 1934	1901	Jaffa
2512031	Neinhaus, Margarete	Aug. 1, 1935	1913	Jaffa
1170246	Roehrich, Georg F. v.	July 01, 1932	1908	Haifa
5505573	Roehrich, Gustav von	Jan. 1, 1938	1905	Haifa
1369202	Schwarz, Erwin	Dec. 1, 1932	1905	Jaffa
574848	Tietz, Fritz Wilhelm	July 01, 1931	1900	Jaffa
5600118	Uhlherr, Werner	Oct. 1, 1937	1913	Jaffa
2189970	Wieland, Wilhelm	Jan. 10, 1934	1900	Jerusalem

Address/Country	Occupation	NS post	Source
Kima, Nairobi, Kenya	Engineer	Party member	Membership records, USHMM.
Eldoret, Kenya	Farmer	Party member	Membership records, USHMM.
Kakamega, Kenya	Farmer	Party member	Membership records, USHMM.
Eldoret, Kenya	Clerk	Party member	Membership records, USHMM.
Soy, Kenya	Farmer	Party member	Membership records, USHMM.
Eldoret, Kenya	Auto mechanic	Party member	Membership records, USHMM.
Kitale, Kenya	Farmer	Party member	Membership records, USHMM.
Arusha, Tanganyika	Construction worker	Party member	Membership records, USHMM.
Nairobi, Kenya	Architect	Party member	Membership records, USHMM.
Tangier, Span. Morocco	Consulate secretary	Party member	Membership records, USHMM.
Jacoli, Argentina	Farmer	Party member	Membership records, USHMM.
Farm Maguliwa, Tanganyika	Planter	Party member	Membership records, USHMM.
Istanbul, Turkey	Housewife	Party member	Membership records, USHMM.
Tangier, Span. Morocco	Attaché	Party member	Membership records, USHMM.
Mlingotini, Tanganyika	Machinist	Party member	Membership records, USHMM.
Alexandria, Egypt	Bank clerk	Party member	Membership records, USHMM.
Mexico	Traveling salesman	Party member	Membership records, USHMM.
Mexico	Farmer	Party member	Membership records, USHMM.
Cairo, Egypt		Party member	Membership records, USHMM.
Cairo, Egypt	Merchant	Party member	Membership records, USHMM.
Nairobi, Kenya	Clerk	Party member	Membership records, USHMM.
Pto. Monte Carlo, Argentina	Mate planter	Party member	Membership records, USHMM.

Abbreviations

AGdFA	Arbeitsgemeinschaft der deutschen Frau im Ausland (Work Group of the German Woman Abroad)
AO	Auslands-Organisation (Overseas Organization)
BArch	Bundesarchiv
BDC	Berlin Document Center
BDM	Bund deutscher Mädel (League of German Girls)
BPRO	British Public Record Office
C.I.D.	Criminal Investigation Department
CZA	Central Zionist Archives
DAF	Deutsche Arbeitsfront (German Labor Front)
DJ	Deutsches Jungvolk (German Young People)
DNB	Deutsches Nachrichtenbüro (German News Agency)
DZ	*Deutsche Zeitung* (German Newspaper)
EvGB	Evangelischer Gemeindebrief (Newsletter of the German Protestant Community)
EZA	Evangelisches Zentralarchiv Berlin (Central Archives of the Protestant Church, Berlin)
FO	Foreign Office
GPH	The Gebhardt-Paulus-Hoffmann families
HJ	Hitler Jugend (Hitler Youth)
Hl.	Heilig (holy)
ISTA	Israel State Archive
JV	Jungvolk (Young People)
KdF	Kraft durch Freude (Strength through Joy)
Kor.	Korintherbrief (Neues Testament), Letter to the Corinthians
NNM	*Neueste Nachrichten aus dem Morgenlande* (Lastest News from the Orient)
NS	National Socialist
NSDAP	Nationalsozialistische Deutsche Arbeiterpartei (National Socialist German Workers' Party)
NSKK	Nationalsozialistisches Kraftfahrerkorps (NS Motor Corps)
NSLB	Nationalsozialistischer Lehrerbund (NS Teachers' Alliance)
NSV	Nationalsozialistische Volkswohlfahrt (NS People's Welfare Organization)
OGL	Ortsgruppenleiter (leader of a local group of the NSDAP)
OGW	Ortsgruppenwalter (local group warden of the DAF)
PA AA	Politisches Archiv des Auswärtigen Amtes (Political Archive of the Foreign Office, Germany)

P.T.A.	Palestinian Telegraphic Agency
RAD	Reichsarbeitsdienst (Reich Labor Service)
RSHA	Reichssicherheits-Hauptamt (Reich Central Security Office)
SA	Sturmabteilung (Storm Detachment)
SD	Sicherheitsdienst (Security Service)
SS	Schutzstaffel (Protection Squadrons)
TGA	Archiv der Tempelgesellschaft in Deutschland (Archives of the Temple Society, Germany)
USHMM	United States Holocaust Memorial Museum (Washington D.C.)
WHW	Winterhilfswerk (Winter Relief Organization)
YMCA	Young Men's Christian Association
YVA	Yad Vashem Archives, Jerusalem

Bibliography

Archives

Bundesarchiv Berlin
NS 19 – Persönlicher Stab Reichsführer-SS: NS 19/186.
PK – Partei-Korrespondenz: PK/L0160, PK/Q106, PK/B0335, PK/T0026, PK(ehem. BDC)1200/0054/99.
R 58 – Reichssicherheitshauptamt: R 58/6401, R 58/6381, R 58/7076, R 58/954, R 58/563.

Central Zionist Archives, Jerusalem
S25: Political Department.
S25/4060: Untergrundaktivitäten der Nazis in Palästina.
S25/6583: Verhandlungen der Jewish Agency mit dem deutschen Generalkonsulat in Jerusalem.
S25/10971: Aufgezeichnete Telefongespräche des Waisenhauses Schneller (in Hebrew).
S25, 1012/22608: Die Fünfte Kolonne 1940.
S25, 1012/22475: Geheime Memoranden, in der Hauptsache über die deutsche Gemeinde in Palästina, übermittelt von einem Araber.

Evangelisches Zentralarchiv Berlin:
EZA 5, 56: Documents of the German Protestant Community and Lutheran Church of the Redeemer in Jerusalem.

Israel State Archives (ISTA), Jerusalem
821/1-פ: The beginnings of the NSDAP in Palestine, correspondence Karl Ruff, 1931–1932.
821/2-פ: NSDAP/AO, circulars, correspondence, etc., 1933.
821/3-פ: Cornelius Schwarz, private.
821/4-פ: Cornelius Schwarz, correspondence 1935-1938.
821/5-פ: Monthly reports of the local NS group in Jerusalem 1933–1935.
821/6-פ: Cornelius Schwarz, correspondence.
821/7-פ: Bethlehem-Waldheim, correspondence 1935–1936.
821/8-פ: NSLB 1937–1938.
821/9-פ: NSLB.
821/11-פ: DAF Palestine, correspondence 1936–1937.
821/13-פ: DAF Palestine, 1935–1937.
822/3-פ: Reports: Waldheim 1934–1937.
822/4-פ: Monthly reports of the Hitler Youth, Jaffa-Sarona 1935–1939.
822/6-פ: Monthly reports of the Hitler Youth, Jerusalem, Jaffa 1935–1938.
822/9-פ: Hitler Youth, Haifa, protocols, August 1938–August 1939.
822/15-פ: NSDAP Palestine, Karl Ruff, 1934.
823/2-פ: Arbeitsgemeinschaft der Deutschen Frau im Ausland.
823/3-פ: Mitteilungsblatt der Leitung der Auslands-Organisation der NSDAP 1934–1937.
823/4-פ: Die Deutsche Arbeitsfront 1938–1939.
823/6-פ: DAF-Sarona 1938–1939.
823/8-פ: Vertrauensmann für Palästina (confidential NS agent), correspondence 1933.
497/1049-פ: Celebrations.

525/1377-פ: Schools.
527/1429-פ: German institutions.
528/1426-פ: Syrisches Waisenhaus und andere deutsche Anstalten.
1879/1-פ: LJF Palästina, 1934–1936 (Leadership of Hitler Youth in Palestine).
1036/4-פ: German consulate in Jerusalem, correspondence.
1036/11-פ: Press.
1046/2-פ: Miscellaneous.
1046/18-פ: NSDAP 1939.
1063/14-פ: Deutschtum und deutsche Anstalten.
3136/11-פ: DNB – Pressedienst.
3160/9-פ: Franz Reichert, DNB.
3162/10-פ: Gottloeb Frank.
3162/19-פ: H. Wolff, Generalkonsul.
3169/6-פ: NSDAP – Sarona.
3169/7-פ: NSDAP
3174/27-פ: VDA – Volksbund Deutschtum im Ausland.
6/19-תת: Treatment of German foreigners.
18/19-תת: Documents of the NSDAP.

Jerusalemsverein, Berlin
Correspondence, annual and other reports of German Protestant communities in Palestine:
B 536, B 557

Politisches Archiv des Auswärtigen Amts (PA AA), Berlin
Rechtsabteilung, Akten betreffend Zivilgefangenenaustausch Palästina
R 41527: Erster Austausch, 1941.
R 41528: Erster Austausch, 1941.
R 41529: Zweiter Austausch, November 1942.
R 41530: Zweiter Austausch, November 1942.
R 41531: Zweiter Austausch und Nachaustauschtransport, 1942/43.
R 41532: Dritter Austausch, Korrespondenz 1943/44.
R 41533: Dritter Austausch, Korrespondenz 1943/44.
R 41853: Deutsche Internierte in Palästina, 1939–1940.
R 41854: Lager Akko.
R 41855: Deutsche Internierte in Palästina, 1941–1944.
R 78357: Nationalsozialismus, Faschismus und ähnliche Bestrebungen (1935).
R 78355: Das Deutschtum in Palästina (January 1927–March 1934).
R 104790: Deutschtum im Ausland (1936–1939).
R 104791: Judenfragen.
R 28877: Palästina (March 1937–Feb. 1941).
R 41242: Deutsche Kriegsgefangene in Palästina – Lager – (1941–1943).
R 100852: Judenfragen allgemein.
Private Correspondenz des Siegfried Blumenthal, Tel Aviv, 5 Nov. 1936.

Schumacher Institute, Haifa
Karl Ruff et al.: Correspondence, bills, business letters, etc. (P-RK-63, P-RK-66, P-LK-01).

Tempelgesellschaft-Archiv (TGA), Stuttgart
-576b_1: Report by Nikolai Schmidt.

US Holocaust Memorial Museum, Washington D.C:
Documentary: *Transport 222* by N. Ben Nathan, c. 1990.
Microfilms: British Public Record Office London, FO 371/21887+21888, FO 371/23237+23238 (expulsion of Reichert and Vollhardt), FO 371/23222 (expulsion of Reichert and Vollhardt), KV 2/400-402.

Nazi Party Membership Records, Part 1-4, submitted by the War Department to the Subcommittee on War Mobilization of the Committee on Military Affairs, United States Senate, U.S. Government Printing Office, Washington, D.C., 1947.

Yad Vashem Archives, Jerusalem:
R 3: NSDAP Palestine.
P 19: Carl Lutz, Swiss Vice Consul.

Journals, Periodicals, Newsletters, Newspapers

Der Armen- und Krankenfreund. Eine Zeitschrift für die weibliche Diakonie der evangelischen Kirche. Organ der deutschen Reichs-Konferenz evangelischer Mädchenerziehungsheime, 1933–1940.
Auslanddeutschtum und evangelische Kirche. Jahrbuch, edited by Ernst Schubert. Munich. 1932–1939.
Blumenthals Neuste Nachrichten (formerly Private Correspondenz des Siegfried Blumenthal). Tel Aviv. 1938.
Evangelisches Gemeindeblatt für Palästina. Jerusalem. 1927–1938.
Gemeindebrief der Evangelischen Gemeinde Deutscher Sprache zu Jerusalem. 1998–2005.
Haaretz. Tel Aviv. 29 Oct. 1999; 28 Feb. 2008.
Das Heilige Land. Organ des Deutschen Vereins vom Hl. Lande. Cologne. 1931–1938.
DZ — Deutsche Zeitung für Guatemala und das übrige Mittelamerika. Deutsches Auslandsinstitut. Stuttgart.
Front der Heimat. Published by Gau-Propaganda-Amt Oberdonau. Linz. 1939.
Hochland. Monatsschrift für alle Gebiete des Wissens/der Literatur u. Kunst. Edited by Karl Muth. Kempten. 1932–1939.
Israelitisches Familienblatt. Hamburg. 1933.
Jerusalem Post. 9 Oct. 1998.
Jewish Quarterly Review. 95/2. 2005.
Journal of Contemporary History. 12. 1977.
Journal of Contemporary History. 26/1. 1991.
Mitteilungsblatt der Leitung der Auslandsorganisation der NSDAP. 1934–1937.
Nachrichten-Blatt für die Teilnehmer und Foerderer des Deutschen Vereins vom Hl. Lande. Cologne. Oct. 1935.
Nachrichtendienst der NS-Frauenschaft. 1935.
Neueste Nachrichten aus dem Morgenlande. 1933–1939.

Palestine Bulletin/Palestine Post. Jerusalem. 1930–1948.
Der Tagesspiegel. 16 Apr. 2006.
Die Tageszeitung (TAZ). 4 Nov. 2006.
Times (London). 19 Nov. 1942.
Tirgumim. Übersetzung der wichtigsten Nachrichten aus der Presse. Haifa. 1936–1939.
Die Warte des Tempels. 1930–1939.
Vorschläge zur NS-Schulungsarbeit im Ausland. Nov. 1936.
Wiener Neueste Nachrichten. 14 Nov. 1942.
Wiener Mittag. 14 Nov. 1942.
Wochenzeitung. Guatemala. 1932–1941.
Yediot Achronot. Tel Aviv. 1 Oct. 1999; 3 Mar. 2006.

Published Sources, Secondary Accounts

Albrecht, Dieter, ed. *Katholische Kirche und Nationalsozialismus. Ausgewählte Aufsätze von Ludwig Volk. Veröffentlichungen der Kommission für Zeitgeschichte*. Part B: Research. Vol. 46. Mainz, 1987.

Arendt, Hans-Jürgen, Sabine Hering, and Leonie Wagner, eds. *Nationalsozialistische Frauenpolitik vor 1933. Dokumentation*. Frankfurt a.M., 1995.

Bacharach, Walter Zvi. "The Catholic Anti-Jewish Prejudice, Hitler and the Jews." In *Probing the Depths of German Antisemitism. German Society and the Persecution of the Jews, 1933–1941*, edited by David Bankier. New York, 2000. 415–30.

Bahat, L: "Hitler Boulevard at the Corner of Kaplan." [in Hebrew] *Yediot Achronot* (Tel Aviv). March 3, 2006.

Balke, Ralf. *Hakenkreuz im Heiligen Land. Die NSDAP-Landesgruppe Palästina*. Erfurt, 2001.

Bankier, David, ed. *Probing the Depths of German Antisemitism. German Society and the Persecution of the Jews, 1933–1941*. New York, 2000.

Bauer, Yehuda. "Overall Explanations, German Society and the Jews or: Some Thoughts about Context." In *Probing the Depths of German Antisemitism. German Society and the Persecution of the Jews, 1933–1941*, edited by David Bankier. New York, 2000. 3–18.

Baumann, Shaul. *Die Deutsche Glaubensbewegung und ihr Gründer Jakob Wilhelm Hauer (1881–1962)*. Marburg, 2005.

Benz, Wolfgang, Hermann Graml, and Hermann Weiß. *Enzyklopädie des Nationalsozialismus*. Munich, 1997.

Berger, M. *Vorschulerziehung im Nationalsozialismus. Recherchen zur Situation des Kindergartenwesens 1933–1945*. Weinheim, 1986.

Black, Edwin. *The Transfer Agreement. The Dramatic Story of the Pact between the Third Reich and Jewish Palestine*. New York, 1999.

Blumhagen, H. *Südwestafrika einst und jetzt*. Berlin, 1934.

Brasz, Chaya. *Transport 222: Bergen-Belsen—Palestine—July 1944*. Jerusalem, 1994.

Breitman, Richard "American Diplomatic Records Regarding German Public Opinion during the Nazi Regime." In *Probing the Depths of German Antisemitism. German Society and the Persecution of the Jews, 1933–1941*, edited by David Bankier. New York, 2000. 501–10.

Brenner, Lenni, ed. *51 Documents: Zionist Collaboration with the Nazis*. Fort Lee, N.J., 2002.

Buettner, Ursula. "The Jewish Problem Becomes a Christian Problem. German Protestants and the Persecution of the Jews in the Third Reich." In *Probing the Depths of German Antisemitism. German Society and the Persecution of the Jews, 1933–1941*, edited by David Bankier. New York, 2000. 431–62.

Carmel, Alex. *Die Siedlungen der württembergischen Templer in Palästina 1868–1918. Ihre lokalpolitischen und internationalen Probleme*. Stuttgart, 1973.

Carmel, Alex. *Palästina-Chronik 1853 bis 1882. Deutsche Zeitungsberichte vom Krimkrieg bis zur ersten jüdischen Einwanderungswelle*. Ulm, 1978.

Carmel, Alex. *Christen als Pioniere im Heiligen Land. Ein Beitrag zur Geschichte der Pilgermission und des Wiederaufbaus Palästinas im 19. Jahrhundert*. Basel, 1981.

Carmel, Alex. *Palästina-Chronik 1883 bis 1914. Deutsche Zeitungsberichte von der ersten jüdischen Einwanderungswelle bis zum Ersten Weltkrieg*. Ulm, 1983.

Carmel, Alex. "Der Missionar Theodor Fliedner als Pionier deutscher Palästina-Arbeit." *Jahrbuch des Instituts für Deutsche Geschichte* 14 (1985): 191–220.

Carmel, Alex. "Der Kaiser reist ins Heilige Land. Realität und Legende." In *Dem Erlöser der Welt zur Ehre. Festschrift zum hundertjährigen Jubiläum der Einweihung der evangelischen Erlöserkirche in Jerusalem*, edited by Karl-Heinz Ronecker on behalf of the Jerusalem-Stiftung and Jerusalemsverein. Leipzig, 1998. 116–35.

Carmel, Alex. "What's this? Making Fun of Nazis?" [in Hebrew]. *Haaretz* (Tel Aviv). 29 Oct. 1999.

Carmel, Alex. "Der christliche Beitrag zum Wiederaufbau Palästinas im 19. Jahrhundert." In *Seht, wir gehen hinauf nach Jerusalem. Festschrift zum 150jährigen Jubiläum von Talitha Kumi und des Jerusalemsvereins*, edited by Almuth Nothnagle, Hans-Jürgen Abromeit, and Frank Foerster. Leipzig, 2000. 17–30.

Carmel, Alex. and E. Jakob Eisler. *Der Kaiser reist ins Heilige Land. Die Palästinareise Wilhelm II*. Stuttgart, 1999.

Conze, Eckart, Norbert Frei, Peter Hayes, and Moshe Zimmermann. *Das Amt und die Vergangenheit: Deutsche Diplomaten im Dritten Reich und in der Bundesrepublik*. Munich, 2010.

Cramer, Valmar. *Ein Jahrhundert deutscher katholischer Palästinamission 1855–1955*. Cologne, 1956.

Dachs, Gisela, ed. *Jüdischer Almanach des Leo Baeck Instituts: Die Jeckes*. Frankfurt a.M., 2005.

Davis, Douglas. "From Auschwitz to Sainthood." *Jerusalem Post*, October 9, 1998.

Dietrich, Donald J. *Catholic Citizens in the Third Reich. Psycho-Social Principles and Moral Reasoning*. New Brunswick, N.J., 1988.

Documents on German Foreign Policy, 1918–1945. Series D, Vol. 13: *The War Years. June 23, 1941 to December 11, 1941*. London 1964.

Döring, Johannes. "Die Amtszeit des Propstes Döring. 1938–1954. Um den Zweiten Weltkrieg und die Teilung des Landes." In *Jerusalem. Geschichte einer Gemeinde*, edited by Hans Wilhelm Hertzberg. Kassel 1965. 93–112.

Doerry, Martin. *Übergangsmenschen. Die Mentalität der Wilhelminer und die Krise des Kaiserreichs*. Weinheim and Munich, 1986.

Dolev, Gania, ed. "Chronicle of a Utopia. The Templers in the Holy Land 1868–1948." Catalogue. Exhibition curator: Sara Turel, Eretz Israel Museum, Tel Aviv, 2006.

Ehrich, Emil. *Die Auslands-Organisation der NSDAP*. Berlin 1937.

Eisler, E. Jakob. "'Kirchler' im Heiligen Land. Die evangelischen Gemeinden in den württembergischen Siedlungen Palästinas." In *Dem Erlöser der Welt zur Ehre. Festschrift zum hundertjährigen Jubiläum der Einweihung der evangelischen Erlöserkirche in Jerusalem*, edited by

Karl-Heinz Ronecker, on behalf of the Jerusalem-Stiftung and Jerusalemsverein. Leipzig, 1998. 81–100.

Eisler, E. Jakob. *Peter Martin Metzler (1824–1907). Ein christlicher Missionar im Heiligen Land.* Haifa, 1999.

Eisler, Jakob. *Der deutsche Beitrag zum Aufstieg Jaffas 1850–1914: zur Geschichte Palästinas im 19. Jahrhundert.* Wiesbaden, 1997.

Eisler, Jakob, Norbert Haag, and Sabine Holtz. *Kultureller Wandel in Palästina im frühen 20. Jahrhundert. Eine Bilddokumentation.* Epfendorf, 2003.

Elan, Shlomo. *Deutsche in Jerusalem von der Mitte des 19. Jahrhunderts bis zum 1. Weltkrieg.* Wertheim a.M., 1984.

Eppinger, Richard Otto (2005): "Die Zypern-Gruppe. Tagebuch-Notizen vom Ende des Siedlungswerks der Templer in Palästina." In *Der besondere Beitrag.* Beilage der *Warte des Tempels,* (Stuttgart), December 2005.

Falbaum, Berl, ed. *Shanghai Remembered: Stories of Jews Who Escaped to Shanghai from Nazi Europe.* Royal Oak, Mich., 2005.

Fandel, Thomas. *Konfession und Nationalsozialismus. Evangelische und katholische Pfarrer in der Pfalz 1930–1939.* Paderborn, 1997.

Farias, Victor. *Die Nazis in Chile.* Berlin, 2002.

Felgentreff, Ruth. "Diakonisse Theodore Barkhausen, 18. August 1869–1. November 1959." In *Mitteilungen aus Ökumene und Auslandsarbeit,* edited by Kirchenamt der Ev. Kirche in Deutschland. Breklum, 2002. 1–56.

Flanagan, Ben and Donald Bloxham. *Remembering Belsen. Eyewitnesses Record the Liberation.* London, 2005.

Foerster, Frank. *Mission im Heiligen Land. Der Jerusalems-Verein zu Berlin 1852–1945.* Gütersloh, 1991.

Friedman, Isaiah. "Germany and Zionism, 1897–1918." In *Germany and the Middle East: Past, Present and Future,* edited by Haim Goren. Jerusalem, 2003. 61–68.

"From Bergen Belsen to Freedom. The story of the exchange of Jewish inmates of Bergen-Belsen with German Templers from Palestine. A symposium in memory of Dr. Haim Pazner." Yad Vashem, Jerusalem, 1986.

Fugmann, Markus. *Moderner Antisemitismus.* Frankfurt a.M., 1998.

"Fünfzig Jahre Kaiserswerther Diakonissen-Arbeit im heiligen Lande. Festschrift zur Jubelfeier der Diakonissen-Anstalten in Jerusalem am 4. Mai 1901." Kaiserswerth/Rhein, 1901.

Geldbach, Erich. "The German Protestant Network in the Holy Land." In *With Eyes toward Zion—III: Western Societies and the Holy Land,* edited by Moshe Davis, and Yehoshua Ben-Arieh. New York, 1991. 150–69.

Geldermann, Barbara. "'Jewish Refugees Should be Welcomed and Assisted here!' Shanghai: Exile and Return." *Yearbook of the Leo Baeck Institute* 19 (1999): 227–43.

Gensicke, Klaus. *Der Mufti von Jerusalem, Amin el-Husseini, und die Nationalsozialisten.* Frankfurt a.M., 1988.

Glenk, Helmut. *From Desert Sands to Golden Oranges. The History of the German Settlement of Sarona in Palestine 1871–1947.* Victoria, 2005.

Godman, Peter. *Hitler and the Vatican. Inside the Secret Archives that Reveal the New Story of the Nazis and the Church.* New York, 2004.

Goldman, Dan. "The Architecture of the Templers in their Colonies in Eretz-Israel, 1868–1948, and their Settlements in the United States, 1860–1925." Ph.D. diss., University of Cincinnati, Ohio, 2003.

Goren, Haim. Vom "Flaggenstreit" zum "Hospizwettstreit": das katholische Deutschland und Frankreich in Palästina am Ende des 19. Jahrhunderts. *Jahrbuch des Deutschen Evangelischen Instituts für Altertumswissenschaft des Heiligen Landes*. 7 (2001): 35–50.

Goren, Haim. "Ziehet hin und erforscht das Land." *Die deutsche Palästinaforschung im 19. Jahrhundert*. Göttingen, 2003.

Goren, Haim. "Debating the Jews of Palestine — German Discourses of Colonization, 1840–1883. In *Leipziger Beiträge zur jüdischen Geschichte und Kultur*, edited by Dan Diner. Leipzig, 2003. 217–38.

Goren, Haim, ed. *Germany and the Middle East. Past, Present and Future*. Jerusalem, 2003.

Gotto, Klaus, Hans Günter Hockerts, and Konrad Repgen. "Nationalsozialistische Herausforderung und kirchliche Antwort. Eine Bilanz." In *Die Katholiken und das Dritte Reich*, edited by Klaus Gotto and Konrad Repgen. Mainz, 1990.

Grover, Warren. *Nazis in Newark*. New Brunswick, N.J., 2003.

Hagemann, Albrecht. *Südafrika und das "Dritte Reich." Rassenpolitische Affinität und machtpolitische Rivalität*. Frankfurt a.M., 1989.

Hall, Trevor. *Enduring the Hour. A British Soldier in Palestine 1946–1947*. Lincolnshire, 2005.

Harris, James. *The People Speak! Anti-Semitism and Emancipation in Nineteenth Century Bavaria*. Ann Arbor, 1994.

Herrmann, Simon H. *Austauschlager Bergen-Belsen. Geschichte eines Austauschtransports*. Tel Aviv, 1944.

Herrmann, Hugo. Palästina. Unpublished manuscript, Leo Baeck Institute Jerusalem, 1935.

Hertzberg, Hans Wilhelm, ed. *Jerusalem. Geschichte einer Gemeinde*. Kassel, 1965.

Heym, Stefan. *Nazis in U.S.A. An Expose of Hitler's Aims and Agents in the U.S.A.* New York, 1938.

Hillenbrand, Klaus. "Der Ausgetauschte," *Die Tageszeitung (TAZ)*, 4 Nov. 2006.

Hillenbrand, Klaus. *Der Ausgetauschte. Die außergewöhnliche Rettung des Israel Sumer Korman*. Frankfurt a.M., 2010.

Hoffmann, Brigitte. "Unsere Verantwortung in der Welt." In *Der besondere Beitrag. Beilage der Warte des Tempels*, Stuttgart 2 (1995): 7–14.

Hoffmann, Joseph Paul. "The Price of Flight: German Jews, the Nazi Regime and the Finance of the Ha'avarah Agreement, 1933–1939." Ph.D. diss. Columbian College of Arts and Sciences at the George Washington University, Washington, D.C., 2002.

Hoffmann, Paul E. "Zusammenbruch und Wiederaufbau. Die Arbeit des Jerusalemsvereins und Kaiserswerth nach dem 2. Weltkrieg." In *Seht, wir gehen hinauf nach Jerusalem. Festschrift zum 150jährigen Jubiläum von Talitha Kumi und des Jerusalemsvereins*, edited by Almut Nothnagle, Hans-Jürgen Abromeit, and Frank Foerster, eds. Leipzig, 2000. 213–67.

Hübinger, Gangolf. "Kulturprotestantismus, Bürgerkirche und liberaler Revisionismus im wilhelminischen Deutschland." In *Religion und Gesellschaft im 19. Jahrhundert*, edited by Wolfgang Schieder. Stuttgart, 1993. 272–99.

Hornung, Richard. "Reminiscence from the Middle East." (21 Mar. 2002, Adelaide, Australia). *Adelaide Institute Newsletter*, no. 159 (May 2002).

Israel, Alec. *The Monasteries and Convents of the Holy Land*. Jerusalem, 2002.

Jacobsen, Hans Adolf. *Nationalsozialistische Aussenpolitik, 1933–1938*. Frankfurt a.M., 1968.

Kampffmeyer, G. "Die Stellung der Araber zu den Gegenwartsproblemen Palästinas." In *Zeitschrift des Deutschen Palästina-Vereins*, edited by Martin Noth. (1930): 248–59.

Kaplan, Marion. "Jewish Daily Life in Wartime Germany." In *Probing the Depths of German Antisemitism. German Society and the Persecution of the Jews, 1933–1941*, edited by David Bankier. New York, 2000. 395–414.

Kark, Ruth and Naftali Thalmann. "Technological Innovation in Palestine: The role of the German Templers." In *Germany and the Middle East. Past, Present and Future*, edited by Haim Goren. Jerusalem, 2003. 201–24.

Karpel, Dalia. "Swastika in Jerusalem." *Haaretz*, Feb. 28, 2008.

Klingemann Karl . "Die Kaiserswerther Arbeit im Ausland und das Auslanddeutschtum." In *Auslanddeutschtum und evangelische Kirche. Jahrbuch*, edited by Ernst Schubert. (1934): 126–42.

Klinksiek, Dorothee. *Die Frau im NS-Staat*. Stuttgart, 1982.

Kohler, Oliver. "Mehr als ein Anhängsel. Das Grundstück 'Dormition' und die katholische Dimension des 31. Oktober 1898." In *Dem Erlöser der Welt zur Ehre. Festschrift zum hundertjährigen Jubiläum der Einweihung der evangelischen Erlöserkirche in Jerusalem*, edited by Karl-Heinz Ronecker on behalf of the Jerusalem-Stiftung and Jerusalemsverein. Leipzig, 1998. 136–53.

Kolb, Eberhard. *Bergen-Belsen. Geschichte des "Aufenthaltslagers"*. Hannover 1962

Kolb, Eberhard. *Bergen-Belsen. Vom "Aufenthaltslager" zum Konzentrationslager 1943–1945*. Göttingen, 1996.

Kremer, Hannes. "Neuwertung 'überlieferter' Brauchformen?." *Die neue Gemeinschaft* 3 (1937): 3005a–c.

Kroyanker, David. *The German Colony and Emek Refaim Street*. Jerusalem, 2008.

Kulka, Otto and Aron Rodrigue. "The German Population and the Jews in the Third Reich. Recent Publications and Trends in Research on German Society and the Jewish Question." *Yad Vashem Studies* 16 (1984): 421–36.

Kulka, Otto. "The German Population and the Jews: State of Research and New Perspectives." In *Probing the Depths of German Antisemitism. German Society and the Persecution of the Jews, 1933–1941*, edited by David Bankier. New York, 2000. 271–81.

Lackmann, Thomas. "Hitlers Todesschwadron vor Palästina. Spektakulärer Fund deutscher Historiker: Wie die SS die Juden im Nahen Osten ermorden wollte." *Der Tagesspiegel*, April 16, 2006.

Lauterer, H.-M. *Liebestätigkeit für die Volksgemeinschaft. Der Kaiserswerther Verband deutscher Diakonissenmutterhäuser in den ersten Jahren des NS-Regimes*. Göttingen, 1994.

Lewy, Günter. *The Catholic Church and Nazi Germany*. Cambridge, Mass., 2000.

Lill, Rudolf. "NS-Ideologie und katholische Kirche." In *Die Katholiken und das Dritte Reich*, edited by Klaus Gotto and Konrad Repgen. Mainz, 1990.

Löffler, Roland. "Die Gemeinden des Jerusalemsvereins in Palästina im Kontext des kirchlichen und politischen Zeitgeschehens in der Mandatszeit." In *Seht, wir gehen hinauf nach Jerusalem. Festschrift zum 150jährigen Jubiläum von Talitha Kumi und des Jerusalemsvereins*, edited by Almut Nothnagle, Hans-Jürgen Abromeit, and Frank Foerster. Leipzig, 2000. 185–212.

Löffler, Roland. (2008): *Protestanten in Palästina: Religionspolitik, sozialer Protestantismus und Mission in den deutschen evangelischen und anglikanischen Institutionen des Heiligen Landes 1917–1939*. Stuttgart, 2008.

Lückhoff, Martin (1998): Anglikaner und Protestanten im Heiligen Land. Das gemeinsame Bistum Jerusalem (1841-1886). Wiesbaden, 1998.

Lumans, Valdis O. (1993): Himmler's Auxiliaries. The Volksdeutsche Mittelstelle and the German National Minorities of Europe, 1933-1945. Chapel Hill, London, 1993.

Mallmann, Klaus-Michael and Martin Cüppers. "'Beseitigung der jüdisch-nationalen Heimstätte in Palästina.' Das Einsatzkommando bei der Panzerarmee Afrika 1942." In *Deutsche, Juden,*

Völkermord. Der Holocaust als Geschichte und Gegenwart, edited by Jürgen Matthäus and K.-M. Mallmann. Darmstadt, 2006. 153–76.

Mallmann, Klaus-Michael and Martin Cüppers. *Halbmond und Hakenkreuz. Das Dritte Reich, die Araber und Palästina*. Darmstadt, 2006.

McCann, Frank D. "Vargas and the Destruction of the Brazilian Integralista and Nazi Parties." *The Americas* 26, no. 1 (July 1969): 15–34.

McKale, Donald M. "The Nazi Party in the Far East, 1931–45. *Journal of Contemporary History* 12 (1977): 291–311.

McKale, Donald M. *The Swastika Outside Germany*. Kent State, Ohio, 1977.

Michman, Dan. "Täteraussagen und Geschichtswissenschaft. Der Fall Dieter Wisliceny und der Entscheidungsprozeß zur 'Endlösung.'" In *Deutsche, Juden, Völkermord. Der Holocaust als Geschichte und Gegenwart*, edited by Jürgen Matthäus and K.-M. Mallmann. Darmstadt, 2006. 205–22.

Modras, Ronald. *The Catholic Church and Antisemitism. Poland, 1933–1939*. Chur 1994.

Morris, Benny. *Righteous Victims. A History of the Zionist-Arab Conflict, 1881–2001*. New York, 2001.

Mosse, George L. *Die Geschichte des Rassismus in Europa*. Frankfurt a.M., 2006.

Müller, Jürgen. *Nationalsozialismus in Lateinamerika: Auslandsorganisation der NSDAP in Argentinien, Brasilien, Chile and Mexiko, 1931–1945*. Stuttgart, 1997.

Nafi, Basheer M. "The Arabs and the Axis: 1933–1940." *Arab Studies Quarterly* 19, no. 2 (1997): 1–24.

Nicosia, Francis R., ed. *Central Zionist Archives, Jerusalem 1933–1939*. Archives of the Holocaust. An International Series, edited by Sybil Milton and Henry Friedlander, 3. New York, 1990.

Nicosia, Francis R., ed. *Central Zionist Archives, Jerusalem 1939–1945*. Archives of the Holocaust. An International Series, edited by Sybil Milton and Henry Friedlander, 4. New York, 1990.

Nicosia, Francis R.. *The Third Reich and the Palestine Question*. London, 2000.

Nieren, Günther. Arbeitsfeld Palästina. Die Geschichte des Jerusalemsvereins. Unpublished manuscript, 1967.

Niewyk, Donald and Francis Nicosia, eds. *Columbia Guide to the Holocaust*. New York, 2000.

Pappé, Ilan. *A History of Modern Palestine. One Land. Two Peoples*. Cambridge, 2004.

Paulus, Rudolf F. *Kurze Geschichte der Württembergischen Familie Paulus/Hoffmann*. Stuttgart, 2000.

Perkins, John. "The Swastika Down Under: Nazi Activities in Australia, 1933–39." *Journal of Contemporary History* 26, no. 1 (1991): 111–29.

Perry, Yaron. *"Mount Hope.". Deutsch-Amerikanische Siedlungen in Palästina 1850–1858*. Haifa, 1995.

Rahden, Till van. "Ideologie und Gewalt. Neuerscheinungen über den Antisemitismus in der deutschen Geschichte des 19. und frühen 20. Jahrhunderts." *Neue Politische Literatur* 41 (1996): 11–29.

Raheb, Mitri. *Das reformatorische Erbe unter den Palästinensern. Zur Entstehung der Evangelisch-Lutherischen Kirche in Jordanien*. Gütersloh, 1999.

Rattner, Anna and Lola Blonder. *1938 — Zuflucht Palästina. Zwei Frauen berichten*. Wien, 1989.

Reimesch, Fritz Heinz. "Auslanddeutschtum und Deutscher Rundfunk." In *Auslanddeutschtum und evangelische Kirche, Jahrbuch*, edited by Ernst Schubert (1935): 69–83.

Rhein, Christoph. "Eine Kindheit in Jerusalem." In *Dem Erlöser der Welt zur Ehre. Festschrift zum hundertjährigen Jubiläum der Einweihung der evangelischen Erlöserkirche in Jerusalem*, edited by Karl-Heinz Ronecker on behalf of the Jerusalem-stiftung and Jerusalemsverein. Leipzig, 1998. 222–28.

Rhein, Ernst. "Die Amtszeit des Propstes Rhein, 1930–1938: Zwischen Festigung und drohenden Vorzeichen." In *Jerusalem. Geschichte einer Gemeinde*, edited by Hans Wilhelm Hertzberg. Kassel, 1965. 76–92.

Ross, James R. *Escape to Shanghai: A Jewish Community in China*. New York, 1994.

Ruff, Gottlieb Samuel. "Aus der Jugendzeit eines alten Templers. Erinnerungen von Gottlieb Samuel Ruff (1890–1983) an die Tempelgemeinde in Haifa (gegr. 1869)." *Beitrag Beilage der Warte des Tempels* 17 (2010): 1–24.

Sakakini, Hala. *Jerusalem and I. A Personal Record*. 2nd ed. Amman, 1990.

Sauer, Paul. *Uns rief das Heilige Land. Die Tempelgesellschaft im Wandel der Zeit*. Stuttgart, 1985.

Sauer, Paul. "Vom Land um den Asperg — im Namen Gottes nach Palästina und Australien." Lecture, October 20, 1995, Burgstetten.

Schaser, Angelika. "Das Engagement des Bundes Deutscher Frauenvereine für das 'Auslandsdeutschtum': Weibliche 'Kulturaufgabe' und nationale Politik vom Ersten Weltkrieg bis 1933." In *Nation, Politik und Geschlecht. Frauenbewegungen und Nationalismus in der Moderne*, edited by Ute Planert. New York, 2000. 254–74.

Schechtman, Joseph B. *The Mufti and the Führer: The rise and fall of Haj Amin el-Husseini*. New York, 1965.

Scheck, Raffael. "Zwischen Volksgemeinschaft und Frauenrechten: Das Verhältnis rechtsbürgerlicher Politikerinnen zur NSDAP 1930–1933. In *Nation, Politik und Geschlecht. Frauenbewegungen und Nationalismus in der Moderne*, edited by Ute Planert. New York, 2000. 234–53.

Schmidt, H. (1952): "The Nazi Party in Palestine and the Levant 1932–9." *International Affairs* 28, no. 4 (1952): 460–69.

Schubert, Ernst, ed. *Auslanddeutschtum und evangelische Kirche. Jahrbuch*. Munich, 1932–1939.

Schulze, Rainer. "Keeping very clear of any 'Kuh-Handel.' The British Foreign Office and the Rescue of Jews from Bergen-Belsen." *Holocaust and Genocide Studies* 19, no. 2 (2005): 226–51.

Schwarz, Simone. *Chile im Schatten faschistischer Bewegungen. Der Einfluß europäischer und chilenischer Strömungen in den 30er und 70er Jahren*. Frankfurt a.M., 1997.

Segev, Tom. *One Palestine Complete. Jews and Arabs under the British Mandate*. London, 2001.

Snyder, Louis L. *Encyclopedia of the Third Reich*. New York, 1979.

Stern, Carola and Inge Brodersen, eds. *Eine Erdbeere für Hitler. Deutschland unterm Hakenkreuz*. 2nd ed. Frankfurt a.M., 2005.

Temkin, Moshe. "The History of the Hitler Youth in Jerusalem. [in Hebrew]. *Yediot Achronot* (Tel Aviv). Oct. 1, 1999, 52–57.

Tempelgesellschaft Deutschland, ed. *Damals in Palästina – Templer erzählen vom Leben in ihren Gemeinden*. Stuttgart, 1990.

Volkov, Shulamit. *Antisemitismus als kultureller Code*. 2nd ed. Munich, 2000.

Wassermann-Deininger, Gertrud. Wir haben hier keine bleibende Statt. Geschichte der Familie Deininger in Palästina 1868–1948. Self publication, 1982.

Wawrzyn, Heidemarie. *Vaterland statt Menschenrecht. Formen der Judenfeindschaft in den Frauenbewegungen des Deutschen Kaiserreiches*. Marburg, 1999.

Wawrzyn, Heidemarie. *Ham and Eggs in Palestine. The Auguste Victoria Foundation 1898–1939*. Marburg, 2005.

Weller, Alfred. "Gedanken über die Haltung der Tempelgesellschaft zum Nationalsozialismus." Lecture, 1948, edited by Brigitte Hoffnung. In *Der besondere Beitrag. Beilage der Warte des Tempels* 2 (1995): 3–7.
Wiesenthal, Simon. *Großmufti — Großagent der Achse*. Salzburg, 1946.
Wickert, Christl. "Popular Attitudes to National Socialist Antisemitism: Denunciations for Insidious Offenses and Racial Ignominy." In *Probing the Depths of German Antisemitism. German Society and the Persecution of the Jews, 1933–1941*, edited by David Bankier. New York, 2000. 282–92.
Wistrich, Robert S. *Antisemitism. The Longest Hatred*. London, 1992.
Wistrich, Robert S. *Antisemitism in the New Europe*. Oxford, 1994.
Yahil, Leni. "The Double Consciousness of the Nazi Mind and Practice." In *Probing the Depths of German Antisemitism. German Society and the Persecution of the Jews, 1933–1941*, edited by David Bankier. New York, 2000. 36–53.

Websites

http://baltimore.indymedia.org/newswire/display/5200/index.php.
http://www.ushmm.org (Shanghai Ghetto).
http://www.sonntagsblatt-bayern.de/archiv01/17/ woche2.htm ("Interniert am Ende der Welt" by Thomas Greif).
http://www.dhm.de/lemo/html/nazi/innenpolitik/mutterkreuz/
http://www.wikipedia.org/wiki/Mutterkreuz/
http://www.waldorfanswers.org/AnthroposophyDuringNaziTimes.htm (Mar. 10, 2006).
http://www.carmelite.com/saints/edith1.shtml (Aug. 7, 2007).
http://www.teachers.ash.org.au/dnutting/germanaustralia/e/palestine3.htm (May 28, 2008).
http://www.paulbogdanor.com/holocaust/mideast.pdf (14 Oct. 2012).

Documentaries

Rommels Schatz, ZDF, Zweites Deutsches Fernsehen, May 2007.
Rommels Krieg, ZDF, Zweites Deutsches Fernsehen, May 2007.
Transport 222 by N. Ben Nathan, c. 1990.
The True Story. The Templers — Secrets in Tel Aviv, Israeli TV, Channel 1, spring 2007.

Correspondence and Interviews

Dr. [first name unknown] Segal, conversation with author, Jerusalem, autumn 2005.
Peter Gewitsch, correspondence with author, Haifa, 2005.
Ron Lahav to Heidemarie Wawrzyn, 2 Oct. 2006.
Brigitte Kneher, Temple Society Germany, correspondence with author, 3 and 12 Nov. 2006; 22 Apr. 2008.
Peter Lange, Temple Society Germany, correspondence with author, 28 Apr. 2008.
Helen Benninga, interview by Heidemarie Wawrzyn, Jerusalem, 13 Oct. 2007.

Index

www.ingramcontent.com/pod-product-compliance
Lightning Source LLC
Chambersburg PA
CBHW052127270326
41930CB00012B/2785

* 9 7 8 3 1 1 0 4 8 5 6 7 7 *